MR. STANDFAST

JOHN BUCHAN

1st WORLD
LIBRARY
Literary Society

Mr. Standfast

John Buchan

© 1st World Library, 2007
PO Box 2211
Fairfield, IA 52556
www.1stworldlibrary.com
First Edition

LCCN: 2007924145

Softcover ISBN: 978-1-4218-4285-1
Hardcover ISBN: 978-1-4218-4187-8
eBook ISBN: 978-1-4218-4383-4

Purchase *"Mr. Standfast"*
as a traditional bound book at:
www.1stWorldLibrary.com/purchase.asp?ISBN=978-1-4218-4285-1

1st World Library is a literary, educational organization
dedicated to:

- Creating a free internet library of downloadable ebooks

- Hosting writing competitions and offering book
  publishing scholarships.

Interested in more 1st World Library books?
contact: literacy@1stworldlibrary.com
Check us out at: www.1stworldlibrary.com

1st World Library Literary Society

Giving Back to the World

"If you want to work on the core problem, it's early school literacy."

- James Barksdale, former CEO of Netscape

"No skill is more crucial to the future of a child, or to a democratic and prosperous society, than literacy."

- Los Angeles Times

Literacy... means far more than learning how to read and write... The aim is to transmit... knowledge and promote social participation."

- UNESCO

"Literacy is not a luxury, it is a right and a responsibility. If our world is to meet the challenges of the twenty-first century we must harness the energy and creativity of all our citizens."

- President Bill Clinton

"Parents should be encouraged to read to their children, and teachers should be equipped with all available techniques for teaching literacy, so the varying needs and capacities of individual kids can be taken into account."

- Hugh Mackay

TO THAT MOST GALLANT COMPANY
THE OFFICERS AND MEN
OF THE
SOUTH AFRICAN INFANTRY BRIGADE
on the Western Front

CONTENTS

NOTE

The earlier adventures of Richard Hannay, to which occasional reference is made in this narrative, are recounted in The Thirty-Nine Steps and Greenmantle.

J. B.

PART I

CHAPTER ONE

THE WICKET-GATE

I spent one-third of my journey looking out of the window of a first-class carriage, the next in a local motor-car following the course of a trout stream in a shallow valley, and the last tramping over a ridge of downland through great beech-woods to my quarters for the night. In the first part I was in an infamous temper; in the second I was worried and mystified; but the cool twilight of the third stage calmed and heartened me, and I reached the gates of Fosse Manor with a mighty appetite and a quiet mind.

As we slipped up the Thames valley on the smooth Great Western line I had reflected ruefully on the thorns in the path of duty. For more than a year I had never been out of khaki, except the months I spent in hospital. They gave me my battalion before the Somme, and I came out of that weary battle after the first big September fighting with a crack in my head and a D.S.O. I had received a C.B. for the Erzerum business, so what with these and my Matabele and South African medals and the Legion of Honour, I had a chest like the High Priest's breastplate. I rejoined in January, and got a brigade on the eve of Arras. There we had a star turn, and took about as many prisoners as we put infantry over the top. After that we were hauled out for a month, and subsequently planted in a bad bit on the Scarpe with a hint that we would soon be used for a big push. Then suddenly I was ordered home to report to the War Office, and passed on by them to Bullivant and his merry men. So here I was sitting in a railway carriage in a grey tweed suit, with a neat new suitcase on the rack labelled C.B. The initials stood for Cornelius Brand, for that was my name now. And an old boy in the corner was asking me questions and wondering audibly why I wasn't fighting, while a young blood of a second lieutenant with a wound stripe was eyeing me with scorn.

The old chap was one of the cross-examining type, and after he had borrowed my matches he set to work to find out all about me. He was a tremendous fire-eater, and a bit of a pessimist about our slow progress in the west. I told him I came from South Africa and was a mining engineer.

'Been fighting with Botha?' he asked.

'No,' I said. 'I'm not the fighting kind.' The second lieutenant screwed up his nose.

'Is there no conscription in South Africa?'

'Thank God there isn't,' I said, and the old fellow begged permission to tell me a lot of unpalatable things. I knew his kind and didn't give much for it. He was the sort who, if he had been under fifty, would have crawled on his belly to his tribunal to get exempted, but being over age was able to pose as a patriot. But I didn't like the second lieutenant's grin, for he seemed a good class of lad. I looked steadily out of the window for the rest of the way, and wasn't sorry when I got to my station.

I had had the queerest interview with Bullivant and Macgillivray. They asked me first if I was willing to serve again in the old game, and I said I was. I felt as bitter as sin, for I had got fixed in the military groove, and had made good there. Here was I - a brigadier and still under forty, and with another year of the war there was no saying where I might end. I had started out without any ambition, only a great wish to see the business finished. But now I had acquired a professional interest in the thing, I had a nailing good brigade, and I had got the hang of our new kind of war as well as any fellow from Sandhurst and Camberley. They were asking me to scrap all I had learned and start again in a new job. I had to agree, for discipline's discipline, but I could have knocked their heads together in my vexation.

What was worse they wouldn't, or couldn't, tell me anything about what they wanted me for. It was the old game of running me in blinkers. They asked me to take it on trust and put myself unreservedly in their hands. I would get my instructions later, they said.

I asked if it was important.

Bullivant narrowed his eyes. 'If it weren't, do you suppose we could have wrung an active brigadier out of the War Office? As it was, it was like drawing teeth.'

'Is it risky?' was my next question.

'in the long run - damnably,' was the answer.

'And you can't tell me anything more?'

'Nothing as yet. You'll get your instructions soon enough. You know both of us, Hannay, and you know we wouldn't waste the time of a good man on folly. We are going to ask you for something which will make a big call on your patriotism. It will be a difficult and arduous task, and it may be a very grim one before you get to the end of it, but we believe you can do it, and that no one else can ... You know us pretty well. Will you let us judge for you?'

I looked at Bullivant's shrewd, kind old face and Macgillivray's steady eyes. These men were my friends and wouldn't play with Me.

'All right,' I said. 'I'm willing. What's the first step?'

'Get out of uniform and forget you ever were a soldier. Change your name. Your old one, Cornelis Brandt, will do, but you'd better spell it "Brand" this time. Remember that you are an engineer just back from South Africa, and that you don't care a rush about the war. You can't understand what all the fools are fighting about, and you think we might have peace at once by a little friendly business talk. You needn't be pro-German - if you like you can be rather severe on the Hun. But you must be in deadly earnest about a speedy peace.'

I expect the corners of my mouth fell, for Bullivant burst out laughing.

'Hang it all, man, it's not so difficult. I feel sometimes inclined to argue that way myself, when my dinner doesn't agree with me. It's not so hard as to wander round the Fatherland abusing Britain, which was your last job.'

'I'm ready,' I said. 'But I want to do one errand on my own first. I must see a fellow in my brigade who is in a shell-shock hospital in the Cotswolds. Isham's the name of the place.'

The two men exchanged glances. 'This looks like fate,' said Bullivant. 'By all means go to Isham. The place where your work begins is only a couple of miles off. I want you to spend next Thursday night as the guest of two maiden ladies called Wymondham at Fosse Manor. You will go down there as a lone South African visiting a sick friend. They are hospitable souls and entertain many angels unawares.'

'And I get my orders there?'

'You get your orders, and you are under bond to obey them.' And Bullivant and Macgillivray smiled at each other.

I was thinking hard about that odd conversation as the small Ford car, which I had wired for to the inn, carried me away from the suburbs of the county town into a land of rolling hills and green water-meadows. It was a gorgeous afternoon and the blossom of early June was on every tree. But I had no eyes for landscape and the summer, being engaged in reprobating Bullivant and cursing my fantastic fate. I detested my new part and looked forward to naked shame. It was bad enough for anyone to have to pose as a pacifist, but for me, strong as a bull and as sunburnt as a gipsy and not looking my forty years, it was a black disgrace. To go into Germany as an anti-British Afrikander was a stoutish adventure, but to lounge about at home talking rot was a very different-sized job. My stomach rose at the thought of it, and I had pretty well decided to wire to Bullivant and cry off. There are some things that no one has a right to ask of any white man.

When I got to Isham and found poor old Blaikie I didn't feel happier. He had been a friend of mine in Rhodesia, and after the German South-West affair was over had come home to a Fusilier battalion, which was in my brigade at Arras. He had been buried by a big crump just before we got our second objective, and was dug out without a scratch on him, but as daft as a hatter. I had heard he was mending, and had promised his family to look him up the first chance I got. I found him sitting on a garden seat, staring steadily before him like a lookout at sea. He knew me all right and cheered up for a second, but very soon he was back at his staring, and every word he uttered was like the careful speech of a drunken man. A bird flew out of a bush, and I could see him holding himself tight to keep from screaming. The best I could do was to put a hand on his shoulder and stroke him as one strokes a frightened horse. The sight of the price my old friend had paid didn't put me in love with pacificism.

We talked of brother officers and South Africa, for I wanted to keep his thoughts off the war, but he kept edging round to it.

'How long will the damned thing last?' he asked.

'Oh, it's practically over,' I lied cheerfully. 'No more fighting for you and precious little for me. The Boche is done in all right ... What you've got to do, my lad, is to sleep fourteen hours in the twenty-four and spend half the rest catching trout. We'll have a shot at the grouse-bird together this autumn and we'll get some of the old gang to join us.'

Someone put a tea-tray on the table beside us, and I looked up to see the very prettiest girl I ever set eyes on. She seemed little more than a child, and before the war would probably have still ranked as a flapper. She wore the neat blue dress and apron of a V.A.D. and her white cap was set on hair like spun gold. She smiled demurely as she arranged the tea-things, and I thought I had never seen eyes at once so merry and so grave. I stared after her as she walked across the lawn, and I remember noticing that she moved with the free grace of an athletic boy.

'Who on earth's that?' I asked Blaikie.

'That? Oh, one of the sisters,' he said listlessly. 'There are squads of them. I can't tell one from another.'

Nothing gave me such an impression of my friend's sickness as the fact that he should have no interest in something so fresh and jolly as that girl. Presently my time was up and I had to go, and as I looked back I saw him sunk in his chair again, his eyes fixed on vacancy, and his hands gripping his knees.

The thought of him depressed me horribly. Here was I condemned to some rotten buffoonery in inglorious safety, while the salt of the earth like Blaikie was paying the ghastliest price. From him my thoughts flew to old Peter Pienaar, and I sat down on a roadside wall and read his last letter. It nearly made me howl. Peter, you must know, had shaved his beard and joined the Royal Flying Corps the summer before when we got back from the Greenmantle affair. That was the only kind of reward he wanted, and, though he was absurdly over age, the authorities allowed it. They were wise not to stickle about rules, for Peter's eyesight and nerve were as good as those of any boy of twenty. I knew he would do well, but I was not prepared for his immediately blazing success. He got his pilot's certificate in record time and went out to France; and presently even we foot-sloggers, busy shifting ground before the Somme, began to hear rumours of his doings. He developed a perfect genius for air-fighting. There were plenty better trick-flyers, and plenty who knew more about the science of the game, but there was no one with quite Peter's genius for an actual scrap. He was as full of dodges a couple of miles up in the sky as he had been among the rocks of the Berg. He apparently knew how to hide in the empty air as cleverly as in the long grass of the Lebombo Flats. Amazing yarns began to circulate among the infantry about this new airman, who could take cover below one plane of an enemy squadron while all the rest were looking for him. I remember talking about him with the South Africans when we were out resting next door to them after the bloody Delville Wood business. The day before we had seen a good battle in the clouds when the Boche plane had crashed, and a Transvaal machine-gun officer brought the report that the British airman had been Pienaar. 'Well done, the old takhaar!' he cried, and started to yarn about Peter's methods. It appeared that Peter had a theory that every man has a blind spot, and that he knew just how to find that blind spot in the world of air. The best cover, he maintained, was not in cloud or a wisp of fog, but in the unseeing patch in the eye of your enemy. I recognized that talk for the real thing. It was on a par with Peter's doctrine of 'atmosphere' and 'the double bluff' and all the other principles that his queer old mind had cogitated out of his rackety life.

By the end of August that year Peter's was about the best-known figure in the Flying Corps. If the reports had mentioned names he would have been a national hero, but he was only 'Lieutenant Blank', and the newspapers, which expatiated on his deeds, had to praise the Service and not the man. That was right enough, for half the magic of our Flying Corps was its freedom from advertisement. But the British Army knew all about him, and the men in the trenches used to discuss him as if he were a crack football-player. There was a very big German airman called Lensch, one of the Albatross heroes, who about the end of August claimed to have destroyed thirty-two Allied machines. Peter had then only seventeen planes to his credit, but he was rapidly increasing his score. Lensch was a mighty man of valour and a good sportsman after his fashion. He was amazingly quick at manoeuvring his machine in the actual fight, but Peter was supposed to be better at forcing the kind of fight he wanted. Lensch, if you like, was the tactician and Peter the strategist. Anyhow the two were out to get each other. There were plenty of fellows who saw the campaign as a struggle not between Hun and Briton, but between Lensch and Pienaar.

The 15th September came, and I got knocked out and went to hospital. When I was fit to read the papers again and receive letters, I found to my consternation that Peter had been downed. It happened at the end of October when the southwest gales badly handicapped our airwork. When our bombing or reconnaissance jobs behind the enemy lines were completed, instead of being able to glide back into safety, we had to fight our way home slowly against a head-wind exposed to Archies and Hun planes. Somewhere east of Bapaume on a return journey Peter fell in with Lensch - at least the German Press gave Lensch the credit. His petrol tank was shot to bits and he was forced to descend in a wood near Morchies. 'The celebrated British airman, Pinner,' in the words of the German communique, was made prisoner.

I had no letter from him till the beginning of the New Year, when I was preparing to return to France. It was a very contented letter. He seemed to have been fairly well treated, though he had always a low standard of what he expected from the world in the way of comfort. I inferred that his captors had not identified in the brilliant airman the Dutch miscreant who a year before had broken out of a German jail. He had discovered the pleasures of reading and had perfected himself in an art which he had once practised indifferently. Somehow or other he had got a Pilgrim's Progress, from which he seemed to extract enormous pleasure. And then at the end, quite casually, he mentioned that he had been badly wounded and that his left leg would never be much use again.

After that I got frequent letters, and I wrote to him every week and sent him every kind of parcel I could think of. His letters used to make me both ashamed and happy. I had always banked on old Peter, and here he was behaving like an early Christian martyr - never a word of complaint, and just as cheery as if it were a winter morning on the high veld and we were off to ride down springbok. I knew what the loss of a leg must mean to him, for bodily fitness had always been his pride. The rest of life must have unrolled itself before him very drab and dusty to the grave. But he wrote as if he were on the top of his form and kept commiserating me on the discomforts of my job. The picture of that patient, gentle old fellow, hobbling about his compound and puzzling over his Pilgrim's Progress, a cripple for life after five months of blazing glory, would have stiffened the back of a jellyfish.

This last letter was horribly touching, for summer had come and the smell of the woods behind his prison reminded Peter of a place in the Woodbush, and one could read in every sentence the ache of exile. I sat on that stone wall and considered how trifling were the crumpled leaves in my bed of life compared with the thorns Peter and Blaikie had to lie on. I thought of Sandy far off in Mesopotamia, and old Blenkiron groaning with dyspepsia somewhere in America, and I considered that they were the kind of fellows who did their jobs without complaining. The result was that when I got up to go on I had recovered a manlier temper. I wasn't going to shame my friends or pick and choose my duty. I would trust myself to Providence, for, as Blenkiron used to say, Providence was all right if you gave him a chance. It was not only Peter's letter that steadied and calmed me. Isham stood high up in a fold of the hills away from the main valley, and the road I was taking brought me over the ridge and back to the stream-side. I climbed through great beechwoods, which seemed in the twilight like some green place far below the sea, and then over a short stretch of hill pasture to the rim of the vale. All about me were little fields enclosed with walls of grey stone and full of dim sheep. Below were dusky woods around what I took to be Fosse Manor, for the great Roman Fosse Way, straight as an arrow, passed over the hills to the south and skirted its grounds. I could see the stream slipping among its water-meadows and could hear the plash of the weir. A tiny village settled in a crook of the hill, and its church-tower sounded seven with a curiously sweet chime. Otherwise there was no noise but the twitter of small birds and the night wind in the tops of the beeches.

In that moment I had a kind of revelation. I had a vision of what I had been fighting for, what we all were fighting for. It was peace, deep and holy and ancient, peace older than the oldest wars, peace which would endure when all our swords were hammered into ploughshares. It was more; for in that hour England first took hold of me. Before my country had been South Africa, and when I thought of home it had been the wide sun-steeped spaces of the veld or some scented glen of the Berg. But now I realized that I had a new home. I understood what a precious thing this little England was, how old and kindly and comforting, how wholly worth striving for. The freedom of an acre of her soil was cheaply bought by the blood of the best of us. I knew what it meant to be a poet, though for the life of me I could not have made a line of verse. For in that hour I had a prospect as if from a hilltop which made all the present troubles of the road seem of no account. I saw not only victory after war, but a new and happier world after victory, when I should inherit something of this English peace and wrap myself in it till the end of my days.

Very humbly and quietly, like a man walking through a cathedral, I went down the hill to the Manor lodge, and came to a door in an old red-brick facade, smothered in magnolias which smelt like hot lemons in the June dusk. The car from the inn had brought on my baggage, and presently I was dressing in a room which looked out on a water-garden. For the first time for more than a year I put on a starched shirt and a dinner-jacket, and as I dressed I could have sung from pure lightheartedness. I was in for some arduous job, and sometime that evening in that place I should get my marching orders. Someone would arrive - perhaps Bullivant - and read me the riddle. But whatever it was, I was ready for it, for my whole being had found a new purpose. Living in the trenches, you are apt to get your horizon narrowed down to the front line of enemy barbed wire on one side and the nearest rest billets on the other. But now I seemed to see beyond the fog to a happy country.

High-pitched voices greeted my ears as I came down the broad staircase, voices which scarcely accorded with the panelled walls and the austere family portraits; and when I found my hostesses in the hall I thought their looks still less in keeping with the house. Both ladies were on the wrong side of forty, but their dress was that of young girls. Miss Doria Wymondham was tall and thin with a mass of nondescript pale hair confined by a black velvet fillet. Miss Claire Wymondham was shorter and plumper and had done her best by ill-applied cosmetics to make herself look like a foreign demi-mondaine. They greeted me with the friendly casualness which I had long ago discovered was the right English manner towards your guests; as if they had just strolled in and billeted themselves, and you were quite glad to see them but mustn't be asked to trouble yourself further. The next second they were cooing like pigeons round a picture which a young man was holding up in the lamplight.

He was a tallish, lean fellow of round about thirty years, wearing grey flannels and shoes dusty from the country roads. His thin face was sallow as if from living indoors, and he had rather more hair on his head than most of us. In the glow of the lamp his features were very clear, and I examined them with interest, for, remember, I was expecting a stranger to give me orders. He had a long, rather strong chin and an obstinate mouth with peevish lines about its corners. But the remarkable feature was his eyes. I can best describe them by saying that they looked hot - not fierce or angry, but so restless that they seemed to ache physically and to want sponging with cold water.

They finished their talk about the picture - which was couched in a jargon of which I did not understand one word - and Miss Doria turned to me and the young man.

'My cousin Launcelot Wake - Mr Brand.'

We nodded stiffly and Mr Wake's hand went up to smooth his hair in a self-conscious gesture.

'Has Barnard announced dinner? By the way, where is Mary?'

'She came in five minutes ago and I sent her to change,' said Miss Claire. 'I won't have her spoiling the evening with that horrid uniform. She may masquerade as she likes out-of-doors, but this house is for civilized people.'

The butler appeared and mumbled something. 'Come along,' cried Miss Doria, 'for I'm sure you are starving, Mr Brand. And Launcelot has bicycled ten miles.'

The dining-room was very unlike the hall. The panelling had been stripped off, and the walls and ceiling were covered with a dead-black satiny paper on which hung the most monstrous pictures in large dull-gold frames. I could only see them dimly, but they seemed to be a mere riot of ugly colour. The young man nodded towards them. 'I see you have got the Degousses hung at last,' he said.

'How exquisite they are!' cried Miss Claire. 'How subtle and candid and brave! Doria and I warm our souls at their flame.'

Some aromatic wood had been burned in the room, and there was a queer sickly scent about. Everything in that place was strained and uneasy and abnormal - the candle shades on the table, the mass of faked china fruit in the centre dish, the gaudy hangings and the nightmarish walls. But the food was magnificent. It was the best dinner I had eaten since 1914. 'Tell me, Mr Brand,' said Miss Doria, her long white face propped on a much-beringed hand. 'You are one of us? You are in revolt against this crazy war?'

'Why, yes,' I said, remembering my part. 'I think a little common-sense would settle it right away.'

'With a little common-sense it would never have started,' said Mr Wake.

'Launcelot's a C.O., you know,' said Miss Doria.

I did not know, for he did not look any kind of soldier ... I was just about to ask him what he commanded, when I remembered that the letters stood also for 'Conscientious Objector,' and stopped in time.

At that moment someone slipped into the vacant seat on my right hand. I turned and saw the V.A.D. girl who had brought tea to Blaikie that afternoon at the hospital.

'He was exempted by his Department,' the lady went on, 'for he's a Civil Servant, and so he never had a chance of testifying in court, but no one has done better work for our cause. He is on the committee of the L.D.A., and questions have been asked about him in Parliament.'

The man was not quite comfortable at this biography. He glanced nervously at me and was going to begin some kind of explanation, when Miss Doria cut him short. 'Remember our rule, Launcelot. No turgid war controversy within these walls.'

I agreed with her. The war had seemed closely knit to the Summer landscape for all its peace, and to the noble old chambers of the Manor. But in that demented modish dining-room it was shriekingly incongruous.

Then they spoke of other things. Mostly of pictures or common friends, and a little of books. They paid no heed to me, which was fortunate, for I know nothing about these matters and didn't understand half the language. But once

Miss Doria tried to bring me in. They were talking about some Russian novel - a name like Leprous Souls - and she asked me if I had read it. By a curious chance I had. It had drifted somehow into our dug-out on the Scarpe, and after we had all stuck in the second chapter it had disappeared in the mud to which it naturally belonged. The lady praised its 'poignancy' and 'grave beauty'. I assented and congratulated myself on my second escape - for if the question had been put to me I should have described it as God-forgotten twaddle.

I turned to the girl, who welcomed me with a smile. I had thought her pretty in her V.A.D. dress, but now, in a filmy black gown and with her hair no longer hidden by a cap, she was the most ravishing thing you ever saw. And I observed something else. There was more than good looks in her young face. Her broad, low brow and her laughing eyes were amazingly intelligent. She had an uncanny power of making her eyes go suddenly grave and deep, like a glittering river narrowing into a pool.

'We shall never be introduced,' she said, 'so let me reveal myself. I'm Mary Lamington and these are my aunts ... Did you really like Leprous Souls?'

It was easy enough to talk to her. And oddly enough her mere presence took away the oppression I had felt in that room. For she belonged to the out-of-doors and to the old house and to the world at large. She belonged to the war, and to that happier world beyond it - a world which must be won by going through the struggle and not by shirking it, like those two silly ladies.

I could see Wake's eyes often on the girl, while he boomed and oraculated and the Misses Wymondham prattled. Presently the conversation seemed to leave the flowery paths of art and to verge perilously near forbidden topics. He began to abuse our generals in the field. I could not choose but listen. Miss Lamington's brows were slightly bent, as if in disapproval, and my own temper began to rise.

He had every kind of idiotic criticism - incompetence, faint-heartedness, corruption. Where he got the stuff I can't imagine, for the most grousing Tommy, with his leave stopped, never put together such balderdash. Worst of all he asked me to agree with him.

It took all my sense of discipline. 'I don't know much about the subject,' I said, 'but out in South Africa I did hear that the British leading was the weak point. I expect there's a good deal in what you say.'

It may have been fancy, but the girl at my side seemed to whisper 'Well done!'

Wake and I did not remain long behind before joining the ladies; I purposely cut it short, for I was in mortal fear lest I should lose my temper and spoil everything. I stood up with my back against the mantelpiece for as long as a man may smoke a cigarette, and I let him yarn to me, while I looked steadily at his face. By this time I was very clear that Wake was not the fellow to give me my instructions. He wasn't playing a game. He was a perfectly honest crank, but not a fanatic, for he wasn't sure of himself. He had somehow lost his self-respect and was trying to argue himself back into it. He had considerable brains, for the reasons he gave for differing from most of his countrymen were good so far as they went. I shouldn't have cared to take him on in public argument. If you had told me about such a fellow a week before I should have been sick at the thought of him. But now I didn't dislike him. I was bored by him and I was also tremendously sorry for him. You could see he was as restless as a hen.

When we went back to the hall he announced that he must get on the road, and commandeered Miss Lamington to help him find his bicycle. It appeared he was staying at an inn a dozen miles off for a couple of days' fishing, and the news somehow made me like him better. Presently the ladies of the house departed to bed for their beauty sleep and I was left to my own devices.

For some time I sat smoking in the hall wondering when the messenger would arrive. It was getting late and there seemed to be no preparation in the house to receive anybody. The butler came in with a tray of drinks and I asked him if he expected another guest that night.

'I 'adn't 'eard of it, sir,' was his answer. 'There 'asn't been a telegram that I know of, and I 'ave received no instructions.'

I lit my pipe and sat for twenty minutes reading a weekly paper. Then I got up and looked at the family portraits. The moon coming through the lattice invited me out-of-doors as a cure for my anxiety. It was after eleven o'clock, and I was still without any knowledge of my next step. It is a maddening business to be screwed up for an unpleasant job and to have the wheels of the confounded thing tarry.

Outside the house beyond a flagged terrace the lawn fell away, white in the moonshine, to the edge of the stream, which here had expanded into a miniature lake. By the water's edge was a little formal garden with grey stone parapets which now gleamed like dusky marble. Great wafts of scent rose from it, for the lilacs were scarcely over and the may was in full blossom. Out from the shade of it came suddenly a voice like a nightingale.

It was singing the old song 'Cherry Ripe', a common enough thing which I had chiefly known from barrel-organs. But heard in the scented moonlight it seemed to hold all the lingering magic of an elder England and of this hallowed countryside. I stepped inside the garden bounds and saw the head of the girl Mary.

She was conscious of my presence, for she turned towards me.

'I was coming to look for you,' she said, 'now that the house is quiet. I have something to say to you, General Hannay.'

She knew my name and must be somehow in the business.

John Buchan

The thought entranced me. 'Thank God I can speak to you freely,' I cried. 'Who and what are you - living in that house in that kind of company?'

'My good aunts!' She laughed softly. 'They talk a great deal about their souls, but they really mean their nerves. Why, they are what you call my camouflage, and a very good one too.'

'And that cadaverous young prig?'

'Poor Launcelot! Yes - camouflage too - perhaps something a little more. You must not judge him too harshly.'

'But ... but -' I did not know how to put it, and stammered in my eagerness. 'How can I tell that you are the right person for me to speak to? You see I am under orders, and I have got none about you.'

'I will give You Proof,' she said. 'Three days ago Sir Walter Bullivant and Mr Macgillivray told you to come here tonight and to wait here for further instructions. You met them in the little smoking-room at the back of the Rota Club. You were bidden take the name of Cornelius Brand, and turn yourself from a successful general into a pacifist South African engineer. Is that correct?'

'Perfectly.'

'You have been restless all evening looking for the messenger to give you these instructions. Set your mind at ease. No messenger is coming. You will get your orders from me.'

'I could not take them from a more welcome source,' I said.

'Very prettily put. If you want further credentials I can tell you much about your own doings in the past three years. I can explain to you who don't need the explanation, every step in the business of the Black Stone. I think I could draw a pretty accurate map of your journey to Erzerum. You have a letter from Peter Pienaar in your pocket - I can tell you its contents. Are you willing to trust me?'

'With all my heart,' I said.

'Good. Then my first order will try you pretty hard. For I have no orders to give you except to bid you go and steep yourself in a particular kind of life. Your first duty is to get "atmosphere", as your friend Peter used to say. Oh, I will tell you where to go and how to behave. But I can't bid you do anything, only live idly with open eyes and ears till you have got the "feel" of the situation.'

She stopped and laid a hand on my arm.

'It won't be easy. It would madden me, and it will be a far heavier burden for a man like you. You have got to sink down deep into the life of the half-baked, the people whom this war hasn't touched or has touched in the wrong way, the people who split hairs all day and are engrossed in what you and I would call selfish little fads. Yes. People like my aunts and Launcelot, only for the most part in a different social grade. You won't live in an old manor like this, but among gimcrack little "arty" houses. You will hear everything you regard as sacred laughed at and condemned, and every kind of nauseous folly acclaimed, and you must hold your tongue and pretend to agree. You will have nothing in the world to do except to let the life soak into you, and, as I have said, keep your eyes and ears open.'

'But you must give me some clue as to what I should be looking for?'

'My orders are to give you none. Our chiefs - yours and mine - want you to go where you are going without any kind of parti pris. Remember we are still in the intelligence stage of the affair. The time hasn't yet come for a plan of campaign, and still less for action.'

John Buchan

'Tell me one thing,' I said. 'Is it a really big thing we're after?'

'A - really - big - thing,' she said slowly and very gravely. 'You and I and some hundred others are hunting the most dangerous man in all the world. Till we succeed everything that Britain does is crippled. If we fail or succeed too late the Allies may never win the victory which is their right. I will tell you one thing to cheer you. It is in some sort a race against time, so your purgatory won't endure too long.'

I was bound to obey, and she knew it, for she took my willingness for granted.

From a little gold satchel she selected a tiny box, and opening it extracted a thing like a purple wafer with a white St Andrew's Cross on it.

'What kind of watch have you? Ah, a hunter. Paste that inside the lid. Some day you may be called on to show it ... One other thing. Buy tomorrow a copy of the Pilgrim's Progress and get it by heart. You will receive letters and messages some day and the style of our friends is apt to be reminiscent of John Bunyan ... The car will be at the door tomorrow to catch the ten-thirty, and I will give you the address of the rooms that have been taken for you ... Beyond that I have nothing to say, except to beg you to play the part well and keep your temper. You behaved very nicely at dinner.'

I asked one last question as we said good night in the hall. 'Shall I see you again?'

'Soon, and often,' was the answer. 'Remember we are colleagues.'

I went upstairs feeling extraordinarily comforted. I had a perfectly beastly time ahead of me, but now it was all glorified and coloured with the thought of the girl who had sung 'Cherry Ripe' in the garden. I commended the wisdom of that old serpent Bullivant in the choice of his intermediary, for I'm hanged if I would have taken such orders from anyone else.

CHAPTER TWO

'THE VILLAGE NAMED MORALITY'

UP on the high veld our rivers are apt to be strings of pools linked by muddy trickles - the most stagnant kind of watercourse you would look for in a day's journey. But presently they reach the edge of the plateau and are tossed down into the flats in noble ravines, and roll thereafter in full and sounding currents to the sea. So with the story I am telling. It began in smooth reaches, as idle as a mill-pond; yet the day soon came when I was in the grip of a torrent, flung breathless from rock to rock by a destiny which I could not control. But for the present I was in a backwater, no less than the Garden City of Biggleswick, where Mr Cornelius Brand, a South African gentleman visiting England on holiday, lodged in a pair of rooms in the cottage of Mr Tancred Jimson.

The house - or 'home' as they preferred to name it at Biggleswick - was one of some two hundred others which ringed a pleasant Midland common. It was badly built and oddly furnished; the bed was too short, the windows did not fit, the doors did not stay shut; but it was as clean as soap and water and scrubbing could make it. The three-quarters of an acre of garden were mainly devoted to the culture of potatoes, though under the parlour window Mrs Jimson had a plot of sweet-smelling herbs, and lines of lank sunflowers fringed the path that led to the front door. It was Mrs Jimson who received me as I descended from the station fly - a large red woman with hair bleached by constant exposure to weather, clad in a gown which, both in shape and material, seemed to have been modelled on a chintz curtain. She was a good kindly soul, and as proud as Punch of her house.

'We follow the simple life here, Mr Brand,' she said. 'You must take us as you find us.'

I assured her that I asked for nothing better, and as I unpacked in my fresh little bedroom with a west wind blowing in at the window I considered that I had seen worse quarters.

I had bought in London a considerable number of books, for I thought that, as I would have time on my hands, I might as well do something about my education. They were mostly English classics, whose names I knew but which I had never read, and they were all in a little flat-backed series at a shilling apiece. I arranged them on top of a chest of drawers, but I kept the Pilgrim's Progress beside my bed, for that was one of my working tools and I had got to get it by heart.

Mrs Jimson, who came in while I was unpacking to see if the room was to my liking, approved my taste. At our midday dinner she wanted to discuss books with me, and was so full of her own knowledge that I was able to conceal my ignorance.

'We are all labouring to express our personalities,' she informed me. 'Have you found your medium, Mr Brand? is it to be the pen or the pencil? Or perhaps it is music? You have the brow of an artist, the frontal "bar of Michelangelo", you remember!'

I told her that I concluded I would try literature, but before writing anything I would read a bit more.

It was a Saturday, so Jimson came back from town in the early afternoon. He was a managing clerk in some shipping office, but you wouldn't have guessed it from his appearance. His city clothes were loose dark-grey flannels, a soft collar, an orange tie, and a soft black hat. His wife went down the road to meet him, and they returned hand-in-hand, swinging their arms like a couple of schoolchildren. He had a skimpy red beard streaked with grey, and mild blue eyes behind strong glasses. He was the most friendly creature in the world, full of rapid questions, and eager to make me feel one of the family. Presently he got into a tweed Norfolk jacket, and started to cultivate his garden. I took off my coat and lent him a hand, and when he stopped to rest from his labours - which was every five minutes, for he had no kind of physique - he would mop his brow and rub his spectacles and declaim about the good smell of the earth and the joy of getting close to Nature.

Once he looked at my big brown hands and muscular arms with a kind of wistfulness. 'You are one of the doers, Mr Brand,' he said, 'and I could find it in my heart to envy you. You have seen Nature in wild forms in far countries. Some day I hope you will tell us about your life. I must be content with my little corner, but happily there are no territorial limits for the mind. This modest dwelling is a watch-tower from which I look over all the world.'

After that he took me for a walk. We met parties of returning tennis-players and here and there a golfer. There seemed to be an abundance of young men, mostly rather weedy-looking, but with one or two well-grown ones who should have been fighting. The names of some of them Jimson mentioned with awe. An unwholesome youth was Aronson, the great novelist; a sturdy, bristling fellow with a fierce moustache was Letchford, the celebrated leader-writer of the Critic. Several were pointed out to me as artists who had gone one better than anybody else, and a vast billowy creature was described as the leader of the new Orientalism in England. I noticed that these people, according to Jimson, were all 'great', and that they all dabbled in something 'new'. There were quantities of young women, too, most of them rather badly dressed and inclining to untidy hair. And there were several decent couples taking the air like house-holders of an evening all the world Over. Most of these last were Jimson's friends, to whom he introduced me. They were his own class - modest folk, who sought for a coloured background to their prosaic city lives and found it in this odd settlement.

At supper I was initiated into the peculiar merits of Biggleswick.

'It is one great laboratory of thought,' said Mrs Jimson. 'It is glorious to feel that you are living among the eager, vital people who are at the head of all the newest movements, and that the intellectual history of England is being made in our studies and gardens. The war to us seems a remote and secondary affair. As someone has said, the great fights of the world are all fought in the mind.'

A spasm of pain crossed her husband's face. 'I wish I could feel it far away. After all, Ursula, it is the sacrifice of the young that gives people like us leisure and peace to think. Our duty is to do the best which is permitted to us, but that duty is a poor thing compared with what our young soldiers are giving! I may be quite wrong about the war ... I know I can't argue with Letchford. But I will not pretend to a superiority I do not feel.'

I went to bed feeling that in Jimson I had struck a pretty sound fellow. As I lit the candles on my dressing-table I observed that the stack of silver which I had taken out of my pockets when I washed before supper was top-heavy. It had two big coins at the top and sixpences and shillings beneath. Now it is one of my oddities that ever since I was a small boy I have arranged my loose coins symmetrically, with the smallest uppermost. That made me observant and led me to notice a second point. The English classics on the top of the chest of drawers were not in the order I had left them. Izaak Walton had got to the left of Sir Thomas Browne, and the poet Burns was wedged disconsolately between two volumes of Hazlitt. Moreover a receipted bill which I had stuck in the Pilgrim's Progress to mark my place had been moved. Someone had been going through my belongings.

A moment's reflection convinced me that it couldn't have been

John Buchan

Mrs Jimson. She had no servant and did the housework herself, but my things had been untouched when I left the room before supper, for she had come to tidy up before I had gone downstairs. Someone had been here while we were at supper, and had examined elaborately everything I possessed. Happily I had little luggage, and no papers save the new books and a bill or two in the name of Cornelius Brand - The inquisitor, whoever he was, had found nothing ... The incident gave me a good deal of comfort. It had been hard to believe that any mystery could exist in this public place, where people lived brazenly in the open, and wore their hearts on their sleeves and proclaimed their opinions from the rooftops. Yet mystery there must be, or an inoffensive stranger with a kit-bag would not have received these strange attentions. I made a practice after that of sleeping with my watch below my pillow, for inside the case was Mary Lamington's label. Now began a period of pleasant idle receptiveness. Once a week it was my custom to go up to London for the day to receive letters and instructions, if any should come. I had moved from my chambers in Park Lane, which I leased under my proper name, to a small flat in Westminster taken in the name of Cornelius Brand. The letters addressed to Park Lane were forwarded to Sir Walter, who sent them round under cover to my new address. For the rest I used to spend my mornings reading in the garden, and I discovered for the first time what a pleasure was to be got from old books. They recalled and amplified that vision I had seen from the Cotswold ridge, the revelation of the priceless heritage which is England. I imbibed a mighty quantity of history, but especially I liked the writers, like Walton, who got at the very heart of the English countryside. Soon, too, I found the Pilgrim's Progress not a duty but a delight. I discovered new jewels daily in the honest old story, and my letters to Peter began to be as full of it as Peter's own epistles. I loved, also, the songs of the Elizabethans, for they reminded me of the girl who had sung to me in the June night.

In the afternoons I took my exercise in long tramps along the good dusty English roads. The country fell away from Biggleswick into a plain of wood and pasture-land, with low hills on the horizon. The Place was sown with villages, each with its green and pond and ancient church. Most, too, had inns, and there I had many a draught of cool nutty ale, for the inn at Biggleswick was a reformed place which sold nothing but washy cider. Often, tramping home in the dusk, I was so much in love with the land that I could have sung with the pure joy of it. And in the evening, after a bath, there would be supper, when a rather fagged Jimson struggled between sleep and hunger, and the lady, with an artistic mutch on her untidy head, talked ruthlessly of culture.

Bit by bit I edged my way into local society. The Jimsons were a great help, for they were popular and had a nodding acquaintance with most of the inhabitants. They regarded me as a meritorious aspirant towards a higher life, and I was paraded before their friends with the suggestion of a vivid, if Philistine, past. If I had any gift for writing, I would make a book about the inhabitants of Biggleswick. About half were respectable citizens who came there for country air and low rates, but even these had a touch of queerness and had picked up the jargon of the place. The younger men were mostly Government clerks or writers or artists. There were a few widows with flocks of daughters, and on the outskirts were several bigger houses - mostly houses which had been there before the garden city was planted. One of them was brand-new, a staring villa with sham-antique timbering, stuck on the top of a hill among raw gardens. It belonged to a man called Moxon Ivery, who was a kind of academic pacificist and a great god in the place. Another, a quiet Georgian manor house, was owned by a London publisher, an ardent Liberal whose particular branch of business compelled him to keep in touch with the new movements. I used to see him hurrying to the station swinging a little black bag and returning at night with the fish for dinner.

I soon got to know a surprising lot of people, and they were the rummiest birds you can imagine. For example, there were the Weekeses, three girls who lived with their mother in a house so artistic that you broke your head whichever way you turned in it. The son of the family was a conscientious objector who had refused to do any sort of work whatever, and had got quodded for his pains. They were immensely proud of him and used to relate his sufferings in Dartmoor with a gusto which I thought rather heartless. Art was their great subject, and I am afraid they found me pretty heavy going. It was their fashion never to admire anything that was obviously beautiful, like a sunset or a pretty woman, but to find surprising loveliness in things which I thought hideous. Also they talked a language that was beyond me. This kind of conversation used to happen. - miss WEEKES: 'Don't you admire Ursula Jimson?' SELF: 'Rather!' miss w.: 'She is so John-esque in her lines.' SELF: 'Exactly!' miss w.: 'And Tancred, too - he is so full of nuances.' SELF: 'Rather!' miss w.: 'He suggests one of Degousse's countrymen.' SELF: 'Exactly!'

They hadn't much use for books, except some Russian ones, and I acquired merit in their eyes for having read Leprous Souls. If you talked to them about that divine countryside, you found they didn't give a rap for it and had never been a mile beyond the village. But they admired greatly the sombre effect of a train going into Marylebone station on a rainy day.

But it was the men who interested me most. Aronson, the novelist, proved on acquaintance the worst kind of blighter. He considered himself a genius whom it was the duty of the country to support, and he sponged on his wretched relatives and anyone who would lend him money. He was always babbling about his sins, and pretty squalid they were. I should like to have flung him among a few good old-fashioned full-blooded sinners of my acquaintance; they would have scared him considerably. He told me that he sought 'reality' and 'life' and 'truth', but it was hard to see how he could know much about them, for he spent half the day in bed smoking cheap cigarettes, and the rest sunning himself in the admiration of half-witted girls. The creature was tuberculous in mind and body, and the only novel of his I read, pretty well turned my stomach. Mr Aronson's strong point was jokes about the war. If he heard of any acquaintance who had joined up or was even doing war work his merriment knew no bounds. My fingers used to itch to box the little wretch's ears.

Letchford was a different pair of shoes. He was some kind of a man, to begin with, and had an excellent brain and the worst manners conceivable. He contradicted everything you said, and looked out for an argument as other people look for their dinner. He was a double-engined, high-speed pacificist, because he was the kind of cantankerous fellow who must always be in a minority. if Britain had stood out of the war he would have been a raving militarist, but since she was in it he had got to find reasons why she was wrong. And jolly good reasons they were, too. I couldn't have met his arguments if I had wanted to, so I sat docilely at his feet. The world was all crooked for Letchford, and God had created him with two left hands. But the fellow had merits. He had a couple of jolly children whom he adored, and he would walk miles with me on a Sunday, and spout poetry about the beauty and greatness of England. He was forty-five; if he had been thirty and in my battalion I could have made a soldier out of him.

There were dozens more whose names I have forgotten, but they had one common characteristic. They were puffed up with spiritual pride, and I used to amuse myself with finding their originals in the Pilgrim's Progress. When I tried to judge them by the standard of old Peter, they fell woefully short. They shut out the war from their lives, some out of funk, some out of pure levity of mind, and some because they were really convinced that the thing was all wrong. I think I grew rather popular in my role of the seeker after truth, the honest colonial who was against the war by instinct and was looking for instruction in the matter. They regarded me as a convert from an alien world of action which they secretly dreaded, though they affected to despise it. Anyhow they talked to me very freely, and before long I had all the pacifist arguments by heart. I made out that there were three schools. One objected to war altogether, and this had few adherents except Aronson and Weekes, C.O., now languishing in Dartmoor. The second thought that the Allies' cause was tainted, and that Britain had contributed as much as Germany to the catastrophe. This included all the adherents of the L.D.A. - or League of Democrats against Aggression - a very proud body. The third and much the largest, which embraced everybody else, held that we had fought long enough and that the business could now be settled by negotiation, since Germany had learned her lesson. I was myself a modest member of the last school, but I was gradually working my way up to the second, and I hoped with luck to qualify for the first. My acquaintances approved my progress. Letchford said I had a core of fanaticism in my slow nature, and that I would end by waving the red flag.

Spiritual pride and vanity, as I have said, were at the bottom of most of them, and, try as I might, I could find nothing very dangerous in it all. This vexed me, for I began to wonder if the mission which I had embarked on so solemnly were not going to be a fiasco. Sometimes they worried me beyond endurance. When the news of Messines came nobody took the slightest interest, while I was aching to tooth every detail of the great fight. And when they talked on military affairs, as Letchford and others did sometimes, it was difficult to keep from sending them all to the devil, for their amateur cocksureness would have riled job. One had got to batten down the recollection of our fellows out there who were sweating blood to keep these fools snug. Yet I found it impossible to be angry with them for long, they were so babyishly innocent. Indeed, I couldn't help liking them, and finding a sort of quality in them. I had spent three years among soldiers, and the British regular, great follow that he is, has his faults. His discipline makes him in a funk of red-tape and any kind of superior authority. Now these people were quite honest and in a perverted way courageous. Letchford was, at any rate. I could no more have done what he did and got hunted off platforms by the crowd and hooted at by women in the streets than I could have written his leading articles.

All the same I was rather low about my job. Barring the episode of the ransacking of my effects the first night, I had not a suspicion of a clue or a hint of any mystery. The place and the people were as open and bright as a Y.M.C.A. hut. But one day I got a solid wad of comfort. In a corner of Letchford's paper, the Critic, I found a letter which was one of the steepest pieces of invective I had ever met with. The writer gave tongue like a beagle pup about the prostitution, as he called it, of American republicanism to the vices of European aristocracies. He declared that Senator La Follette was a much-misunderstood patriot, seeing that he alone spoke for the toiling millions who had no other friend. He was mad with President Wilson, and he prophesied a great awakening when Uncle Sam got up against John Bull in Europe and found out the kind of standpatter he was. The letter was signed 'John S. Blenkiron' and dated 'London, 3 July-'

The thought that Blenkiron was in England put a new complexion on my business. I reckoned I would see him soon, for he wasn't the man to stand still in his tracks. He had taken up the role he had played before he left in December 1915, and very right too, for not more than half a dozen people knew of the Erzerum affair, and to the British public he was only the man who had been fired out of the Savoy for talking treason. I had felt a bit lonely before, but now somewhere within the four corners of the island the best companion God ever made was writing nonsense with his tongue in his old cheek.

There was an institution in Biggleswick which deserves mention. On the south of the common, near the station, stood a red-brick building called the Moot Hall, which was a kind of church for the very undevout population. Undevout in the ordinary sense, I mean, for I had already counted twenty-seven varieties of religious conviction, including three Buddhists, a Celestial Hierarch, five Latter-day Saints, and about ten varieties of Mystic whose names I could never remember. The hall had been the gift of the publisher I have spoken of, and twice a week it was used for lectures and debates. The place was managed by a committee and was surprisingly popular, for it gave all the bubbling intellects a chance of airing their views. When you asked where somebody was and were told he was 'at Moot,' the answer was spoken in the respectful tone in which you would mention a sacrament.

I went there regularly and got my mind broadened to cracking point. We had all the stars of the New Movements. We had Doctor Chirk, who lectured on 'God', which, as far as I could make out, was a new name he had invented for himself. There was a woman, a terrible woman, who had come back from Russia with what she called a 'message of healing'. And to my joy, one night there was a great buck nigger who had a lot to say about 'Africa for the Africans'. I had a few words with him in Sesutu afterwards, and rather spoiled his visit. Some of the people were extraordinarily good, especially one jolly old fellow who talked about English folk songs and dances, and wanted us to set up a Maypole. In the debates which generally followed I began to join, very coyly at first, but presently with some confidence. If my time at Biggleswick did nothing else it taught me to argue on my feet.

The first big effort I made was on a full-dress occasion, when Launcelot Wake came down to speak. Mr Ivery was in the chair - the first I had seen of him - a plump middle-aged man, with a colourless face and nondescript features. I was not interested in him till he began to talk, and then I sat bolt upright and took notice. For he was the genuine silver-tongue, the sentences flowing from his mouth as smooth as butter and as neatly dovetailed as a parquet floor. He had a sort of man-of-the-world manner, treating his opponents with condescending geniality, deprecating all passion and exaggeration and making you feel that his urbane statement must be right, for if he had wanted he could have put the case so much higher. I watched him, fascinated, studying his face carefully; and the thing that struck me was that there was nothing in it - nothing, that is to say, to lay hold on. It was simply nondescript, so almightily commonplace that that very fact made it rather remarkable.

Wake was speaking of the revelations of the Sukhomhnov trial in Russia, which showed that Germany had not been responsible for the war. He was jolly good at the job, and put as clear an argument as a first-class lawyer. I had been sweating away at the subject and had all the ordinary case at my fingers' ends, so when I got a chance of speaking I gave them a long harangue, with some good quotations I had cribbed out of the Vossische Zeitung, which Letchford lent me. I felt it was up to me to be extra violent, for I wanted to establish my character with Wake, seeing that he was a friend of Mary and Mary would know that I was playing the game. I got tremendously applauded, far more than the chief speaker, and after the meeting Wake came up to me with his hot eyes, and wrung my hand. 'You're coming on well, Brand,' he said, and then he introduced me to Mr Ivery. 'Here's a second and a better Smuts,' he said.

Ivery made me walk a bit of the road home with him. 'I am struck by your grip on these difficult problems, Mr Brand,' he told me. 'There is much I can tell you, and you may be of great value to our cause.' He asked me a lot of questions about my past, which I answered with easy mendacity. Before we parted he made me promise to come one night to supper.

Next day I got a glimpse of Mary, and to my vexation she cut me dead. She was walking with a flock of bare-headed girls, all chattering hard, and though she saw me quite plainly she turned away her eyes. I had been waiting for my cue, so I did not lift my hat, but passed on as if we were strangers. I reckoned it was part of the game, but that trifling thing annoyed me, and I spent a morose evening.

The following day I saw her again, this time talking sedately with Mr Ivery, and dressed in a very pretty summer gown, and a broad-brimmed straw hat with flowers in it. This time she stopped with a bright smile and held out her hand. 'Mr Brand, isn't it?' she asked with a pretty hesitation. And then, turning to her companion - 'This is Mr Brand. He stayed with us last month in Gloucestershire.'

Mr Ivery announced that he and I were already acquainted. Seen in broad daylight he was a very personable fellow, somewhere between forty-five and fifty, with a middle-aged figure and a curiously young face. I noticed that there were hardly any lines on it, and it was rather that of a very wise child than that of a man. He had a pleasant smile which made his jaw and cheeks expand like indiarubber. 'You are coming to sup with me, Mr Brand,' he cried after me. 'On Tuesday after Moot. I have already written.' He whisked Mary away from me, and I had to content myself with contemplating her figure till it disappeared round a bend of the road.

Next day in London I found a letter from Peter. He had been very solemn of late, and very reminiscent of old days now that he concluded his active life was over. But this time he was in a different mood. 'I think,' he wrote, 'that you and I will meet again soon, my old friend. Do you remember when we went after the big black-maned lion in the Rooirand and couldn't get on his track, and then one morning we woke up and said we would get him today? - and we did, but he very near got you first. I've had a feel these last days that we're both going down into the Valley to meet with Apolyon, and that the devil will give us a bad time, but anyhow we'll be together.'

I had the same kind of feel myself, though I didn't see how Peter and I were going to meet, unless I went out to the Front again and got put in the bag and sent to the same Boche prison. But I had an instinct that my time in Biggleswick was drawing to a close, and that presently I would be in rougher quarters. I felt quite affectionate towards the place, and took all my favourite walks, and drank my own health in the brew of the village inns, with a consciousness of saying goodbye. Also I made haste to finish my English classics, for I concluded I wouldn't have much time in the future for miscellaneous reading.

The Tuesday came, and in the evening I set out rather late for the Moot Hall, for I had been getting into decent clothes after a long, hot stride. When I reached the place it was pretty well packed, and I could only find a seat on the back benches. There on the platform was Ivery, and beside him sat a figure that thrilled every inch of me with affection and a wild anticipation. 'I have now the privilege,' said the chairman, 'of introducing to you the speaker whom we so warmly welcome, our fearless and indefatigable American friend, Mr Blenkiron.'

It was the old Blenkiron, but almightily changed. His stoutness had gone, and he was as lean as Abraham Lincoln. Instead of a puffy face, his cheek-bones and jaw stood out hard and sharp, and in place of his former pasty colour his complexion had the clear glow of health. I saw now that he was a splendid figure of a man, and when he got to his feet every movement had the suppleness of an athlete in training. In that moment I realized that my serious business had now begun. My senses suddenly seemed quicker, my nerves tenser, my brain more active. The big game had started, and he and I were playing it together.

I watched him with strained attention. It was a funny speech, stuffed with extravagance and vehemence, not very well argued and terribly discursive. His main point was that Germany was now in a fine democratic mood and might well be admitted into a brotherly partnership - that indeed she had never been in any other mood, but had been forced into violence by the plots of her enemies. Much of it, I should have thought, was in stark defiance of the Defence of the Realm Acts, but if any wise Scotland Yard officer had listened to it he would probably have considered it harmless because of its contradictions. It was full of a fierce earnestness, and it was full of humour - long-drawn American metaphors at which that most critical audience roared with laughter. But it was not the kind of thing that they were accustomed to, and I could fancy what Wake would have said of it. The conviction grew upon me that Blenkiron was deliberately trying to prove himself an honest idiot. If so, it was a huge success. He produced on one the impression of the type of sentimental revolutionary who ruthlessly knifes his opponent and then weeps and prays over his tomb.

Just at the end he seemed to pull himself together and to try a little argument. He made a great point of the Austrian socialists going to Stockholm, going freely and with their Government's assent, from a country which its critics called an autocracy, while the democratic western peoples held back. 'I admit I haven't any real water-tight proof,' he said, 'but I will bet my bottom dollar that the influence which moved the Austrian Government to allow this embassy of freedom was the influence of Germany herself. And that is the land from which the Allied Pharisees draw in their skirts lest their garments be defiled!'

He sat down amid a good deal of applause, for his audience had not been bored, though I could see that some of them thought his praise of Germany a bit steep. It was all right in Biggleswick to prove Britain in the wrong, but it was a slightly different thing to extol the enemy. I was puzzled about his last point, for it was not of a piece with the rest of his discourse, and I was trying to guess at his purpose. The chairman referred to it in his concluding remarks. 'I am in a position,' he said, 'to bear out all that the lecturer has said. I can go further. I can assure him on the best authority that his surmise is correct, and that Vienna's decision to send delegates to Stockholm was largely dictated by representations from Berlin. I am given to understand that the fact has in the last few days been admitted in the Austrian Press.'

A vote of thanks was carried, and then I found myself shaking hands with Ivery while Blenkiron stood a yard off, talking to one of the Misses Weekes. The next moment I was being introduced.

'Mr Brand, very pleased to meet you,' said the voice I knew so well. 'Mr Ivery has been telling me about you, and I guess we've got something to say to each other. We're both from noo countries, and we've got to teach the old nations a little horse-sense.'

Mr Ivery's car - the only one left in the neighbourhood - carried us to his villa, and presently we were seated in a brightly-lit dining-room. It was not a pretty house, but it had the luxury of an expensive hotel, and the supper we had was as good as any London restaurant. Gone were the old days of fish and toast and boiled milk. Blenkiron squared his shoulders and showed himself a noble trencherman.

'A year ago,' he told our host, 'I was the meanest kind of dyspeptic. I had the love of righteousness in my heart, but I had the devil in my stomach. Then I heard stories about the Robson Brothers, the star surgeons way out west in White Springs, Nebraska. They were reckoned the neatest hands in the world at carving up a man and removing devilments from his intestines. Now, sir, I've always fought pretty shy of surgeons, for I considered that our Maker never intended His handiwork to be reconstructed like a bankrupt Dago railway. But by that time I was feeling so almighty wretched that I could have paid a man to put a bullet through my head. "There's no other way," I said to myself. "Either you forget your religion and your miserable cowardice and get cut up, or it's you for the Golden Shore." So I set my teeth and journeyed to White Springs, and the Brothers had a look at my duodenum. They saw that the darned thing wouldn't do, so they sidetracked it and made a noo route for my noo-trition traffic. It was the cunningest piece of surgery since the Lord took a rib out of the side of our First Parent. They've got a mighty fine way of charging, too, for they take five per cent of a man's income, and it's all one to them whether he's a Meat King or a clerk on twenty dollars a week. I can tell you I took some trouble to be a very rich man last year.'

All through the meal I sat in a kind of stupor. I was trying to assimilate the new Blenkiron, and drinking in the comfort of his heavenly drawl, and I was puzzling my head about Ivery. I had a ridiculous notion that I had seen him before, but, delve as I might into my memory, I couldn't place him. He was the incarnation of the commonplace, a comfortable middle-class sentimentalist, who patronized pacificism out of vanity, but was very careful not to dip his hands too far. He was always damping down Blenkiron's volcanic utterances. 'Of course, as you know, the other side have an argument which I find rather hard to meet ...' 'I can sympathize with patriotism, and even with jingoism, in certain moods, but I always come back to this difficulty.' 'Our opponents are not ill-meaning so much as ill-judging,' - these were the sort of sentences he kept throwing in. And he was full of quotations from private conversations he had had with every sort of person - including members of the Government. I remember that he expressed great admiration for Mr Balfour.

Of all that talk, I only recalled one thing clearly, and I recalled it because Blenkiron seemed to collect his wits and try to argue, just as he had done at the end of his lecture. He was speaking about a story he had heard from someone, who had heard it from someone else, that Austria in the last week of July 1914 had accepted Russia's proposal to hold her hand and negotiate, and that the Kaiser had sent a message to the Tsar saying he agreed. According to his story this telegram had been received in Petrograd, and had been re-written, like Bismarck's Ems telegram, before it reached the Emperor. He expressed his disbelief in the yarn. 'I reckon if it had been true,' he said, 'we'd have had the right text out long ago. They'd have kept a copy in Berlin. All the same I did hear a sort of rumour that some kind of message of that sort was published in a German paper.'

Mr Ivery looked wise. 'You are right,' he said. 'I happen to know that it has been published. You will find it in the Wieser Zeitung.'

'You don't say?' he said admiringly. 'I wish I could read the old tombstone language. But if I could they wouldn't let me have the papers.'

'Oh yes they would.' Mr Ivery laughed pleasantly. 'England has still a good share of freedom. Any respectable person can get a permit to import the enemy press. I'm not considered quite respectable, for the authorities have a narrow definition of patriotism, but happily I have respectable friends.'

Blenkiron was staying the night, and I took my leave as the clock struck twelve. They both came into the hall to see me off, and, as I was helping myself to a drink, and my host was looking for my hat and stick, I suddenly heard Blenkiron's whisper in my ear. 'London ... the day after tomorrow,' he said. Then he took a formal farewell. 'Mr Brand, it's been an honour for me, as an American citizen, to make your acquaintance, sir. I will consider myself fortunate if we have an early reunion. I am stopping at Claridge's Ho-tel, and I hope to be privileged to receive you there.'

CHAPTER THREE

THE REFLECTIONS OF A CURED DYSPEPTIC

Thirty-five hours later I found myself in my rooms in Westminster. I thought there might be a message for me there, for I didn't propose to go and call openly on Blenkiron at Claridge's till I had his instructions. But there was no message - only a line from Peter, saying he had hopes of being sent to Switzerland. That made me realize that he must be pretty badly broken up.

Presently the telephone bell rang. It was Blenkiron who spoke. 'Go down and have a talk with your brokers about the War Loan. Arrive there about twelve o'clock and don't go upstairs till you have met a friend. You'd better have a quick luncheon at your club, and then come to Traill's bookshop in the Haymarket at two. You can get back to Biggleswick by the 5.16.'

I did as I was bid, and twenty minutes later, having travelled by Underground, for I couldn't raise a taxi, I approached the block of chambers in Leadenhall Street where dwelt the respected firm who managed my investments. It was still a few minutes before noon, and as I slowed down a familiar figure came out of the bank next door.

Ivery beamed recognition. 'Up for the day, Mr Brand?' he asked. 'I have to see my brokers,' I said, 'read the South African papers in my club, and get back by the 5.16. Any chance of your company?'

'Why, yes - that's my train. Au revoir. We meet at the station.'
He bustled off, looking very smart with his neat clothes and a
rose in his button-hole.

I lunched impatiently, and at two was turning over some new
books in Traill's shop with an eye on the street-door behind
me. It seemed a public place for an assignation. I had begun to
dip into a big illustrated book on flower-gardens when an
assistant came up. 'The manager's compliments, sir, and he
thinks there are some old works of travel upstairs that might
interest you.' I followed him obediently to an upper floor lined
with every kind of volume and with tables littered with maps
and engravings. 'This way, sir,' he said, and opened a door in
the wall concealed by bogus book-backs. I found myself in a
little study, and Blenkiron sitting in an armchair smoking.

He got up and seized both my hands. 'Why, Dick, this is
better than good noos. I've heard all about your exploits since
we parted a year ago on the wharf at Liverpool. We've both
been busy on our own jobs, and there was no way of keeping
you wise about my doings, for after I thought I was cured I got
worse than hell inside, and, as I told you, had to get the
doctor-men to dig into me. After that I was playing a pretty
dark game, and had to get down and out of decent society.
But, holy Mike! I'm a new man. I used to do my work with a
sick heart and a taste in my mouth like a graveyard, and now I
can eat and drink what I like and frolic round like a colt. I
wake up every morning whistling and thank the good God
that I'm alive, It was a bad day for Kaiser when I got on the
cars for White Springs.'

'This is a rum place to meet,' I said, 'and you brought me by a
roundabout road.'

He grinned and offered me a cigar.

'There were reasons. It don't do for you and me to advertise our acquaintance in the street. As for the shop, I've owned it for five years. I've a taste for good reading, though you wouldn't think it, and it tickles me to hand it out across the counter ... First, I want to hear about Biggleswick.'

'There isn't a great deal to it. A lot of ignorance, a large slice of vanity, and a pinch or two of wrong-headed honesty - these are the ingredients of the pie. Not much real harm in it. There's one or two dirty literary gents who should be in a navvies' battalion, but they're about as dangerous as yellow Kaffir dogs. I've learned a lot and got all the arguments by heart, but you might plant a Biggleswick in every shire and it wouldn't help the Boche. I can see where the danger lies all the same. These fellows talked academic anarchism, but the genuine article is somewhere about and to find it you've got to look in the big industrial districts. We had faint echoes of it in Biggleswick. I mean that the really dangerous fellows are those who want to close up the war at once and so get on with their blessed class war, which cuts across nationalities. As for being spies and that sort of thing, the Biggleswick lads are too callow.'

'Yes,' said Blenkiron reflectively. 'They haven't got as much sense as God gave to geese. You're sure you didn't hit against any heavier metal?'

'Yes. There's a man called Launcelot Wake, who came down to speak once. I had met him before. He has the makings of a fanatic, and he's the more dangerous because you can see his conscience is uneasy. I can fancy him bombing a Prime Minister merely to quiet his own doubts.'

'So,' he said. 'Nobody else?'

I reflected. 'There's Mr Ivery, but you know him better than I. I shouldn't put much on him, but I'm not precisely certain, for I never had a chance of getting to know him.'

'Ivery,' said Blenkiron in surprise. 'He has a hobby for half-baked youth, just as another rich man might fancy orchids or fast trotters. You sure can place him right enough.'

'I dare say. Only I don't know enough to be positive.'

He sucked at his cigar for a minute or so. 'I guess, Dick, if I told you all I've been doing since I reached these shores you would call me a ro-mancer. I've been way down among the toilers. I did a spell as unskilled dilooted labour in the Barrow shipyards. I was barman in a ho-tel on the Portsmouth Road, and I put in a black month driving a taxicab in the city of London. For a while I was the accredited correspondent of the Noo York Sentinel and used to go with the rest of the bunch to the pow-wows of under-secretaries of State and War Office generals. They censored my stuff so cruel that the paper fired me. Then I went on a walking-tour round England and sat for a fortnight in a little farm in Suffolk. By and by I came back to Claridge's and this bookshop, for I had learned most of what I wanted.

'I had learned,' he went on, turning his curious, full, ruminating eyes on me, 'that the British working-man is about the soundest piece of humanity on God's earth. He grumbles a bit and jibs a bit when he thinks the Government are giving him a crooked deal, but he's gotten the patience of job and the sand of a gamecock. And he's gotten humour too, that tickles me to death. There's not much trouble in that quarter for it's he and his kind that's beating the Hun ... But I picked up a thing or two besides that.'

He leaned forward and tapped me on the knee. 'I reverence the British Intelligence Service. Flies don't settle on it to any considerable extent. It's got a mighty fine mesh, but there's one hole in that mesh, and it's our job to mend it. There's a high-powered brain in the game against us. I struck it a couple of years ago when I was hunting Dumba and Albert, and I thought it was in Noo York, but it wasn't. I struck its working again at home last year and located its head office in Europe. So I tried Switzerland and Holland, but only bits of it were there. The centre of the web where the old spider sits is right here in England, and for six months I've been shadowing that spider. There's a gang to help, a big gang, and a clever gang, and partly an innocent gang. But there's only one brain, and it's to match that that the Robson Brothers settled my duodenum.'

I was listening with a quickened pulse, for now at last I was getting to business.

'What is he - international socialist, or anarchist, or what?' I asked.

'Pure-blooded Boche agent, but the biggest-sized brand in the catalogue - bigger than Steinmeier or old Bismarck's Staubier. Thank God I've got him located ... I must put you wise about some things.'

He lay back in his rubbed leather armchair and yarned for twenty minutes. He told me how at the beginning of the war Scotland Yard had had a pretty complete register of enemy spies, and without making any fuss had just tidied them away. After that, the covey having been broken up, it was a question of picking off stray birds. That had taken some doing. There had been all kinds of inflammatory stuff around, Red Masons and international anarchists, and, worst of all, international finance-touts, but they had mostly been ordinary cranks and rogues, the tools of the Boche agents rather than agents themselves. However, by the middle of 1915 most of the stragglers had been gathered in. But there remained loose ends, and towards the close of last year somebody was very busy combining these ends into a net. Funny cases cropped up of the leakage of vital information. They began to be bad about October 1916, when the Hun submarines started on a special racket. The enemy suddenly appeared possessed of a knowledge which we thought to be shared only by half a dozen officers. Blenkiron said he was not surprised at the leakage, for there's always a lot of people who hear things they oughtn't to. What surprised him was that it got so quickly to the enemy.

Then after last February, when the Hun submarines went in for frightfulness on a big scale, the thing grew desperate. Leakages occurred every week, and the business was managed by people who knew their way about, for they avoided all the traps set for them, and when bogus news was released on purpose, they never sent it. A convoy which had been kept a deadly secret would be attacked at the one place where it was helpless. A carefully prepared defensive plan would be checkmated before it could be tried. Blenkiron said that there was no evidence that a single brain was behind it all, for there was no similarity in the cases, but he had a strong impression all the time that it was the work of one man. We managed to close some of the bolt-holes, but we couldn't put our hands near the big ones. 'By this time,' said he, 'I reckoned I was about ready to change my methods. I had been working by what the highbrows call induction, trying to argue up from the deeds to the doer. Now I tried a new lay, which was to calculate down from the doer to the deeds. They call it deduction. I opined that somewhere in this island was a gentleman whom we will call Mr X, and that, pursuing the line of business he did, he must have certain characteristics. I considered very carefully just what sort of personage he must be. I had noticed that his device was apparently the Double Bluff. That is to say, when he had two courses open to him, A and B, he pretended he was going to take B, and so got us guessing that he would try A. Then he took B after all. So I reckoned that his camouflage must correspond to this little idiosyncrasy. Being a Boche agent, he wouldn't pretend to be a hearty patriot, an honest old blood-and-bones Tory. That would be only the Single Bluff. I considered that he would be a pacifist, cunning enough just to keep inside the law, but with the eyes of the police on him. He would write books which would not be allowed to be exported. He would get himself disliked in the popular papers, but all the mugwumps would admire his moral courage. I drew a mighty fine picture to myself of just the man I expected to find. Then I started out to look for him.'

Blenkiron's face took on the air of a disappointed child. 'It was no good. I kept barking up the wrong tree and wore myself out playing the sleuth on white-souled innocents.'

'But you've found him all right,' I cried, a sudden suspicion leaping into my brain.

'He's found,' he said sadly, 'but the credit does not belong to John S. Blenkiron. That child merely muddied the pond. The big fish was left for a young lady to hook.'

'I know,' I cried excitedly. 'Her name is Miss Mary Lamington.'

He shook a disapproving head. 'You've guessed right, my son, but you've forgotten your manners. This is a rough business and we won't bring in the name of a gently reared and pure-minded young girl. If we speak to her at all we call her by a pet name out of the Pilgrim's Progress ... Anyhow she hooked the fish, though he isn't landed. D'you see any light?'

'Ivery,' I gasped.

'Yes. Ivery. Nothing much to look at, you say. A common, middle-aged, pie-faced, golf-playing high-brow, that you wouldn't keep out of a Sunday school. A touch of the drummer, too, to show he has no dealings with your effete aristocracy. A languishing silver-tongue that adores the sound of his own voice. As mild, you'd say, as curds and cream.'

Blenkiron got out of his chair and stood above me. 'I tell you, Dick, that man makes my spine cold. He hasn't a drop of good red blood in him. The dirtiest apache is a Christian gentleman compared to Moxon Ivery. He's as cruel as a snake and as deep as hell. But, by God, he's got a brain below his hat. He's hooked and we're playing him, but Lord knows if he'll ever be landed!'

'Why on earth don't you put him away?' I asked.

'We haven't the proof - legal proof, I mean; though there's buckets of the other kind. I could put up a morally certain case, but he'd beat me in a court of law. And half a hundred sheep would get up in Parliament and bleat about persecution. He has a graft with every collection of cranks in England, and with all the geese that cackle about the liberty of the individual when the Boche is ranging about to enslave the world. No, sir, that's too dangerous a game! Besides, I've a better in hand, Moxon Ivery is the best-accredited member of this State. His dossier is the completest thing outside the Recording Angel's little note-book. We've taken up his references in every corner of the globe and they're all as right as Morgan's balance sheet. From these it appears he's been a high-toned citizen ever since he was in short-clothes. He was raised in Norfolk, and there are people living who remember his father. He was educated at Melton School and his name's in the register. He was in business in Valparaiso, and there's enough evidence to write three volumes of his innocent life there. Then he came home with a modest competence two years before the war, and has been in the public eye ever since. He was Liberal candidate for a London constitooency and he has decorated the board of every institootion formed for the amelioration of mankind. He's got enough alibis to choke a boa constrictor, and they're water-tight and copper-bottomed, and they're mostly damned lies ... But you can't beat him at that stunt. The man's the superbest actor that ever walked the earth. You can see it in his face. It isn't a face, it's a mask. He could make himself look like Shakespeare or Julius Caesar or Billy Sunday or Brigadier-General Richard Hannay if he wanted to. He hasn't got any personality either - he's got fifty, and there's no one he could call his own. I reckon when the devil gets the handling of him at last he'll have to put sand on his claws to keep him from slipping through.'

Blenkiron was settled in his chair again, with one leg hoisted over the side.

'We've closed a fair number of his channels in the last few months. No, he don't suspect me. The world knows nothing of its greatest men, and to him I'm only a Yankee peace-crank, who gives big subscriptions to loony societies and will travel a hundred miles to let off steam before any kind of audience. He's been to see me at Claridge's and I've arranged that he shall know all my record. A darned bad record it is too, for two years ago I was violent pro-British before I found salvation and was requested to leave England. When I was home last I was officially anti-war, when I wasn't stretched upon a bed of pain. Mr Moxon Ivery don't take any stock in John S. Blenkiron as a serious proposition. And while I've been here I've been so low down in the social scale and working in so many devious ways that he can't connect me up ... As I was saying, we've cut most of his wires, but the biggest we haven't got at. He's still sending stuff out, and mighty compromising stuff it is. Now listen close, Dick, for we're coming near your own business.'

It appeared that Blenkiron had reason to suspect that the channel still open had something to do with the North. He couldn't get closer than that, till he heard from his people that a certain Abel Gresson had turned up in Glasgow from the States. This Gresson he discovered was the same as one Wrankester, who as a leader of the Industrial Workers of the World had been mixed up in some ugly cases of sabotage in Colorado. He kept his news to himself, for he didn't want the police to interfere, but he had his own lot get into touch with Gresson and shadow him closely. The man was very discreet but very mysterious, and he would disappear for a week at a time, leaving no trace. For some unknown reason - he couldn't explain why - Blenkiron had arrived at the conclusion that Gresson was in touch with Ivery, so he made experiments to prove it.

'I wanted various cross-bearings to make certain, and I got them the night before last. My visit to Biggleswick was good business.'

'I don't know what they meant,' I said, 'but I know where they came in. One was in your speech when you spoke of the

Austrian socialists, and Ivery took you up about them. The other was after supper when he quoted the Wieser Zeitung.'

'You're no fool, Dick,' he said, with his slow smile. 'You've hit the mark first shot. You know me and you could follow my process of thought in those remarks. Ivery, not knowing me so well, and having his head full of just that sort of argument, saw nothing unusual. Those bits of noos were pumped into Gresson that he might pass them on. And he did pass them on - to Ivery. They completed my chain.'

'But they were commonplace enough things which he might have guessed for himself.'

'No, they weren't. They were the nicest tit-bits of political noos which all the cranks have been reaching after.'

'Anyhow, they were quotations from German papers. He might have had the papers themselves earlier than you thought.'

'Wrong again. The paragraph never appeared in the Wieser Zeitung. But we faked up a torn bit of that noospaper, and a very pretty bit of forgery it was, and Gresson, who's a kind of a scholar, was allowed to have it. He passed it on. Ivery showed it me two nights ago. Nothing like it ever sullied the columns of Boche journalism. No, it was a perfectly final proof ... Now, Dick, it's up to you to get after Gresson.'

'Right,' I said. 'I'm jolly glad I'm to start work again. I'm getting fat from lack of exercise. I suppose you want me to catch Gresson out in some piece of blackguardism and have him and Ivery snugly put away.'

'I don't want anything of the kind,' he said very slowly and distinctly. 'You've got to attend very close to your instructions, I cherish these two beauties as if they were my own white-headed boys. I wouldn't for the world interfere with their comfort and liberty. I want them to go on corresponding with their friends. I want to give them every facility.'

He burst out laughing at my mystified face.

'See here, Dick. How do we want to treat the Boche? Why, to fill him up with all the cunningest lies and get him to act on them. Now here is Moxon Ivery, who has always given them good information. They trust him absolutely, and we would be fools to spoil their confidence. Only, if we can find out Moxon's methods, we can arrange to use them ourselves and send noos in his name which isn't quite so genooine. Every word he dispatches goes straight to the Grand High Secret General Staff, and old Hindenburg and Ludendorff put towels round their heads and cipher it out. We want to encourage them to go on doing it. We'll arrange to send true stuff that don't matter, so as they'll continue to trust him, and a few selected falsehoods that'll matter like hell. It's a game you can't play for ever, but with luck I propose to play it long enough to confuse Fritz's little plans.'

His face became serious and wore the air that our corps commander used to have at the big pow-wow before a push.

'I'm not going to give you instructions, for you're man enough to make your own. But I can give you the general hang of the situation. You tell Ivery you're going North to inquire into industrial disputes at first hand. That will seem to him natural and in line with your recent behaviour. He'll tell his people that you're a guileless colonial who feels disgruntled with Britain, and may come in useful. You'll go to a man of mine in Glasgow, a red-hot agitator who chooses that way of doing his bit for his country. It's a darned hard way and darned dangerous. Through him you'll get in touch with Gresson, and you'll keep alongside that bright citizen. Find out what he is doing, and get a chance of following him. He must never suspect you, and for that purpose you must be very near the edge of the law yourself. You go up there as an unabashed pacifist and you'll live with folk that will turn your stomach. Maybe you'll have to break some of these two-cent rules the

British Government have invented to defend the realm, and it's up to you not to get caught out ... Remember, you'll get no help from me. you've got to wise up about Gresson with the whole forces of the British State arrayed officially against you. I guess it's a steep proposition, but you're man enough to make good.'

As we shook hands, he added a last word. 'You must take your own time, but it's not a case for slouching. Every day that passes Ivery is sending out the worst kind of poison. The Boche is blowing up for a big campaign in the field, and a big effort to shake the nerve and confuse the judgement of our civilians. The whole earth's war-weary, and we've about reached the danger-point. There's pretty big stakes hang on you, Dick, for things are getting mighty delicate.'

I purchased a new novel in the shop and reached St Pancras in time to have a cup of tea at the buffet. Ivery was at the bookstall buying an evening paper. When we got into the carriage he seized my Punch and kept laughing and calling my attention to the pictures. As I looked at him, I thought that he made a perfect picture of the citizen turned countryman, going back of an evening to his innocent home. Everything was right - his neat tweeds, his light spats, his spotted neckcloth, and his Aquascutum.

Not that I dared look at him much. What I had learned made me eager to search his face, but I did not dare show any increased interest. I had always been a little off-hand with him, for I had never much liked him, so I had to keep on the same manner. He was as merry as a grig, full of chat and very friendly and amusing. I remember he picked up the book I had brought off that morning to read in the train - the second volume of Hazlitt's Essays, the last of my English classics - and discoursed so wisely about books that I wished I had spent more time in his company at Biggleswick.

'Hazlitt was the academic Radical of his day,' he said. 'He is always lashing himself into a state of theoretical fury over abuses he has never encountered in person. Men who are up against the real thing save their breath for action.'

That gave me my cue to tell him about my journey to the North. I said I had learned a lot in Biggleswick, but I wanted to see industrial life at close quarters. 'Otherwise I might become like Hazlitt,' I said.

He was very interested and encouraging. 'That's the right way to set about it,' he said. 'Where were you thinking of going?'

I told him that I had half thought of Barrow, but decided to try Glasgow, since the Clyde seemed to be a warm corner.

'Right,' he said. 'I only wish I was coming with you. It'll take you a little while to understand the language. You'll find a good deal of senseless bellicosity among the workmen, for they've got parrot-cries about the war as they used to have parrot-cries about their labour politics. But there's plenty of shrewd brains and sound hearts too. You must write and tell me your conclusions.'

It was a warm evening and he dozed the last part of the journey. I looked at him and wished I could see into the mind at the back of that mask-like face. I counted for nothing in his eyes, not even enough for him to want to make me a tool, and I was setting out to try to make a tool of him. It sounded a forlorn enterprise. And all the while I was puzzled with a persistent sense of recognition. I told myself it was idiocy, for a man with a face like that must have hints of resemblance to a thousand people. But the idea kept nagging at me till we reached our destination.

As we emerged from the station into the golden evening I saw Mary Lamington again. She was with one of the Weekes girls, and after the Biggleswick fashion was bareheaded, so that the sun glinted from her hair. Ivery swept his hat off and made her a pretty speech, while I faced her steady eyes with the expressionlessness of the stage conspirator.

'A charming child,' he observed as we passed on. 'Not without a touch of seriousness, too, which may yet be touched to noble issues.'

I considered, as I made my way to my final supper with the Jimsons, that the said child was likely to prove a sufficiently serious business for Mr Moxon Ivery before the game was out.

John Buchan

CHAPTER FOUR

ANDREW AMOS

I took the train three days later from King's Cross to Edinburgh. I went to the Pentland Hotel in Princes Street and left there a suit-case containing some clean linen and a change of clothes. I had been thinking the thing out, and had come to the conclusion that I must have a base somewhere and a fresh outfit. Then in well-worn tweeds and with no more luggage than a small trench kit-bag, I descended upon the city of Glasgow.

I walked from the station to the address which Blenkiron had given me. It was a hot summer evening, and the streets were filled with bareheaded women and weary-looking artisans. As I made my way down the Dumbarton Road I was amazed at the number of able-bodied fellows about, considering that you couldn't stir a mile on any British front without bumping up against a Glasgow battalion. Then I realized that there were such things as munitions and ships, and I wondered no more.

A stout and dishevelled lady at a close-mouth directed me to Mr Amos's dwelling. 'Twa stairs up. Andra will be in noo, havin' his tea. He's no yin for overtime. He's generally hame on the chap of six.' I ascended the stairs with a sinking heart, for like all South Africans I have a horror of dirt. The place was pretty filthy, but at each landing there were two doors with well-polished handles and brass plates. On one I read the name of Andrew Amos.

A man in his shirt-sleeves opened to me, a little man, without a collar, and with an unbuttoned waistcoat. That was all I saw of him in the dim light, but he held out a paw like a gorilla's and drew me in.

The sitting-room, which looked over many chimneys to a pale yellow sky against which two factory stalks stood out sharply, gave me light enough to observe him fully. He was about five feet four, broad-shouldered, and with a great towsy head of grizzled hair. He wore spectacles, and his face was like some old-fashioned Scots minister's, for he had heavy eyebrows and whiskers which joined each other under his jaw, while his chin and enormous upper lip were clean-shaven. His eyes were steely grey and very solemn, but full of smouldering energy. His voice was enormous and would have shaken the walls if he had not had the habit of speaking with half-closed lips. He had not a sound tooth in his head.

A saucer full of tea and a plate which had once contained ham and eggs were on the table. He nodded towards them and asked me if I had fed.

'Ye'll no eat onything? Well, some would offer ye a dram, but this house is staunch teetotal. I door ye'll have to try the nearest public if ye're thirsty.'

I disclaimed any bodily wants, and produced my pipe, at which he started to fill an old clay. 'Mr Brand's your name?' he asked in his gusty voice. 'I was expectin' ye, but Dod! man ye're late!'

He extricated from his trousers pocket an ancient silver watch, and regarded it with disfavour. 'The dashed thing has stoppit. What do ye make the time, Mr Brand?'

He proceeded to prise open the lid of his watch with the knife he had used to cut his tobacco, and, as he examined the works, he turned the back of the case towards me. On the inside I saw pasted Mary Lamington's purple-and-white wafer.

I held my watch so that he could see the same token. His keen eyes, raised for a second, noted it, and he shut his own with a snap and returned it to his pocket. His manner lost its wariness and became almost genial.

'Ye've come up to see Glasgow, Mr Brand? Well, it's a steerin' bit, and there's honest folk bides in it, and some not so honest. They tell me ye're from South Africa. That's a long gait away, but I ken something aboot South Africa, for I had a cousin's son oot there for his lungs. He was in a shop in Main Street, Bloomfountain. They called him Peter Dobson. Ye would maybe mind of him.'

Then he discoursed of the Clyde. He was an incomer, he told me, from the Borders, his native place being the town of Galashiels, or, as he called it, 'Gawly'. 'I began as a powerloom tuner in Stavert's mill. Then my father dee'd and I took up his trade of jiner. But it's no world nowadays for the sma' independent business, so I cam to the Clyde and learned a shipwright's job. I may say I've become a leader in the trade, for though I'm no an official of the Union, and not likely to be, there's no man's word carries more weight than mine. And the Goavernment kens that, for they've sent me on commissions up and down the land to look at wuds and report on the nature of the timber. Bribery, they think it is, but Andrew Amos is not to be bribit. He'll have his say about any Goavernment on earth, and tell them to their face what he thinks of them. Ay, and he'll fight the case of the workingman against his oppressor, should it be the Goavernment or the fatted calves they ca' Labour Members. Ye'll have heard tell o' the shop stewards, Mr Brand?'

I admitted I had, for I had been well coached by Blenkiron in the current history of industrial disputes.

'Well, I'm a shop steward. We represent the rank and file against office-bearers that have lost the confidence o' the workingman. But I'm no socialist, and I would have ye keep mind of that. I'm yin o' the old Border radicals, and I'm not like to change. I'm for individual liberty and equal rights and chances for all men. I'll no more bow down before a Dagon of a Goavernment official than before the Baal of a feckless Tweedside laird. I've to keep my views to mysel', for thae young lads are all drucken-daft with their wee books about Cawpital and Collectivism and a wheen long senseless words I wouldna fyle my tongue with. Them and their socialism! There's more gumption in a page of John Stuart Mill than in all that foreign trash. But, as I say, I've got to keep a quiet sough, for the world is gettin' socialism now like the measles. It all comes of a defective eddication.'

'And what does a Border radical say about the war?' I asked.

He took off his spectacles and cocked his shaggy brows at me. 'I'll tell ye, Mr Brand. All that was bad in all that I've ever wrestled with since I cam to years o' discretion - Tories and lairds and manufacturers and publicans and the Auld Kirk - all that was bad, I say, for there were orra bits of decency, ye'll find in the Germans full measure pressed down and running over. When the war started, I considered the subject calmly for three days, and then I said: "Andra Amos, ye've found the enemy at last. The ones ye fought before were in a manner o' speakin' just misguided friends. It's either you or the Kaiser this time, my man!"'

His eyes had lost their gravity and had taken on a sombre ferocity. 'Ay, and I've not wavered. I got a word early in the business as to the way I could serve my country best. It's not been an easy job, and there's plenty of honest folk the day will give me a bad name. They think I'm stirrin' up the men at home and desertin' the cause o' the lads at the front. Man, I'm keepin' them straight. If I didna fight their battles on a sound economic isshue, they would take the dorts and be at the mercy of the first blagyird that preached revolution. Me and my like are safety-valves, if ye follow me. And dinna you make ony mistake, Mr Brand. The men that are agitating for a rise in wages are not for peace. They're fighting for the lads overseas as much as for themselves. There's not yin in a thousand that wouldna sweat himself blind to beat the Germans. The Goavernment has made mistakes, and maun be made to pay for them. If it were not so, the men would feel like a moose in a trap, for they would have no way to make their grievance felt. What for should the big man double his profits and the small man be ill set to get his ham and egg on Sabbath mornin'? That's the meaning o' Labour unrest, as they call it, and it's a good thing, says I, for if Labour didna get its leg over the traces now and then, the spunk o' the land would be dead in it, and Hindenburg could squeeze it like a rotten aipple.'

I asked if he spoke for the bulk of the men.

'For ninety per cent in ony ballot. I don't say that there's not plenty of riff-raff - the pint-and-a-dram gentry and the soft-heads that are aye reading bits of newspapers, and muddlin' their wits with foreign whigmaleeries. But the average man on the Clyde, like the average man in ither places, hates just three things, and that's the Germans, the profiteers, as they call them, and the Irish. But he hates the Germans first.'

'The Irish!' I exclaimed in astonishment.

'Ay, the Irish,' cried the last of the old Border radicals. 'Glasgow's stinkin' nowadays with two things, money and Irish. I mind the day when I followed Mr Gladstone's Home Rule policy, and used to threep about the noble, generous, warm-hearted sister nation held in a foreign bondage. My Goad! I'm not speakin' about Ulster, which is a dour, ill-natured den, but our own folk all the same. But the men that will not do a hand's turn to help the war and take the chance of our necessities to set up a bawbee rebellion are hateful to Goad and man. We treated them like pet lambs and that's the thanks we get. They're coming over here in thousands to tak the jobs of the lads that are doing their duty. I was speakin' last week to a widow woman that keeps a wee dairy down the Dalmarnock Road. She has two sons, and both in the airmy, one in the Cameronians and one a prisoner in Germany. She was telling me that she could not keep goin' any more, lacking the help of the boys, though she had worked her fingers to the bone. "Surely it's a crool job, Mr Amos," she says, "that the Goavernment should tak baith my laddies, and I'll maybe never see them again, and let the Irish gang free and tak the bread frae our mouth. At the gasworks across the road they took on a hundred Irish last week, and every yin o' them as young and well set up as you would ask to see. And my wee Davie, him that's in Germany, had aye a weak chest, and Jimmy was troubled wi' a bowel complaint. That's surely no justice!". ...'

He broke off and lit a match by drawing it across the seat of his trousers. 'It's time I got the gas lichtit. There's some men coming here at half-ten.'

As the gas squealed and flickered in the lighting, he sketched for me the coming guests. 'There's Macnab and Niven, two o' my colleagues. And there's Gilkison of the Boiler-fitters, and a lad Wilkie - he's got consumption, and writes wee bits in the papers. And there's a queer chap o' the name o' Tombs - they tell me he comes frae Cambridge, and is a kind of a professor there - anyway he's more stuffed wi' havers than an egg wi' meat. He telled me he was here to get at the heart o' the workingman, and I said to him that he would hae to look a bit further than the sleeve o' the workin'-man's jaicket. There's no muckle in his head, poor soul. Then there'll be Tam Norie, him that edits our weekly paper - Justice for All. Tam's a humorist and great on Robert Burns, but he hasna the balance o' a dwinin' teetotum ... Ye'll understand, Mr Brand, that I keep my mouth shut in such company, and don't express my own views more than is absolutely necessary. I criticize whiles, and that gives me a name of whunstane common-sense, but I never let my tongue wag. The feck o' the lads comin' the night are not the real workingman - they're just the froth on the pot, but it's the froth that will be useful to you. Remember they've heard tell o' ye already, and ye've some sort o' reputation to keep up.'

John Buchan

'Will Mr Abel Gresson be here?' I asked.

'No,' he said. 'Not yet. Him and me havena yet got to the point O' payin' visits. But the men that come will be Gresson's friends and they'll speak of ye to him. It's the best kind of introduction ye could seek.'

The knocker sounded, and Mr Amos hastened to admit the first comers. These were Macnab and Wilkie: the one a decent middle-aged man with a fresh-washed face and a celluloid collar-, the other a round-shouldered youth, with lank hair and the large eyes and luminous skin which are the marks of phthisis. 'This is Mr Brand boys, from South Africa,' was Amos's presentation. Presently came Niven, a bearded giant, and Mr Norie, the editor, a fat dirty fellow smoking a rank cigar. Gilkison of the Boiler-fitters, when he arrived, proved to be a pleasant young man in spectacles who spoke with an educated voice and clearly belonged to a slightly different social scale. Last came Tombs, the Cambridge 'professor, a lean youth with a sour mouth and eyes that reminded me of Launcelot Wake.

'Ye'll no be a mawgnate, Mr Brand, though ye come from South Africa,' said Mr Norie with a great guffaw.

'Not me. I'm a working engineer,' I said. 'My father was from Scotland, and this is my first visit to my native country, as my friend Mr Amos was telling you.'

The consumptive looked at me suspiciously. 'We've got two-three of the comrades here that the cawpitalist Government expelled from the Transvaal. If ye're our way of thinking, ye will maybe ken them.'

I said I would be overjoyed to meet them, but that at the time of the outrage in question I had been working on a mine a thousand miles further north.

Then ensued an hour of extraordinary talk. Tombs in his

sing-song namby-pamby University voice was concerned to get information. He asked endless questions, chiefly of Gilkison, who was the only one who really understood his language. I thought I had never seen anyone quite so fluent and so futile, and yet there was a kind of feeble violence in him like a demented sheep. He was engaged in venting some private academic spite against society, and I thought that in a revolution he would be the class of lad I would personally conduct to the nearest lamp-post. And all the while Amos and Macnab and Niven carried on their own conversation about the affairs of their society, wholly impervious to the tornado raging around them.

It was Mr Norie, the editor, who brought me into the discussion.

'Our South African friend is very blate,' he said in his boisterous way. 'Andra, if this place of yours wasn't so damned teetotal and we had a dram apiece, we might get his tongue loosened. I want to hear what he's got to say about the war. You told me this morning he was sound in the faith.'

'I said no such thing,' said Mr Amos. 'As ye ken well, Tam Norie, I don't judge soundness on that matter as you judge it. I'm for the war myself, subject to certain conditions that I've often stated. I know nothing of Mr Brand's opinions, except that he's a good democrat, which is more than I can say of some o' your friends.'

'Hear to Andra,' laughed Mr Norie. 'He's thinkin' the inspector in the Socialist State would be a waur kind of awristocrat then the Duke of Buccleuch. Weel, there's maybe something in that. But about the war he's wrong. Ye ken my views, boys. This war was made by the cawpitalists, and it has been fought by the workers, and it's the workers that maun have the ending of it. That day's comin' very near. There are those that want to spin it out till Labour is that weak it can be pit in chains for the rest o' time. That's the manoeuvre we're out to prevent. We've got to beat the Germans, but it's the workers that has the right to judge when the enemy's beaten and not the cawpitalists. What do you say, Mr Brand?'

Mr Norie had obviously pinned his colours to the fence, but he gave me the chance I had been looking for. I let them have my views with a vengeance, and these views were that for the sake of democracy the war must be ended. I flatter myself I put my case well, for I had got up every rotten argument and I borrowed largely from Launcelot Wake's armoury. But I didn't put it too well, for I had a very exact notion of the impression I wanted to produce. I must seem to be honest and in earnest, just a bit of a fanatic, but principally a hard-headed business-man who knew when the time had come to make a deal. Tombs kept interrupting me with imbecile questions, and I had to sit on him. At the end Mr Norie hammered with his pipe on the table.

'That'll sort ye, Andra. Ye're entertain' an angel unawares. What do ye say to that, my man?'

Mr Amos shook his head. 'I'll no deny there's something in it, but I'm not convinced that the Germans have got enough of a wheepin'.' Macnab agreed with him; the others were with me. Norie was for getting me to write an article for his paper, and the consumptive wanted me to address a meeting.

'Wull ye say a' that over again the morn's night down at our hall in Newmilns Street? We've got a lodge meeting o' the I.W.B., and I'll make them pit ye in the programme.' He kept his luminous eyes, like a sick dog's, fixed on me, and I saw that I had made one ally. I told him I had come to Glasgow to learn and not to teach, but I would miss no chance of testifying to my faith.

'Now, boys, I'm for my bed,' said Amos, shaking the dottle from his pipe. 'Mr Tombs, I'll conduct ye the morn over the Brigend works, but I've had enough clavers for one evening. I'm a man that wants his eight hours' sleep.'

The old fellow saw them to the door, and came back to me with the ghost of a grin in his face.

'A queer crowd, Mr Brand! Macnab didna like what ye said. He had a laddie killed in Gallypoly, and he's no lookin' for peace this side the grave. He's my best friend in Glasgow. He's an elder in the Gaelic kirk in the Cowcaddens, and I'm what ye call a free-thinker, but we're wonderful agreed on the fundamentals. Ye spoke your bit verra well, I must admit. Gresson will hear tell of ye as a promising recruit.' 'It's a rotten job,' I said.

'Ay, it's a rotten job. I often feel like vomiting over it mysel'. But it's no for us to complain. There's waur jobs oot in France for better men ... A word in your ear, Mr Brand. Could ye not look a bit more sheepish? Ye stare folk ower straight in the een, like a Hieland sergeant-major up at Maryhill Barracks.' And he winked slowly and grotesquely with his left eye.

He marched to a cupboard and produced a black bottle and glass. 'I'm blue-ribbon myself, but ye'll be the better of something to tak the taste out of your mouth. There's Loch Katrine water at the pipe there ... As I was saying, there's not much ill in that lot. Tombs is a black offence, but a dominie's a dominie all the world over. They may crack about their Industrial Workers and the braw things they're going to do, but there's a wholesome dampness about the tinder on Clydeside. They should try Ireland.'

Supposing,' I said, 'there was a really clever man who wanted to help the enemy. You think he could do little good by stirring up trouble in the shops here?'

'I'm positive.'

'And if he were a shrewd fellow, he'd soon tumble to that?'

'Ay.' 'Then if he still stayed on here he would be after bigger game - something really dangerous and damnable?'

Amos drew down his brows and looked me in the face. 'I see what ye're ettlin' at. Ay! That would be my conclusion. I came to it weeks syne about the man ye'll maybe meet the morn's night.'

Then from below the bed he pulled a box from which he drew a handsome flute. 'Ye'll forgive me, Mr Brand, but I aye like a tune before I go to my bed. Macnab says his prayers, and I have a tune on the flute, and the principle is just the same.'

So that singular evening closed with music - very sweet and true renderings of old Border melodies like 'My Peggy is a young thing', and 'When the kye come hame'. I fell asleep with a vision of Amos, his face all puckered up at the mouth and a wandering sentiment in his eye, recapturing in his dingy world the emotions of a boy.

 The widow-woman from next door, who acted as house-keeper, cook, and general factotum to the establishment, brought me shaving water next morning, but I had to go without a bath. When I entered the kitchen I found no one there, but while I consumed the inevitable ham and egg, Amos arrived back for breakfast. He brought with him the morning's paper. 'The Herald says there's been a big battle at Eepers,' he announced.

I tore open the sheet and read of the great attack Of 31 July which was spoiled by the weather. 'My God!' I cried. 'They've got St Julien and that dirty Frezenberg ridge ... and Hooge ... and Sanctuary Wood. I know every inch of the damned place. ...'

'Mr Brand,' said a warning voice, 'that'll never do. If our friends last night heard ye talk like that ye might as well tak the train back to London ... They're speakin' about ye in the yards this morning. Ye'll get a good turnout at your meeting the night, but they're sayin' that the polis will interfere. That mightna be a bad thing, but I trust ye to show discretion, for ye'll not be muckle use to onybody if they jyle ye in Duke

Street. I hear Gresson will be there with a fraternal message from his lunatics in America ... I've arranged that ye go down to Tam Norie this afternoon and give him a hand with his bit paper. Tam will tell ye the whole clash o' the West country, and I look to ye to keep him off the drink. He's aye arguin' that writin' and drinkin' gang thegither, and quotin' Robert Burns, but the creature has a wife and five bairns dependin' on him.'

I spent a fantastic day. For two hours I sat in Norie's dirty den, while he smoked and orated, and, when he remembered his business, took down in shorthand my impressions of the Labour situation in South Africa for his rag. They were fine breezy impressions, based on the most whole-hearted ignorance, and if they ever reached the Rand I wonder what my friends there made of Cornelius Brand, their author. I stood him dinner in an indifferent eating-house in a street off the Broomielaw, and thereafter had a drink with him in a public-house, and was introduced to some of his less reputable friends.

About tea-time I went back to Amos's lodgings, and spent an hour or so writing a long letter to Mr Ivery. I described to him everybody I had met, I gave highly coloured views of the explosive material on the Clyde, and I deplored the lack of clearheadedness in the progressive forces. I drew an elaborate picture of Amos, and deduced from it that the Radicals were likely to be a bar to true progress. 'They have switched their old militancy,' I wrote, 'on to another track, for with them it is a matter of conscience to be always militant.' I finished up with some very crude remarks on economics culled from the table-talk of the egregious Tombs. It was the kind of letter which I hoped would establish my character in his mind as an industrious innocent.

Seven o'clock found me in Newmilns Street, where I was seized upon by Wilkie. He had put on a clean collar for the occasion and had partially washed his thin face. The poor fellow had a cough that shook him like the walls of a power-house when the dynamos are going.

He was very apologetic about Amos. 'Andra belongs to a past worrld,' he said. 'He has a big reputation in his society, and he's a fine fighter, but he has no kind of Vision, if ye understand me. He's an auld Gladstonian, and that's done and damned in Scotland. He's not a Modern, Mr Brand, like you and me. But tonight ye'll meet one or two chaps that'll be worth your while to ken. Ye'll maybe no go quite as far as them, but ye're on the same road. I'm hoping for the day when we'll have oor Councils of Workmen and Soldiers like the Russians all over the land and dictate our terms to the pawrasites in Pawrliament. They tell me, too, the boys in the trenches are comin' round to our side.'

We entered the hall by a back door, and in a little waiting-room I was introduced to some of the speakers. They were a scratch lot as seen in that dingy place. The chairman was a shop-steward in one of the Societies, a fierce little rat of a man, who spoke with a cockney accent and addressed me as 'Comrade'. But one of them roused my liveliest interest. I heard the name of Gresson, and turned to find a fellow of about thirty-five, rather sprucely dressed, with a flower in his buttonhole. 'Mr Brand,' he said, in a rich American voice which recalled Blenkiron's. 'Very pleased to meet you, sir. We have Come from remote parts of the globe to be present at this gathering.' I noticed that he had reddish hair, and small bright eyes, and a nose with a droop like a Polish jew's.

As soon as we reached the platform I saw that there was going to be trouble. The hall was packed to the door, and in all the front half there was the kind of audience I expected to see - working-men of the political type who before the war would have thronged to party meetings. But not all the crowd at the back had come to listen. Some were scallawags, some looked like better-class clerks out for a spree, and there was a fair quantity of khaki. There were also one or two gentlemen not strictly sober.

The chairman began by putting his foot in it. He said we were there tonight to protest against the continuation of the war and to form a branch of the new British Council of Workmen and Soldiers. He told them with a fine mixture of metaphors that we had got to take the reins into our own hands, for the men who were running the war had their own axes to grind and were marching to oligarchy through the blood of the workers. He added that we had no quarrel with Germany half as bad as we had with our own capitalists. He looked forward to the day when British soldiers would leap from their trenches and extend the hand of friendship to their German comrades.

'No me!' said a solemn voice. 'I'm not seekin' a bullet in my wame,' - at which there was laughter and cat-calls.

Tombs followed and made a worse hash of it. He was determined to speak, as he would have put it, to democracy in its own language, so he said 'hell' several times, loudly but without conviction. Presently he slipped into the manner of the lecturer, and the audience grew restless. 'I propose to ask myself a question -' he began, and from the back of the hall came - 'And a damned sully answer ye'll get.' After that there was no more Tombs.

I followed with extreme nervousness, and to my surprise got a fair hearing. I felt as mean as a mangy dog on a cold morning, for I hated to talk rot before soldiers - especially before a couple of Royal Scots Fusiliers, who, for all I knew, might have been in my own brigade. My line was the plain, practical, patriotic man, just come from the colonies, who looked at things with fresh eyes, and called for a new deal. I was very moderate, but to justify my appearance there I had to put in a wild patch or two, and I got these by impassioned attacks on the Ministry of Munitions. I mixed up a little mild praise of the Germans, whom I said I had known all over the world for decent fellows. I received little applause, but no marked dissent, and sat down with deep thankfulness.

The next speaker put the lid on it. I believe he was a noted

John Buchan

agitator, who had already been deported. Towards him there was no lukewarmness, for one half of the audience cheered wildly when he rose, and the other half hissed and groaned. He began with whirlwind abuse of the idle rich, then of the middle-classes (he called them the 'rich man's flunkeys'), and finally of the Government. All that was fairly well received, for it is the fashion of the Briton to run down every Government and yet to be very averse to parting from it. Then he started on the soldiers and slanged the officers ('gentry pups' was his name for them), and the generals, whom he accused of idleness, of cowardice, and of habitual intoxication. He told us that our own kith and kin were sacrificed in every battle by leaders who had not the guts to share their risks. The Scots Fusiliers looked perturbed, as if they were in doubt of his meaning. Then he put it more plainly. 'Will any soldier deny that the men are the barrage to keep the officers' skins whole?'

'That's a bloody lee,' said one of the Fusilier jocks.

The man took no notice of the interruption, being carried away by the torrent of his own rhetoric, but he had not allowed for the persistence of the interrupter. The jock got slowly to his feet, and announced that he wanted satisfaction. 'If ye open your dirty gab to blagyird honest men, I'll come up on the platform and wring your neck.'

At that there was a fine old row, some crying out 'Order', some 'Fair play', and some applauding. A Canadian at the back of the hall started a song, and there was an ugly press forward. The hall seemed to be moving up from the back, and already men were standing in all the passages and right to the edge of the platform. I did not like the look in the eyes of these new-comers, and among the crowd I saw several who were obviously plain-clothes policemen.

The chairman whispered a word to the speaker, who continued when the noise had temporarily died down. He kept off the army and returned to the Government, and for a little sluiced out pure anarchism. But he got his foot in it again, for he pointed to the Sinn Feiners as examples of manly independence. At that, pandemonium broke loose, and he never had another look in. There were several fights going on in the hall between the public and courageous supporters of the orator.

Then Gresson advanced to the edge of the platform in a vain endeavour to retrieve the day. I must say he did it uncommonly well. He was clearly a practised speaker, and for a moment his appeal 'Now, boys, let's cool down a bit and talk sense,' had an effect. But the mischief had been done, and the crowd was surging round the lonely redoubt where we sat. Besides, I could see that for all his clever talk the meeting did not like the look of him. He was as mild as a turtle dove, but they wouldn't stand for it. A missile hurtled past my nose, and I saw a rotten cabbage envelop the baldish head of the ex-deportee. Someone reached out a long arm and grabbed a chair, and with it took the legs from Gresson. Then the lights suddenly went out, and we retreated in good order by the platform door with a yelling crowd at our heels.

It was here that the plain-clothes men came in handy. They held the door while the ex-deportee was smuggled out by some side entrance. That class of lad would soon cease to exist but for the protection of the law which he would abolish. The rest of us, having less to fear, were suffered to leak into Newmilns Street. I found myself next to Gresson, and took his arm. There was something hard in his coat pocket.

Unfortunately there was a big lamp at the point where we emerged, and there for our confusion were the Fusilier jocks. Both were strung to fighting pitch, and were determined to have someone's blood. Of me they took no notice, but Gresson had spoken after their ire had been roused, and was marked out as a victim. With a howl of joy they rushed for him.

I felt his hand steal to his side-pocket. 'Let that alone, you fool,' I growled in his ear.

'Sure, mister,' he said, and the next second we were in the thick of it.

It was like so many street fights I have seen - an immense crowd which surged up around us, and yet left a clear ring. Gresson and I got against the wall on the side-walk, and faced the furious soldiery. My intention was to do as little as possible, but the first minute convinced me that my companion had no idea how to use his fists, and I was mortally afraid that he would get busy with the gun in his pocket. It was that fear that brought me into the scrap. The jocks were sportsmen every bit of them, and only one advanced to the combat. He hit Gresson a clip on the jaw with his left, and but for the wall would have laid him out. I saw in the lamplight the vicious gleam in the American's eye and the twitch of his hand to his pocket. That decided me to interfere and I got in front of him.

This brought the second jock into the fray. He was a broad, thickset fellow, of the adorable bandy-legged stocky type that I had seen go through the Railway Triangle at Arras as though it were blotting-paper. He had some notion of fighting, too, and gave me a rough time, for I had to keep edging the other fellow off Gresson.

'Go home, you fool,' I shouted. 'Let this gentleman alone. I don't want to hurt you.'

The only answer was a hook-hit which I just managed to guard, followed by a mighty drive with his right which I dodged so that he barked his knuckles on the wall. I heard a yell of rage, and observed that Gresson seemed to have kicked his assailant on the shin. I began to long for the police.

Then there was that swaying of the crowd which betokens the approach of the forces of law and order. But they were too late to prevent trouble. In self-defence I had to take my jock seriously, and got in my blow when he had overreached himself and lost his balance. I never hit anyone so unwillingly in my life. He went over like a poled ox, and measured his length on the causeway.

I found myself explaining things politely to the constables. 'These men objected to this gentleman's speech at the meeting, and I had to interfere to protect him. No, no! I don't want to charge anybody. It was all a misunderstanding.' I helped the stricken jock to rise and offered him ten bob for consolation.

He looked at me sullenly and spat on the ground. 'Keep your dirty money,' he said. 'I'll be even with ye yet, my man - you and that red-headed scab. I'll mind the looks of ye the next time I see ye.' Gresson was wiping the blood from his cheek with a silk handkerchief. 'I guess I'm in your debt, Mr Brand,' he said. 'You may bet I won't forget it.'

I returned to an anxious Amos. He heard my story in silence and his only comment was -'Well done the Fusiliers!'

'It might have been worse, I'll not deny,' he went on. 'Ye've established some kind of a claim upon Gresson, which may come in handy ... Speaking about Gresson, I've news for ye. He's sailing on Friday as purser in the Tobermory. The Tobermory's a boat that wanders every month up the West Highlands as far as Stornoway. I've arranged for ye to take a trip on that boat, Mr Brand.'

I nodded. 'How did you find out that?' I asked.

'It took me some finding,' he said dryly, 'but I've ways and means. Now I'll not trouble ye with advice, for ye ken your job as well as me. But I'm going north myself the morn to look after some of the Ross-shire wuds, and I'll be in the way of getting telegrams at the Kyle. Ye'll keep that in mind. Keep in mind, too, that I'm a great reader of the Pilgrim's Progress and that I've a cousin of the name of Ochterlony.'

John Buchan

CHAPTER FIVE

VARIOUS DOINGS IN THE WEST

The Tobermory was no ship for passengers. Its decks were littered with a hundred oddments, so that a man could barely walk a step without tacking, and my bunk was simply a shelf in the frowsty little saloon, where the odour of ham and eggs hung like a fog. I joined her at Greenock and took a turn on deck with the captain after tea, when he told me the names of the big blue hills to the north. He had a fine old copper-coloured face and side-whiskers like an archbishop, and, having spent all his days beating up the western seas, had as many yarns in his head as Peter himself.

'On this boat,' he announced, 'we don't ken what a day may bring forth. I may put into Colonsay for twa hours and bide there three days. I get a telegram at Oban and the next thing I'm awa ayont Barra. Sheep's the difficult business. They maun be fetched for the sales, and they're dooms slow to lift. So ye see it's not what ye call a pleasure trip, Maister Brand.'

Indeed it wasn't, for the confounded tub wallowed like a fat sow as soon as we rounded a headland and got the weight of the south-western wind. When asked my purpose, I explained that I was a colonial of Scots extraction, who was paying his first visit to his fatherland and wanted to explore the beauties of the West Highlands. I let him gather that I was not rich in this world's goods.

'Ye'll have a passport?' he asked. 'They'll no let ye go north o' Fort William without one.'

Amos had said nothing about passports, so I looked blank.

'I could keep ye on board for the whole voyage,' he went on, 'but ye wouldna be permitted to land. If ye're seekin' enjoyment, it would be a poor job sittin' on this deck and admirin' the works O' God and no allowed to step on the pier-head. Ye should have applied to the military gentlemen in Glesca. But ye've plenty o' time to make up your mind afore we get to Oban. We've a heap o' calls to make Mull and Islay way.'

The purser came up to inquire about my ticket, and greeted me with a grin.

'Ye're acquaint with Mr Gresson, then?' said the captain. 'Weel, we're a cheery wee ship's company, and that's the great thing on this kind o' job.'

I made but a poor supper, for the wind had risen to half a gale, and I saw hours of wretchedness approaching. The trouble with me is that I cannot be honestly sick and get it over. Queasiness and headache beset me and there is no refuge but bed. I turned into my bunk, leaving the captain and the mate smoking shag not six feet from my head, and fell into a restless sleep. When I woke the place was empty, and smelt vilely of stale tobacco and cheese. My throbbing brows made sleep impossible, and I tried to ease them by staggering upon deck. I saw a clear windy sky, with every star as bright as a live coal, and a heaving waste of dark waters running to ink-black hills. Then a douche of spray caught me and sent me down the companion to my bunk again, where I lay for hours trying to make a plan of campaign.

I argued that if Amos had wanted me to have a passport he would have provided one, so I needn't bother my head about that. But it was my business to keep alongside Gresson, and if

John Buchan

the boat stayed a week in some port and he went off ashore, I must follow him. Having no passport I would have to be always dodging trouble, which would handicap my movements and in all likelihood make me more conspicuous than I wanted. I guessed that Amos had denied me the passport for the very reason that he wanted Gresson to think me harmless. The area of danger would, therefore, be the passport country, somewhere north of Fort William.

But to follow Gresson I must run risks and enter that country. His suspicions, if he had any, would be lulled if I left the boat at Oban, but it was up to me to follow overland to the north and hit the place where the Tobermory made a long stay. The confounded tub had no plans; she wandered about the West Highlands looking for sheep and things; and the captain himself could give me no time-table of her voyage. It was incredible that Gresson should take all this trouble if he did not know that at some place - and the right place - he would have time to get a spell ashore. But I could scarcely ask Gresson for that information, though I determined to cast a wary fly over him. I knew roughly the Tobermory's course - through the Sound of Islay to Colonsay; then up the east side of Mull to Oban; then through the Sound of Mull to the islands with names like cocktails, Rum and Eigg and Coll; then to Skye; and then for the Outer Hebrides. I thought the last would be the place, and it seemed madness to leave the boat, for the Lord knew how I should get across the Minch. This consideration upset all my plans again, and I fell into a troubled sleep without coming to any conclusion.

Morning found us nosing between Jura and Islay, and about midday we touched at a little port, where we unloaded some cargo and took on a couple of shepherds who were going to Colonsay. The mellow afternoon and the good smell of salt and heather got rid of the dregs of my queasiness, and I spent a profitable hour on the pier-head with a guide-book called Baddely's Scotland, and one of Bartholomew's maps. I was beginning to think that Amos might be able to tell me something, for a talk with the captain had suggested that the

Tobermory would not dally long in the neighbourhood of Rum and Eigg. The big droving season was scarcely on yet, and sheep for the Oban market would be lifted on the return journey. In that case Skye was the first place to watch, and if I could get wind of any big cargo waiting there I would be able to make a plan. Amos was somewhere near the Kyle, and that was across the narrows from Skye. Looking at the map, it seemed to me that, in spite of being passportless, I might be able somehow to make my way up through Morvern and Arisaig to the latitude of Skye. The difficulty would be to get across the strip of sea, but there must be boats to beg, borrow or steal.

I was poring over Baddely when Gresson sat down beside me. He was in a good temper, and disposed to talk, and to my surprise his talk was all about the beauties of the countryside. There was a kind of apple-green light over everything; the steep heather hills cut into the sky like purple amethysts, while beyond the straits the western ocean stretched its pale molten gold to the sunset. Gresson waxed lyrical over the scene. 'This just about puts me right inside, Mr Brand. I've got to get away from that little old town pretty frequent or I begin to moult like a canary. A man feels a man when he gets to a place that smells as good as this. Why in hell do we ever get messed up in those stone and lime cages? I reckon some day I'll pull my freight for a clean location and settle down there and make little poems. This place would about content me. And there's a spot out in California in the Coast ranges that I've been keeping my eye on.' The odd thing was that I believe he meant it. His ugly face was lit up with a serious delight.

He told me he had taken this voyage before, so I got out Baddely and asked for advice. 'I can't spend too much time on holidaying,' I told him, 'and I want to see all the beauty spots. But the best of them seem to be in the area that this fool British Government won't let you into without a passport. I suppose I shall have to leave you at Oban.'

'Too bad,' he said sympathetically. 'Well, they tell me there's

John Buchan

some pretty sights round Oban.' And he thumbed the guide-book and began to read about Glencoe.

I said that was not my purpose, and pitched him a yarn about Prince Charlie and how my mother's great-grandfather had played some kind of part in that show. I told him I wanted to see the place where the Prince landed and where he left for France. 'So far as I can make out that won't take me into the passport country, but I'll have to do a bit of footslogging. Well, I'm used to padding the hoof. I must get the captain to put me off in Morvern, and then I can foot it round the top of Lochiel and get back to Oban through Appin. How's that for a holiday trek?'

He gave the scheme his approval. 'But if it was me, Mr Brand, I would have a shot at puzzling your gallant policemen. You and I don't take much stock in Governments and their two-cent laws, and it would be a good game to see just how far you could get into the forbidden land. A man like you could put up a good bluff on those hayseeds. I don't mind having a bet ...'

'No,' I said. 'I'm out for a rest, and not for sport. If there was anything to be gained I'd undertake to bluff my way to the Orkney Islands. But it's a wearing job and I've better things to think about.' 'So? Well, enjoy yourself your own way. I'll be sorry when you leave us, for I owe you something for that rough-house, and beside there's darned little company in the old moss-back captain.'

That evening Gresson and I swopped yarns after supper to the accompaniment of the 'Ma Goad!' and 'Is't possible?' of captain and mate. I went to bed after a glass or two of weak grog, and made up for the last night's vigil by falling sound asleep. I had very little kit with me, beyond what I stood up in and could carry in my waterproof pockets, but on Amos's advice I had brought my little nickel-plated revolver. This lived by day in my hip pocket, but at night I put it behind my pillow. But when I woke next morning to find us casting anchor in the bay below rough low hills, which I knew to be the island of Colonsay, I could find no trace of the revolver. I searched every inch of the bunk and only shook out feathers from the mouldy ticking. I remembered perfectly putting the thing behind my head before I went to sleep, and now it had vanished utterly. Of course I could not advertise my loss, and I didn't greatly mind it, for this was not a job where I could do much shooting. But it made me think a good deal about Mr Gresson. He simply could not suspect me; if he had bagged my gun, as I was pretty certain he had, it must be because he wanted it for himself and not that he might disarm me. Every way I argued it I reached the same conclusion. In Gresson's eyes I must seem as harmless as a child.

We spent the better part of a day at Colonsay, and Gresson, so far as his duties allowed, stuck to me like a limpet. Before I went ashore I wrote out a telegram for Amos. I devoted a hectic hour to the Pilgrim's Progress, but I could not compose any kind of intelligible message with reference to its text. We had all the same edition - the one in the Golden Treasury series - so I could have made up a sort of cipher by referring to lines and pages, but that would have taken up a dozen telegraph forms and seemed to me too elaborate for the purpose. So I sent this message:

Ochterlony, Post Office, Kyle, I hope to spend part of holiday near you and to see you if boat's programme permits. Are any good cargoes waiting in your neighbourhood? Reply Post Office, Oban.

It was highly important that Gresson should not see this, but it was the deuce of a business to shake him off. I went for a walk in the afternoon along the shore and passed the telegraph office, but the confounded fellow was with me all the time. My only chance was just before we sailed, when he had to go on board to check some cargo. As the telegraph office stood full in view of the ship's deck I did not go near it. But in the back end of the clachan I found the schoolmaster, and got him to promise to send the wire. I also bought off him a couple of well-worn sevenpenny novels.

The result was that I delayed our departure for ten minutes and when I came on board faced a wrathful Gresson. 'Where the hell have you been?' he asked. 'The weather's blowing up dirty and the old man's mad to get off. Didn't you get your legs stretched enough this afternoon?'

I explained humbly that I had been to the schoolmaster to get something to read, and produced my dingy red volumes. At that his brow cleared. I could see that his suspicions were set at rest.

We left Colonsay about six in the evening with the sky behind us banking for a storm, and the hills of Jura to starboard an angry purple. Colonsay was too low an island to be any kind of breakwater against a western gale, so the weather was bad from the start. Our course was north by east, and when we had passed the butt-end of the island we nosed about in the trough of big seas, shipping tons of water and rolling like a buffalo. I know as much about boats as about Egyptian hieroglyphics, but even my landsman's eyes could tell that we were in for a rough night. I was determined not to get queasy again, but when I went below the smell of tripe and onions promised to be my undoing; so I dined off a slab of chocolate and a cabin biscuit, put on my waterproof, and resolved to stick it out on deck.

I took up position near the bows, where I was out of reach of the oily steamer smells. It was as fresh as the top of a mountain, but mighty cold and wet, for a gusty drizzle had set in, and I got the spindrift of the big waves. There I balanced myself, as we lurched into the twilight, hanging on with one hand to a rope which descended from the stumpy mast. I noticed that there was only an indifferent rail between me and the edge, but that interested me and helped to keep off sickness. I swung to the movement of the vessel, and though I was mortally cold it was rather pleasant than otherwise. My notion was to get the nausea whipped out of me by the weather, and, when I was properly tired, to go down and turn in.

I stood there till the dark had fallen. By that time I was an automaton, the way a man gets on sentry-go, and I could have easily hung on till morning. My thoughts ranged about the earth, beginning with the business I had set out on, and presently - by way of recollections of Blenkiron and Peter - reaching the German forest where, in the Christmas of 1915, I had been nearly done in by fever and old Stumm. I remembered the bitter cold of that wild race, and the way the snow seemed to burn like fire when I stumbled and got my face into it. I reflected that sea-sickness was kitten's play to a good bout of malaria.

The weather was growing worse, and I was getting more than spindrift from the seas. I hooked my arm round the rope, for my fingers were numbing. Then I fell to dreaming again, principally about Fosse Manor and Mary Lamington. This so ravished me that I was as good as asleep. I was trying to reconstruct the picture as I had last seen her at Biggleswick station ...

A heavy body collided with me and shook my arm from the rope. I slithered across the yard of deck, engulfed in a whirl of water. One foot caught a stanchion of the rail, and it gave with me, so that for an instant I was more than half overboard. But my fingers clawed wildly and caught in the links of what must have been the anchor chain. They held, though a ton's weight seemed to be tugging at my feet ... Then the old tub rolled back, the waters slipped off, and I was sprawling on a wet deck with no breath in me and a gallon of brine in my windpipe.

I heard a voice cry out sharply, and a hand helped me to my feet. It was Gresson, and he seemed excited.

'God, Mr Brand, that was a close call! I was coming up to find you, when this damned ship took to lying on her side. I guess I must have cannoned into you, and I was calling myself bad names when I saw you rolling into the Atlantic. If I hadn't got a grip on the rope I would have been down beside you. Say, you're not hurt? I reckon you'd better come below and get a glass of rum under your belt. You're about as wet as mother's dish-clouts.'

There's one advantage about campaigning. You take your luck when it comes and don't worry about what might have been. I didn't think any more of the business, except that it had cured me of wanting to be sea-sick. I went down to the reeking cabin without one qualm in my stomach, and ate a good meal of welsh-rabbit and bottled Bass, with a tot of rum to follow up with. Then I shed my wet garments, and slept in my bunk till we anchored off a village in Mull in a clear blue morning.

It took us four days to crawl up that coast and make Oban, for we seemed to be a floating general store for every hamlet in those parts. Gresson made himself very pleasant, as if he wanted to atone for nearly doing me in. We played some poker, and I read the little books I had got in Colonsay, and then rigged up a fishing-line, and caught saithe and lythe and an occasional big haddock. But I found the time pass slowly, and I was glad that about noon one day we came into a bay blocked with islands and saw a clean little town sitting on the hills and the smoke of a railway engine.

I went ashore and purchased a better brand of hat in a tweed store. Then I made a bee-line for the post office, and asked for telegrams. One was given to me, and as I opened it I saw Gresson at my elbow.

It read thus:

> Brand, Post office, Oban. Page 117, paragraph 3. Ochterlony.

I passed it to Gresson with a rueful face.

'There's a piece of foolishness,' I said. 'I've got a cousin who's a

Presbyterian minister up in Ross-shire, and before I knew about this passport humbug I wrote to him and offered to pay him a visit. I told him to wire me here if it was convenient, and the old idiot has sent me the wrong telegram. This was likely as not meant for some other brother parson, who's got my message instead.'

'What's the guy's name?' Gresson asked curiously, peering at the signature.

'Ochterlony. David Ochterlony. He's a great swell at writing books, but he's no earthly use at handling the telegraph. However, it don't signify, seeing I'm not going near him.' I crumpled up the pink form and tossed it on the floor. Gresson and I walked to the Tobermory together.

That afternoon, when I got a chance, I had out my Pilgrim's Progress. Page 117, paragraph 3, read:

> 'Then I saw in my dream, that a little off the road, over against the Silver-mine, stood Demas (gentlemanlike) to call to passengers to come and see: who said to Christian and his fellow, Ho, turn aside hither and I will show you a thing.

At tea I led the talk to my own past life. I yarned about my experiences as a mining engineer, and said I could never get out of the trick of looking at country with the eye of the prospector. 'For instance,' I said, 'if this had been Rhodesia, I would have said there was a good chance of copper in these little kopjes above the town. They're not unlike the hills round the Messina mine.' I told the captain that after the war I was thinking of turning my attention to the West Highlands and looking out for minerals.

'Ye'll make nothing of it,' said the captain. 'The costs are ower big, even if ye found the minerals, for ye'd have to import a' your labour. The West Hielandman is no fond o' hard work. Ye ken the psalm o' the crofter?

O that the peats would cut themselves,
The fish chump on the shore,
And that I in my bed might lie
Henceforth for ever more!'

'Has it ever been tried?' I asked.

'Often. There's marble and slate quarries, and there was word o' coal in Benbecula. And there's the iron mines at Ranna.'

'Where's that?' I asked.

'Up forenent Skye. We call in there, and generally bide a bit. There's a heap of cargo for Ranna, and we usually get a good load back. But as I tell ye, there's few Hielanders working there. Mostly Irish and lads frae Fife and Falkirk way.'

I didn't pursue the subject, for I had found Demas's silvermine. If the Tobermory lay at Ranna for a week, Gresson would have time to do his own private business. Ranna would not be the spot, for the island was bare to the world in the middle of a much-frequented channel. But Skye was just across the way, and when I looked in my map at its big, wandering peninsulas I concluded that my guess had been right, and that Skye was the place to make for.

That night I sat on deck with Gresson, and in a wonderful starry silence we watched the lights die out of the houses in the town, and talked of a thousand things. I noticed - what I had had a hint of before - that my companion was no common man. There were moments when he forgot himself and talked like an educated gentleman: then he would remember, and relapse into the lingo of Leadville, Colorado. In my character of the ingenuous inquirer I set him posers about politics and economics, the kind of thing I might have been supposed to pick up from unintelligent browsing among little books. Generally he answered with some slangy catchword, but occasionally he was interested beyond his discretion, and treated me to a harangue like an equal. I discovered another thing, that he had a craze for poetry, and a capacious memory for it. I forgot how we drifted into the subject, but I remember he quoted some queer haunting stuff which he said was Swinburne, and verses by people I had heard of from Letchford at Biggleswick. Then he saw by my silence that he had gone too far, and fell back into the jargon of the West. He wanted to know about my plans, and we went down into the cabin and had a look at the map. I explained my route, up Morvern and round the head of Lochiel, and back to Oban by the east side of Loch Linnhe.

'Got you,' he said. 'You've a hell of a walk before you. That bug never bit me, and I guess I'm not envying you any. And after that, Mr Brand?'

'Back to Glasgow to do some work for the cause,' I said lightly. 'Just so,' he said with a grin. 'It's a great life if you don't weaken.'

We steamed out of the bay next morning at dawn, and about nine o'clock I got on shore at a little place called Lochaline. My kit was all on my person, and my waterproof's pockets were stuffed with chocolates and biscuits I had bought in Oban. The captain was discouraging. 'Ye'll get your bellyful o' Hieland hills, Mr Brand, afore ye win round the loch head. Ye'll be wishin' yerself back on the Tobermory.' But Gresson speeded me joyfully on my way, and said he wished he were coming with me. He even accompanied me the first hundred yards, and waved his hat after me till I was round the turn of the road.

The first stage in that journey was pure delight. I was thankful to be rid of the infernal boat, and the hot summer scents coming down the glen were comforting after the cold, salt smell of the sea. The road lay up the side of a small bay, at the top of which a big white house stood among gardens. Presently I had left the coast and was in a glen where a brown salmon-river swirled through acres of bog-myrtle. It had its source in a loch, from which the mountain rose steeply - a place so glassy in that August forenoon that every scar and wrinkle of the hillside were faithfully reflected. After that I crossed a low pass to the head of another sea-lock, and, following the map, struck over the shoulder of a great hill and ate my luncheon far up on its side, with a wonderful vista of wood and water below me.

All that morning I was very happy, not thinking about Gresson or Ivery, but getting my mind clear in those wide spaces, and my lungs filled with the brisk hill air. But I noticed one curious thing. On my last visit to Scotland, when I covered more moorland miles a day than any man since Claverhouse, I had been fascinated by the land, and had pleased myself with plans for settling down in it. But now, after three years of war and general rocketing, I felt less drawn to that kind of landscape. I wanted something more green and peaceful and habitable, and it was to the Cotswolds that my memory turned with longing.

I puzzled over this till I realized that in all my Cotswold pictures a figure kept going and coming - a young girl with a cloud of gold hair and the strong, slim grace of a boy, who had sung 'Cherry Ripe' in a moonlit garden. Up on that hillside I understood very clearly that I, who had been as careless of women as any monk, had fallen wildly in love with a child of half my age. I was loath to admit it, though for weeks the conclusion had been forcing itself on me. Not that I didn't revel in my madness, but that it seemed too hopeless a business, and I had no use for barren philandering. But, seated on a rock munching chocolate and biscuits, I faced up to the fact and resolved to trust my luck. After all we were comrades in a big job, and it was up to me to be man enough to win her. The thought seemed to brace any courage that was in me. No task seemed too hard with her approval to gain and her companionship somewhere at the back of it. I sat for a long time in a happy dream, remembering all the glimpses I had had of her, and humming her song to an audience of one black-faced sheep.

On the highroad half a mile below me, I saw a figure on a

bicycle mounting the hill, and then getting off to mop its face at the summit. I turned my Ziess glasses on to it, and observed that it was a country policeman. It caught sight of me, stared for a bit, tucked its machine into the side of the road, and then very slowly began to climb the hillside. Once it stopped, waved its hand and shouted something which I could not hear. I sat finishing my luncheon, till the features were revealed to me of a fat oldish man, blowing like a grampus, his cap well on the back of a bald head, and his trousers tied about the shins with string.

There was a spring beside me and I had out my flask to round off my meal.

'Have a drink,' I said.

His eye brightened, and a smile overran his moist face.

'Thank you, sir. It will be very warrm coming up the brae.'

'You oughtn't to,' I said. 'You really oughtn't, you know. Scorching up hills and then doubling up a mountain are not good for your time of life.'

He raised the cap of my flask in solemn salutation. 'Your very good health.' Then he smacked his lips, and had several cupfuls of water from the spring.

'You will haf come from Achranich way, maybe?' he said in his soft sing-song, having at last found his breath.

'Just so. Fine weather for the birds, if there was anybody to shoot them.'

'Ah, no. There will be few shots fired today, for there are no gentlemen left in Morvern. But I wass asking you, if you come from Achranich, if you haf seen anybody on the road.'

From his pocket he extricated a brown envelope and a bulky

John Buchan

telegraph form. 'Will you read it, sir, for I haf forgot my spectacles?'

It contained a description of one Brand, a South African and a suspected character, whom the police were warned to stop and return to Oban. The description wasn't bad, but it lacked any one good distinctive detail. Clearly the policeman took me for an innocent pedestrian, probably the guest of some moorland shooting-box, with my brown face and rough tweeds and hobnailed shoes.

I frowned and puzzled a little. 'I did see a fellow about three miles back on the hillside. There's a public-house just where the burn comes in, and I think he was making for it. Maybe that was your man. This wire says "South African"; and now I remember the fellow had the look of a colonial.'

The policeman sighed. 'No doubt it will be the man. Perhaps he will haf a pistol and will shoot.'

'Not him,' I laughed. 'He looked a mangy sort of chap, and he'll be scared out of his senses at the sight of you. But take my advice and get somebody with you before you tackle him. You're always the better of a witness.'

'That is so,' he said, brightening. 'Ach, these are the bad times! in old days there wass nothing to do but watch the doors at the flower-shows and keep the yachts from poaching the sea-trout. But now it is spies, spies, and "Donald, get out of your bed, and go off twenty mile to find a German." I wass wishing the war wass by, and the Germans all dead.'

'Hear, hear!' I cried, and on the strength of it gave him another dram.

I accompanied him to the road, and saw him mount his bicycle and zig-zag like a snipe down the hill towards Achranich. Then I set off briskly northward. It was clear that the faster I moved the better. As I went I paid disgusted tribute to the efficiency of the Scottish police. I wondered how on earth they had marked me down. Perhaps it was the Glasgow meeting, or perhaps my association with Ivery at Biggleswick. Anyhow there was somebody somewhere mighty quick at compiling a dossier. Unless I wanted to be bundled back to Oban I must make good speed to the Arisaig coast.

Presently the road fell to a gleaming sea-loch which lay like the blue blade of a sword among the purple of the hills. At the head there was a tiny clachan, nestled among birches and rowans, where a tawny burn wound to the sea. When I entered the place it was about four o'clock in the afternoon, and peace lay on it like a garment. In the wide, sunny street there was no sign of life, and no sound except of hens clucking and of bees busy among the roses. There was a little grey box of a kirk, and close to the bridge a thatched cottage which bore the sign of a post and telegraph office.

For the past hour I had been considering that I had better prepare for mishaps. If the police of these parts had been warned they might prove too much for me, and Gresson would be allowed to make his journey unmatched. The only thing to do was to send a wire to Amos and leave the matter in his hands. Whether that was possible or not depended upon this remote postal authority.

I entered the little shop, and passed from bright sunshine to a twilight smelling of paraffin and black-striped peppermint balls. An old woman with a mutch sat in an arm-chair behind the counter. She looked up at me over her spectacles and smiled, and I took to her on the instant. She had the kind of old wise face that God loves.

Beside her I noticed a little pile of books, one of which was a Bible. Open on her lap was a paper, the United Free Church Monthly. I noticed these details greedily, for I had to make up my mind on the part to play.

'It's a warm day, mistress,' I said, my voice falling into the broad Lowland speech, for I had an instinct that she was not of the Highlands.

She laid aside her paper. 'It is that, sir. It is grand weather for the hairst, but here that's no till the hinner end o' September, and at the best it's a bit scart o' aits.'

'Ay. It's a different thing down Annandale way,' I said.

Her face lit up. 'Are ye from Dumfries, sir?'

'Not just from Dumfries, but I know the Borders fine.'

'Ye'll no beat them,' she cried. 'Not that this is no a guid place and I've muckle to be thankfu' for since John Sanderson - that was ma man - brought me here forty-seeven year syne come Martinmas. But the aulder I get the mair I think o' the bit whaur I was born. It was twae miles from Wamphray on the Lockerbie road, but they tell me the place is noo just a rickle o' stanes.' 'I was wondering, mistress, if I could get a cup of tea in the village.'

'Ye'll hae a cup wi' me,' she said. 'It's no often we see onybody frae the Borders hereaways. The kettle's just on the boil.'

She gave me tea and scones and butter, and black-currant jam, and treacle biscuits that melted in the mouth. And as we ate we talked of many things - chiefly of the war and of the wickedness of the world.

'There's nae lads left here,' she said. 'They a' joined the Camerons, and the feck o' them fell at an awfu' place called Lowse. John and me never had no boys, jist the one lassie that's married on Donald Frew, the Strontian carrier. I used to vex mysel' about it, but now I thank the Lord that in His mercy He spared me sorrow. But I wad hae liked to have had one laddie fechtin' for his country. I whiles wish I was a Catholic and could pit up prayers for the sodgers that are deid. It maun be a great consolation.'

I whipped out the Pilgrim's Progress from my pocket. 'That is the grand book for a time like this.'

'Fine I ken it,' she said. 'I got it for a prize in the Sabbath School when I was a lassie.'

I turned the pages. I read out a passage or two, and then I seemed struck with a sudden memory.

'This is a telegraph office, mistress. Could I trouble you to send a telegram? You see I've a cousin that's a minister in Ross-shire at the Kyle, and him and me are great correspondents. He was writing about something in the Pilgrim's Progress and I think I'll send him a telegram in answer.'

'A letter would be cheaper,' she said.

'Ay, but I'm on holiday and I've no time for writing.'

She gave me a form, and I wrote:

> ochterlony. Post Office, Kyle. - Demas will be at his mine within the week. Strive with him, lest I faint by the way.

'Ye're unco lavish wi' the words, sir,' was her only comment.

We parted with regret, and there was nearly a row when I tried to pay for the tea. I was bidden remember her to one David Tudhole, farmer in Nether Mirecleuch, the next time I passed by Wamphray.

The village was as quiet when I left it as when I had entered. I took my way up the hill with an easier mind, for I had got off the telegram, and I hoped I had covered my tracks. My friend the postmistress would, if questioned, be unlikely to recognize any South African suspect in the frank and homely traveller who had spoken with her of Annandale and the Pilgrim's Progress.

John Buchan

The soft mulberry gloaming of the west coast was beginning to fall on the hills. I hoped to put in a dozen miles before dark to the next village on the map, where I might find quarters. But ere I had gone far I heard the sound of a motor behind me, and a car slipped past bearing three men. The driver favoured me with a sharp glance, and clapped on the brakes. I noted that the two men in the tonneau were carrying sporting rifles.

'Hi, you, sir,' he cried. 'Come here.' The two rifle-bearers - solemn gillies - brought their weapons to attention.

'By God,' he said, 'it's the man. What's your name? Keep him covered, Angus.'

The gillies duly covered me, and I did not like the look of their wavering barrels. They were obviously as surprised as myself.

I had about half a second to make my plans. I advanced with a very stiff air, and asked him what the devil he meant. No Lowland Scots for me now. My tone was that of an adjutant of a Guards' battalion.

My inquisitor was a tall man in an ulster, with a green felt hat on his small head. He had a lean, well-bred face, and very choleric blue eyes. I set him down as a soldier, retired, Highland regiment or cavalry, old style.

He produced a telegraph form, like the policeman.

'Middle height - strongly built - grey tweeds - brown hat - speaks with a colonial accent - much sunburnt. What's your name, sir?'

I did not reply in a colonial accent, but with the hauteur of the British officer when stopped by a French sentry. I asked him again what the devil he had to do with my business. This made him angry and he began to stammer.

'I'll teach you what I have to do with it. I'm a deputy-lieutenant of this county, and I have Admiralty instructions to watch the coast. Damn it, sir, I've a wire here from the Chief Constable describing you. You're Brand, a very dangerous fellow, and we want to know what the devil you're doing here.'

As I looked at his wrathful eye and lean head, which could not have held much brains, I saw that I must change my tone. if I irritated him he would get nasty and refuse to listen and hang me up for hours. So my voice became respectful.

'I beg your pardon, sir, but I've not been accustomed to be pulled up suddenly, and asked for my credentials. My name is Blaikie, Captain Robert Blaikie, of the Scots Fusiliers. I'm home on three weeks' leave, to get a little peace after Hooge. We were only hauled out five days ago.' I hoped my old friend in the shell-shock hospital at Isham would pardon my borrowing his identity.

The man looked puzzled. 'How the devil am I to be satisfied about that? Have you any papers to prove it?'

'Why, no. I don't carry passports about with me on a walking tour. But you can wire to the depot, or to my London address.'

He pulled at his yellow moustache. 'I'm hanged if I know what to do. I want to get home for dinner. I tell you what, sir, I'll take you on with me and put you up for the night. My boy's at home, convalescing, and if he says you're pukka I'll ask your pardon and give you a dashed good bottle of port. I'll trust him and I warn you he's a keen hand.'

There was nothing to do but consent, and I got in beside him with an uneasy conscience. Supposing the son knew the real Blaikie! I asked the name of the boy's battalion, and was told the 10th Seaforths. That wasn't pleasant hearing, for they had been brigaded with us on the Somme. But Colonel Broadbury - for he told me his name - volunteered another piece of news which set my mind at rest. The boy was not yet twenty, and had only been out seven months. At Arras he had got a bit of shrapnel in his thigh, which had played the deuce with the sciatic nerve, and he was still on crutches.

We spun over ridges of moorland, always keeping northward, and brought up at a pleasant white-washed house close to the sea. Colonel Broadbury ushered me into a hall where a small fire of peats was burning, and on a couch beside it lay a slim, pale-faced young man. He had dropped his policeman's manner, and behaved like a gentleman. 'Ted,' he said, 'I've brought a friend home for the night. I went out to look for a suspect and found a British officer. This is Captain Blaikie, of the Scots Fusiliers.'

The boy looked at me pleasantly. 'I'm very glad to meet you, sir. You'll excuse me not getting up, but I've got a game leg.' He was the copy of his father in features, but dark and sallow where the other was blond. He had just the same narrow head, and stubborn mouth, and honest, quick-tempered eyes. It is the type that makes dashing regimental officers, and earns V.C.s, and gets done in wholesale. I was never that kind. I belonged to the school of the cunning cowards.

In the half-hour before dinner the last wisp of suspicion fled from my host's mind. For Ted Broadbury and I were immediately deep in 'shop'. I had met most of his senior officers, and I knew all about their doings at Arras, for his brigade had been across the river on my left. We fought the great fight over again, and yarned about technicalities and slanged the Staff in the way young officers have, the father throwing in questions that showed how mighty proud he was of his son. I had a bath before dinner, and as he led me to the bathroom he apologized very handsomely for his bad manners. 'Your coming's been a godsend for Ted. He was moping a bit in this place. And, though I say it that shouldn't, he's a dashed good boy.'

I had my promised bottle of port, and after dinner I took on the father at billiards. Then we settled in the smoking-room, and I laid myself out to entertain the pair. The result was that they would have me stay a week, but I spoke of the shortness of my leave, and said I must get on to the railway and then back to Fort William for my luggage.

So I spent that night between clean sheets, and ate a Christian breakfast, and was given my host's car to set me a bit on the road. I dismissed it after half a dozen miles, and, following the map, struck over the hills to the west. About midday I topped a ridge, and beheld the Sound of Sleat shining beneath me. There were other things in the landscape. In the valley on the right a long goods train was crawling on the Mallaig railway. And across the strip of sea, like some fortress of the old gods, rose the dark bastions and turrets of the hills of Skye.

John Buchan

CHAPTER SIX

THE SKIRTS OF THE COOLIN

Obviously I must keep away from the railway. If the police were after me in Morvern, that line would be warned, for it was a barrier I must cross if I were to go farther north. I observed from the map that it turned up the coast, and concluded that the place for me to make for was the shore south of that turn, where Heaven might send me some luck in the boat line. For I was pretty certain that every porter and station-master on that tin-pot outfit was anxious to make better acquaintance with my humble self.

I lunched off the sandwiches the Broadburys had given me, and in the bright afternoon made my way down the hill, crossed at the foot of a small fresh-water lochan, and pursued the issuing stream through midge-infested woods of hazels to its junction with the sea. It was rough going, but very pleasant, and I fell into the same mood of idle contentment that I had enjoyed the previous morning. I never met a soul. Sometimes a roe deer broke out of the covert, or an old blackcock startled me with his scolding. The place was bright with heather, still in its first bloom, and smelt better than the myrrh of Arabia. It was a blessed glen, and I was as happy as a king, till I began to feel the coming of hunger, and reflected that the Lord alone knew when I might get a meal. I had still some chocolate and biscuits, but I wanted something substantial.

The distance was greater than I thought, and it was already

twilight when I reached the coast. The shore was open and desolate - great banks of pebbles to which straggled alders and hazels from the hillside scrub. But as I marched northward and turned a little point of land I saw before me in a crook of the bay a smoking cottage. And, plodding along by the water's edge, was the bent figure of a man, laden with nets and lobster pots. Also, beached on the shingle was a boat.

I quickened my pace and overtook the fisherman. He was an old man with a ragged grey beard, and his rig was seaman's boots and a much-darned blue jersey. He was deaf, and did not hear me when I hailed him. When he caught sight of me he never stopped, though he very solemnly returned my good evening. I fell into step with him, and in his silent company reached the cottage.

He halted before the door and unslung his burdens. The place was a two-roomed building with a roof of thatch, and the walls all grown over with a yellow-flowered creeper. When he had straightened his back, he looked seaward and at the sky, as if to prospect the weather. Then he turned on me his gentle, absorbed eyes. 'It will haf been a fine day, sir. Wass you seeking the road to anywhere?'

'I was seeking a night's lodging,' I said. 'I've had a long tramp on the hills, and I'd be glad of a chance of not going farther.'

'We will haf no accommodation for a gentleman,' he said gravely.

'I can sleep on the floor, if you can give me a blanket and a bite of supper.'

'Indeed you will not,' and he smiled slowly. 'But I will ask the wife. Mary, come here!'

An old woman appeared in answer to his call, a woman whose face was so old that she seemed like his mother. In highland places one sex ages quicker than the other.

John Buchan

'This gentleman would like to bide the night. I wass telling him that we had a poor small house, but he says he will not be minding it.'

She looked at me with the timid politeness that you find only in outland places.

'We can do our best, indeed, sir. The gentleman can have Colin's bed in the loft, but he will haf to be doing with plain food. Supper is ready if you will come in now.'

I had a scrub with a piece of yellow soap at an adjacent pool in the burn and then entered a kitchen blue with peat-reek. We had a meal of boiled fish, oatcakes and skim-milk cheese, with cups of strong tea to wash it down. The old folk had the manners of princes. They pressed food on me, and asked me no questions, till for very decency's sake I had to put up a story and give some account of myself.

I found they had a son in the Argylls and a young boy in the Navy. But they seemed disinclined to talk of them or of the war. By a mere accident I hit on the old man's absorbing interest. He was passionate about the land. He had taken part in long-forgotten agitations, and had suffered eviction in some ancient landlords' quarrel farther north. Presently he was pouring out to me all the woes of the crofter - woes that seemed so antediluvian and forgotten that I listened as one would listen to an old song. 'You who come from a new country will not haf heard of these things,' he kept telling me, but by that peat fire I made up for my defective education. He told me of evictions in the year. One somewhere in Sutherland, and of harsh doings in the Outer Isles. It was far more than a political grievance. It was the lament of the conservative for vanished days and manners. 'Over in Skye wass the fine land for black cattle, and every man had his bit herd on the hillside. But the lairds said it wass better for sheep, and then they said it wass not good for sheep, so they put it under deer, and now there is no black cattle anywhere in Skye.' I tell you it was like sad music on the bagpipes hearing that old fellow. The war and all things modern meant nothing to him; he lived among the tragedies of his youth and his prime.

I'm a Tory myself and a bit of a land-reformer, so we agreed well enough. So well, that I got what I wanted without asking for it. I told him I was going to Skye, and he offered to take me over in his boat in the morning. 'It will be no trouble. Indeed no. I will be going that way myself to the fishing.'

I told him that after the war, every acre of British soil would have to be used for the men that had earned the right to it. But that did not comfort him. He was not thinking about the land itself, but about the men who had been driven from it fifty years before. His desire was not for reform, but for restitution, and that was past the power of any Government. I went to bed in the loft in a sad, reflective mood, considering how in speeding our newfangled plough we must break down a multitude of molehills and how desirable and unreplaceable was the life of the moles.

In brisk, shining weather, with a wind from the south-east, we put off next morning. In front was a brown line of low hills, and behind them, a little to the north, that black toothcomb of mountain range which I had seen the day before from the Arisaig ridge.

'That is the Coolin,' said the fisherman. 'It is a bad place where even the deer cannot go. But all the rest of Skye wass the fine land for black cattle.'

As we neared the coast, he pointed out many places. 'Look there, Sir, in that glen. I haf seen six cot houses smoking there, and now there is not any left. There were three men of my own name had crofts on the machars beyond the point, and if you go there you will only find the marks of their bit gardens. You will know the place by the gean trees.' When he put me ashore in a sandy bay between green ridges of bracken, he was still harping upon the past. I got him to take a pound - for the boat and not for the night's hospitality, for he would have beaten me with an oar if I had suggested that. The last I saw of him, as I turned round at the top of the hill, he had still his sail down, and was gazing at the lands which had once been full of human dwellings and now were desolate.

I kept for a while along the ridge, with the Sound of Sleat on my right, and beyond it the high hills of Knoydart and Kintail. I was watching for the Tobermory, but saw no sign of her. A steamer put out from Mallaig, and there were several drifters crawling up the channel and once I saw the white ensign and a destroyer bustled northward, leaving a cloud of black smoke in her wake. Then, after consulting the map, I struck across country, still keeping the higher ground, but, except at odd minutes, being out of sight of the sea. I concluded that my business was to get to the latitude of Ranna without wasting time.

So soon as I changed my course I had the Coolin for company. Mountains have always been a craze of mine, and the blackness and mystery of those grim peaks went to my head. I forgot all about Fosse Manor and the Cotswolds. I forgot, too, what had been my chief feeling since I left Glasgow, a sense of the absurdity of my mission. It had all seemed too far-fetched and whimsical. I was running apparently no great personal risk, and I had always the unpleasing fear that Blenkiron might have been too clever and that the whole thing might be a mare's nest. But that dark mountain mass changed my outlook. I began to have a queer instinct that that was the place, that something might be concealed there, something pretty damnable. I remember I sat on a top for half an hour raking the hills with my glasses. I made out ugly precipices, and glens which lost themselves in primeval blackness. When the sun caught them - for it was a gleamy day - it brought out no colours, only degrees of shade. No mountains I had ever seen - not the Drakensberg or the red kopjes of Damaraland or the cold, white peaks around Erzerum - ever looked so unearthly and uncanny.

Oddly enough, too, the sight of them set me thinking about

Ivery. There seemed no link between a smooth, sedentary being, dwelling in villas and lecture-rooms, and that shaggy tangle of precipices. But I felt there was, for I had begun to realize the bigness of my opponent. Blenkiron had said that he spun his web wide. That was intelligible enough among the half-baked youth of Biggleswick, and the pacifist societies, or even the toughs on the Clyde. I could fit him in all right to that picture. But that he should be playing his game among those mysterious black crags seemed to make him bigger and more desperate, altogether a different kind of proposition. I didn't exactly dislike the idea, for my objection to my past weeks had been that I was out of my proper job, and this was more my line of country. I always felt that I was a better bandit than a detective. But a sort of awe mingled with my satisfaction. I began to feel about Ivery as I had felt about the three devils of the Black Stone who had hunted me before the war, and as I never felt about any other Hun. The men we fought at the Front and the men I had run across in the Greenmantle business, even old Stumm himself, had been human miscreants. They were formidable enough, but you could gauge and calculate their capacities. But this Ivery was like a poison gas that hung in the air and got into unexpected crannies and that you couldn't fight in an upstanding way. Till then, in spite of Blenkiron's solemnity, I had regarded him simply as a problem. But now he seemed an intimate and omnipresent enemy, intangible, too, as the horror of a haunted house. Up on that sunny hillside, with the sea winds round me and the whaups calling, I got a chill in my spine when I thought of him.

I am ashamed to confess it, but I was also horribly hungry. There was something about the war that made me ravenous, and the less chance of food the worse I felt. If I had been in London with twenty restaurants open to me, I should as likely as not have gone off my feed. That was the cussedness of my stomach. I had still a little chocolate left, and I ate the fisherman's buttered scones for luncheon, but long before the evening my thoughts were dwelling on my empty interior.

John Buchan

I put up that night in a shepherd's cottage miles from anywhere. The man was called Macmorran, and he had come from Galloway when sheep were booming. He was a very good imitation of a savage, a little fellow with red hair and red eyes, who might have been a Pict. He lived with a daughter who had once been in service in Glasgow, a fat young woman with a face entirely covered with freckles and a pout of habitual discontent. No wonder, for that cottage was a pretty mean place. It was so thick with peat-reek that throat and eyes were always smarting. It was badly built, and must have leaked like a sieve in a storm. The father was a surly fellow, whose conversation was one long growl at the world, the high prices, the difficulty of moving his sheep, the meanness of his master, and the godforsaken character of Skye. 'Here's me no seen baker's bread for a month, and no company but a wheen ignorant Hielanders that yatter Gawlic. I wish I was back in the Glenkens. And I'd gang the morn if I could get paid what I'm awed.'

However, he gave me supper - a braxy ham and oatcake, and I bought the remnants off him for use next day. I did not trust his blankets, so I slept the night by the fire in the ruins of an arm-chair, and woke at dawn with a foul taste in my mouth. A dip in the burn refreshed me, and after a bowl of porridge I took the road again. For I was anxious to get to some hill-top that looked over to Ranna.

Before midday I was close under the eastern side of the Coolin, on a road which was more a rockery than a path. Presently I saw a big house ahead of me that looked like an inn, so I gave it a miss and struck the highway that led to it a little farther north. Then I bore off to the east, and was just beginning to climb a hill which I judged stood between me and the sea, when I heard wheels on the road and looked back.

It was a farmer's gig carrying one man. I was about half a mile off, and something in the cut of his jib seemed familiar. I got my glasses on him and made out a short, stout figure clad in a mackintosh, with a woollen comforter round its throat. As I watched, it made a movement as if to rub its nose on its sleeve. That was the pet trick of one man I knew. Inconspicuously I slipped through the long heather so as to reach the road ahead of the gig. When I rose like a wraith from the wayside the horse started, but not the driver.

'So ye're there,' said Amos's voice. 'I've news for ye. The Tobermory will be in Ranna by now. She passed Broadford two hours syne. When I saw her I yoked this beast and came up on the chance of foregathering with ye.'

'How on earth did you know I would be here?' I asked in some surprise.

'Oh, I saw the way your mind was workin' from your telegram. And says I to mysel' - that man Brand, says I, is not the chiel to be easy stoppit. But I was feared ye might be a day late, so I came up the road to hold the fort. Man, I'm glad to see ye. Ye're younger and soopler than me, and yon Gresson's a stirrin' lad.'

'There's one thing you've got to do for me,' I said. 'I can't go into inns and shops, but I can't do without food. I see from the map there's a town about six miles on. Go there and buy me anything that's tinned - biscuits and tongue and sardines, and a couple of bottles of whisky if you can get them. This may be a long job, so buy plenty.'

'Whaur'll I put them?' was his only question.

We fixed on a cache, a hundred yards from the highway in a place where two ridges of hill enclosed the view so that only a short bit of road was visible.

'I'll get back to the Kyle,' he told me, 'and a'body there kens Andra Amos, if ye should find a way of sendin' a message or comin' yourself. Oh, and I've got a word to ye from a lady that we ken of. She says, the sooner ye're back in Vawnity Fair the better she'll be pleased, always provided ye've got over the

Hill Difficulty.'

A smile screwed up his old face and he waved his whip in farewell. I interpreted Mary's message as an incitement to speed, but I could not make the pace. That was Gresson's business. I think I was a little nettled, till I cheered myself by another interpretation. She might be anxious for my safety, she might want to see me again, anyhow the mere sending of the message showed I was not forgotten. I was in a pleasant muse as I breasted the hill, keeping discreetly in the cover of the many gullies. At the top I looked down on Ranna and the sea.

There lay the Tobermory busy unloading. It would be some time, no doubt, before Gresson could leave. There was no row-boat in the channel yet, and I might have to wait hours. I settled myself snugly between two rocks, where I could not be seen, and where I had a clear view of the sea and shore. But presently I found that I wanted some long heather to make a couch, and I emerged to get some. I had not raised my head for a second when I flopped down again. For I had a neighbour on the hill-top.

He was about two hundred yards off, just reaching the crest, and, unlike me, walking quite openly. His eyes were on Ranna, so he did not notice me, but from my cover I scanned every line of him. He looked an ordinary countryman, wearing badly cut, baggy knickerbockers of the kind that gillies affect. He had a face like a Portuguese Jew, but I had seen that type before among people with Highland names; they might be Jews or not, but they could speak Gaelic. Presently he disappeared. He had followed my example and selected a hiding-place.

It was a clear, hot day, but very pleasant in that airy place. Good scents came up from the sea, the heather was warm and fragrant, bees droned about, and stray seagulls swept the ridge with their wings. I took a look now and then towards my neighbour, but he was deep in his hidey-hole. Most of the time I kept my glasses on Ranna, and watched the doings of the

Tobermory. She was tied up at the jetty, but seemed in no hurry to unload. I watched the captain disembark and walk up to a house on the hillside. Then some idlers sauntered down towards her and stood talking and smoking close to her side. The captain returned and left again. A man with papers in his hand appeared, and a woman with what looked like a telegram. The mate went ashore in his best clothes. Then at last, after midday, Gresson appeared. He joined the captain at the piermaster's office, and presently emerged on the other side of the jetty where some small boats were beached. A man from the Tobermory came in answer to his call, a boat was launched, and began to make its way into the channel. Gresson sat in the stern, placidly eating his luncheon.

I watched every detail of that crossing with some satisfaction that my forecast was turning out right. About half-way across, Gresson took the oars, but soon surrendered them to the Tobermory man, and lit a pipe. He got out a pair of binoculars and raked my hillside. I tried to see if my neighbour was making any signal, but all was quiet. Presently the boat was hid from me by the bulge of the hill, and I caught the sound of her scraping on the beach.

Gresson was not a hill-walker like my neighbour. It took him the best part of an hour to get to the top, and he reached it at a point not two yards from my hiding-place. I could hear by his labouring breath that he was very blown. He walked straight over the crest till he was out of sight of Ranna, and flung himself on the ground. He was now about fifty yards from me, and I made shift to lessen the distance. There was a grassy trench skirting the north side of the hill, deep and thickly overgrown with heather. I wound my way along it till I was about twelve yards from him, where I stuck, owing to the trench dying away. When I peered out of the cover I saw that the other man had joined him and that the idiots were engaged in embracing each other.

I dared not move an inch nearer, and as they talked in a low voice I could hear nothing of what they said. Nothing except one phrase, which the strange man repeated twice, very emphatically. 'Tomorrow night,' he said, and I noticed that his voice had not the Highland inflection which I looked for. Gresson nodded and glanced at his watch, and then the two began to move downhill towards the road I had travelled that morning.

I followed as best I could, using a shallow dry watercourse of which sheep had made a track, and which kept me well below the level of the moor. It took me down the hill, but some distance from the line the pair were taking, and I had to reconnoitre frequently to watch their movements. They were still a quarter of a mile or so from the road, when they stopped and stared, and I stared with them. On that lonely highway travellers were about as rare as roadmenders, and what caught their eye was a farmer's gig driven by a thick-set elderly man with a woollen comforter round his neck.

I had a bad moment, for I reckoned that if Gresson recognized Amos he might take fright. Perhaps the driver of the gig thought the same, for he appeared to be very drunk. He waved his whip, he jiggoted the reins, and he made an effort to sing. He looked towards the figures on the hillside, and cried out something. The gig narrowly missed the ditch, and then to my relief the horse bolted. Swaying like a ship in a gale, the whole outfit lurched out of sight round the corner of hill where lay my cache. If Amos could stop the beast and deliver the goods there, he had put up a masterly bit of buffoonery.

The two men laughed at the performance, and then they parted. Gresson retraced his steps up the hill. The other man - I called him in my mind the Portuguese Jew - started off at a great pace due west, across the road, and over a big patch of bog towards the northern butt of the Coolin. He had some errand, which Gresson knew about, and he was in a hurry to perform it. It was clearly my job to get after him.

I had a rotten afternoon. The fellow covered the moorland miles like a deer, and under the hot August sun I toiled on his trail. I had to keep well behind, and as much as possible in cover, in case he looked back; and that meant that when he had passed over a ridge I had to double not to let him get too far ahead, and when we were in an open place I had to make wide circuits to keep hidden. We struck a road which crossed a low pass and skirted the flank of the mountains, and this we followed till we were on the western side and within sight of the sea. It was gorgeous weather, and out on the blue water I saw cool sails moving and little breezes ruffling the calm, while I was glowing like a furnace. Happily I was in fair training, and I needed it. The Portuguese Jew must have done a steady six miles an hour over abominable country.

About five o'clock we came to a point where I dared not follow. The road ran flat by the edge of the sea, so that several miles of it were visible. Moreover, the man had begun to look round every few minutes. He was getting near something and wanted to be sure that no one was in his neighbourhood. I left the road accordingly, and took to the hillside, which to my undoing was one long cascade of screes and tumbled rocks. I saw him drop over a rise which seemed to mark the rim of a little bay into which descended one of the big corries of the mountains. It must have been a good half-hour later before I, at my greater altitude and with far worse going, reached the same rim. I looked into the glen and my man had disappeared.

He could not have crossed it, for the place was wider than I had thought. A ring of black precipices came down to within half a mile of the shore, and between them was a big stream - long, shallow pools at the sea end and a chain of waterfalls above. He had gone to earth like a badger somewhere, and I dared not move in case he might be watching me from behind a boulder.

But even as I hesitated he appeared again, fording the stream, his face set on the road we had come. Whatever his errand was he had finished it, and was posting back to his master. For a moment I thought I should follow him, but another instinct prevailed. He had not come to this wild place for the scenery.

Somewhere down in the glen there was something or somebody that held the key of the mystery. It was my business to stay there till I had unlocked it. Besides, in two hours it would be dark, and I had had enough walking for one day.

I made my way to the stream side and had a long drink. The corrie behind me was lit up with the westering sun, and the bald cliffs were flushed with pink and gold. On each side of the stream was turf like a lawn, perhaps a hundred yards wide, and then a tangle of long heather and boulders right up to the edge of the great rocks. I had never seen a more delectable evening, but I could not enjoy its peace because of my anxiety about the Portuguese Jew. He had not been there more than half an hour, just about long enough for a man to travel to the first ridge across the burn and back. Yet he had found time to do his business. He might have left a letter in some prearranged place - in which case I would stay there till the man it was meant for turned up. Or he might have met someone, though I didn't think that possible. As I scanned the acres of rough moor and then looked at the sea lapping delicately on the grey sand I had the feeling that a knotty problem was before me. It was too dark to try to track his steps. That must be left for the morning, and I prayed that there would be no rain in the night.

I ate for supper most of the braxy ham and oatcake I had brought from Macmorran's cottage. It took some self-denial, for I was ferociously hungry, to save a little for breakfast next morning. Then I pulled heather and bracken and made myself a bed in the shelter of a rock which stood on a knoll above the stream. My bed-chamber was well hidden, but at the same time, if anything should appear in the early dawn, it gave me a prospect. With my waterproof I was perfectly warm, and, after smoking two pipes, I fell asleep.

My night's rest was broken. First it was a fox which came and barked at my ear and woke me to a pitch-black night, with scarcely a star showing. The next time it was nothing but a wandering hill-wind, but as I sat up and listened I thought I saw a spark of light near the edge of the sea. It was only for a second, but it disquieted me. I got out and climbed on the top of the rock, but all was still save for the gentle lap of the tide and the croak of some night bird among the crags. The third time I was suddenly quite wide awake, and without any reason, for I had not been dreaming. Now I have slept hundreds of times alone beside my horse on the veld, and I never knew any cause for such awakenings but the one, and that was the presence near me of some human being. A man who is accustomed to solitude gets this extra sense which announces like an alarm-clock the approach of one of his kind.

But I could hear nothing. There was a scraping and rustling on the moor, but that was only the wind and the little wild things of the hills. A fox, perhaps, or a blue hare. I convinced my reason, but not my senses, and for long I lay awake with my ears at full cock and every nerve tense. Then I fell asleep, and woke to the first flush of dawn.

The sun was behind the Coolin and the hills were black as ink, but far out in the western seas was a broad band of gold. I got up and went down to the shore. The mouth of the stream was shallow, but as I moved south I came to a place where two small capes enclosed an inlet. It must have been a fault in the volcanic rock, for its depth was portentous. I stripped and dived far into its cold abysses, but I did not reach the bottom. I came to the surface rather breathless, and struck out to sea, where I floated on my back and looked at the great rampart of crag. I saw that the place where I had spent the night was only a little oasis of green at the base of one of the grimmest corries the imagination could picture. It was as desert as Damaraland. I noticed, too, how sharply the cliffs rose from the level. There were chimneys and gullies by which a man might have made his way to the summit, but no one of them could have been scaled except by a mountaineer.

I was feeling better now, with all the frowsiness washed out of me, and I dried myself by racing up and down the heather. Then I noticed something. There were marks of human feet at

John Buchan

the top of the deep-water inlet - not mine, for they were on the other side. The short sea-turf was bruised and trampled in several places, and there were broken stems of bracken. I thought that some fisherman had probably landed there to stretch his legs.

But that set me thinking of the Portuguese Jew. After breakfasting on my last morsels of food - a knuckle of braxy and a bit of oatcake - I set about tracking him from the place where he had first entered the glen. To get my bearings, I went back over the road I had come myself, and after a good deal of trouble I found his spoor. It was pretty clear as far as the stream, for he had been walking - or rather running - over ground with many patches of gravel on it. After that it was difficult, and I lost it entirely in the rough heather below the crags. All that I could make out for certain was that he had crossed the stream, and that his business, whatever it was, had been with the few acres of tumbled wilderness below the precipices.

I spent a busy morning there, but found nothing except the skeleton of a sheep picked clean by the ravens. It was a thankless job, and I got very cross over it. I had an ugly feeling that I was on a false scent and wasting my time. I wished to Heaven I had old Peter with me. He could follow spoor like a Bushman, and would have riddled the Portuguese jew's track out of any jungle on earth. That was a game I had never learned, for in the old days I had always left it to my natives. I chucked the attempt, and lay disconsolately on a warm patch of grass and smoked and thought about Peter. But my chief reflections were that I had breakfasted at five, that it was now eleven, that I was intolerably hungry, that there was nothing here to feed a grasshopper, and that I should starve unless I got supplies.

It was a long road to my cache, but there were no two ways of it. My only hope was to sit tight in the glen, and it might involve a wait of days. To wait I must have food, and, though it meant relinquishing guard for a matter of six hours, the risk had to be taken. I set off at a brisk pace with a very depressed mind.

From the map it seemed that a short cut lay over a pass in the range. I resolved to take it, and that short cut, like most of its kind, was unblessed by Heaven. I will not dwell upon the discomforts of the journey. I found myself slithering among screes, climbing steep chimneys, and travelling precariously along razor-backs. The shoes were nearly rent from my feet by the infernal rocks,which were all pitted as if by some geological small-pox. When at last I crossed the divide, I had a horrible business getting down from one level to another in a gruesome corrie, where each step was composed of smooth boiler-plates. But at last I was among the bogs on the east side, and came to the place beside the road where I had fixed my cache.

The faithful Amos had not failed me. There were the provisions - a couple of small loaves, a dozen tins, and a bottle of whisky. I made the best pack I could of them in my waterproof, swung it on my stick, and started back, thinking that I must be very like the picture of Christian on the title-page of Pilgrim's Progress.

I was liker Christian before I reached my destination - Christian after he had got up the Hill Difficulty. The morning's walk had been bad, but the afternoon's was worse, for I was in a fever to get back, and, having had enough of the hills, chose the longer route I had followed the previous day. I was mortally afraid of being seen, for I cut a queer figure, so I avoided every stretch of road where I had not a clear view ahead. Many weary detours I made among moss-hags and screes and the stony channels of burns. But I got there at last, and it was almost with a sense of comfort that I flung my pack down beside the stream where I had passed the night.

I ate a good meal, lit my pipe, and fell into the equable mood which follows upon fatigue ended and hunger satisfied. The sun was westering, and its light fell upon the rock-wall above the place where I had abandoned my search for the spoor.

As I gazed at it idly I saw a curious thing.

It seemed to be split in two and a shaft of sunlight came through between. There could be no doubt about it. I saw the end of the shaft on the moor beneath, while all the rest lay in shadow. I rubbed my eyes, and got out my glasses. Then I guessed the explanation. There was a rock tower close against the face of the main precipice and indistinguishable from it to anyone looking direct at the face. Only when the sun fell on it obliquely could it be discovered. And between the tower and the cliff there must be a substantial hollow.

The discovery brought me to my feet, and set me running towards the end of the shaft of sunlight. I left the heather, scrambled up some yards of screes, and had a difficult time on some very smooth slabs, where only the friction of tweed and rough rock gave me a hold. Slowly I worked my way towards the speck of sunlight, till I found a handhold, and swung myself into the crack. On one side was the main wall of the hill, on the other a tower some ninety feet high, and between them a long crevice varying in width from three to six feet. Beyond it there showed a small bright patch of sea.

There was more, for at the point where I entered it there was an overhang which made a fine cavern, low at the entrance but a dozen feet high inside, and as dry as tinder. Here, thought I, is the perfect hiding-place. Before going farther I resolved to return for food. It was not very easy descending, and I slipped the last twenty feet, landing on my head in a soft patch of screes. At the burnside I filled my flask from the whisky bottle, and put half a loaf, a tin of sardines, a tin of tongue, and a packet of chocolate in my waterproof pockets. Laden as I was, it took me some time to get up again, but I managed it, and stored my belongings in a corner of the cave. Then I set out to explore the rest of the crack.

It slanted down and then rose again to a small platform. After that it dropped in easy steps to the moor beyond the tower. If the Portuguese Jew had come here, that was the way by which he had reached it, for he would not have had the time to make my ascent. I went very cautiously, for I felt I was on the eve of a big discovery. The platform was partly hidden from my end by a bend in the crack, and it was more or less screened by an outlying bastion of the tower from the other side. Its surface was covered with fine powdery dust, as were the steps beyond it. In some excitement I knelt down and examined it.

Beyond doubt there was spoor here. I knew the Portuguese jew's footmarks by this time, and I made them out clearly, especially in one corner. But there were other footsteps, quite different. The one showed the rackets of rough country boots, the others were from un-nailed soles. Again I longed for Peter to make certain, though I was pretty sure of my conclusions. The man I had followed had come here, and he had not stayed long. Someone else had been here, probably later, for the un-nailed shoes overlaid the rackets. The first man might have left a message for the second. Perhaps the second was that human presence of which I had been dimly conscious in the night-time.

I carefully removed all traces of my own footmarks, and went back to my cave. My head was humming with my discovery. I remembered Gresson's word to his friend: 'Tomorrow night.' As I read it, the Portuguese Jew had taken a message from Gresson to someone, and that someone had come from somewhere and picked it up. The message contained an assignation for this very night. I had found a point of observation, for no one was likely to come near my cave, which was reached from the moor by such a toilsome climb. There I should bivouac and see what the darkness brought forth. I remember reflecting on the amazing luck which had so far attended me. As I looked from my refuge at the blue haze of twilight creeping over the waters, I felt my pulses quicken with a wild anticipation.

Then I heard a sound below me, and craned my neck round the edge of the tower. A man was climbing up the rock by the way I had come.

John Buchan

CHAPTER SEVEN

I HEAR OF THE WILD BIRDS

I saw an old green felt hat, and below it lean tweed-clad shoulders. Then I saw a knapsack with a stick slung through it, as the owner wriggled his way on to a shelf. Presently he turned his face upward to judge the remaining distance. It was the face of a young man, a face sallow and angular, but now a little flushed with the day's sun and the work of climbing. It was a face that I had first seen at Fosse Manor.

I felt suddenly sick and heartsore. I don't know why, but I had never really associated the intellectuals of Biggleswick with a business like this. None of them but Ivery, and he was different. They had been silly and priggish, but no more - I would have taken my oath on it. Yet here was one of them engaged in black treason against his native land. Something began to beat in my temples when I remembered that Mary and this man had been friends, that he had held her hand, and called her by her Christian name. My first impulse was to wait till he got up and then pitch him down among the boulders and let his German accomplices puzzle over his broken neck.

With difficulty I kept down that tide of fury. I had my duty to do, and to keep on terms with this man was part of it. I had to convince him that I was an accomplice, and that might not be easy. I leaned over the edge, and, as he got to his feet on the ledge above the boiler-plates, I whistled so that he turned his face to me. 'Hullo, Wake,'I said.

He started, stared for a second, and recognized me. He did not seem over-pleased to see me.

'Brand!' he cried. 'How did you get here?'

He swung himself up beside me, straightened his back and unbuckled his knapsack. 'I thought this was my own private sanctuary, and that nobody knew it but me. Have you spotted the cave? It's the best bedroom in Skye.' His tone was, as usual, rather acid.

That little hammer was beating in my head. I longed to get my hands on his throat and choke the smug treason in him. But I kept my mind fixed on one purpose - to persuade him that I shared his secret and was on his side. His off-hand self-possession seemed only the clever screen of the surprised conspirator who was hunting for a plan.

We entered the cave, and he flung his pack into a corner. 'Last time I was here,' he said, 'I covered the floor with heather. We must get some more if we would sleep soft.' In the twilight he was a dim figure, but he seemed a new man from the one I had last seen in the Moot Hall at Biggleswick. There was a wiry vigour in his body and a purpose in his face. What a fool I had been to set him down as no more than a conceited fidneur!

He went out to the shelf again and sniffed the fresh evening. There was a wonderful red sky in the west, but in the crevice the shades had fallen, and only the bright patches at either end told of the sunset. 'Wake,' I said, 'you and I have to understand each other. I'm a friend of Ivery and I know the meaning of this place. I discovered it by accident, but I want you to know that I'm heart and soul with you. You may trust me in tonight's job as if I were Ivery himself.'

He swung round and looked at me sharply. His eyes were hot again, as I remembered them at our first meeting.

'What do you mean? How much do you know?'

The hammer was going hard in my forehead, and I had to pull myself together to answer.

'I know that at the end of this crack a message was left last night, and that someone came out of the sea and picked it up. That someone is coming again when darkness falls, and there will be another message.'

He had turned his head away. 'You are talking nonsense. No submarine could land on this coast.'

I could see that he was trying me. 'This morning,' I said, 'I swam in the deep-water inlet below us. It is the most perfect submarine shelter in Britain.'

He still kept his face from me, looking the way he had come. For a moment he was silent, and then he spoke in the bitter, drawling voice which had annoyed me at Fosse Manor.

'How do you reconcile this business with your principles, Mr Brand? You were always a patriot, I remember, though you didn't see eye to eye with the Government.'

It was not quite what I expected and I was unready. I stammered in my reply. 'It's because I am a patriot that I want peace. I think that ... I mean ...'

'Therefore you are willing to help the enemy to win?'

'They have already won. I want that recognized and the end hurried on.' I was getting my mind clearer and continued fluently. 'The longer the war lasts, the worse this country is ruined. We must make the people realize the truth, and -'

But he swung round suddenly, his eyes blazing.

'You blackguard!' he cried, 'you damnable blackguard!' And he flung himself on me like a wild-cat.

I had got my answer. He did not believe me, he knew me for a spy, and he was determined to do me in. We were beyond finesse now, and back at the old barbaric game. It was his life or mine. The hammer beat furiously in my head as we closed, and a fierce satisfaction rose in my heart. He never had a chance, for though he was in good trim and had the light, wiry figure of the mountaineer, he hadn't a quarter of my muscular strength. Besides, he was wrongly placed, for he had the outside station. Had he been on the inside he might have toppled me over the edge by his sudden assault. As it was, I grappled him and forced him to the ground, squeezing the breath out of his body in the process. I must have hurt him considerably, but he never gave a cry. With a good deal of trouble I lashed his hands behind his back with the belt of my waterproof, carried him inside the cave and laid him in the dark end of it. Then I tied his feet with the strap of his own knapsack. I would have to gag him, but that could wait.

I had still to contrive a plan of action for the night, for I did not know what part he had been meant to play in it. He might be the messenger instead of the Portuguese Jew, in which case he would have papers about his person. If he knew of the cave, others might have the same knowledge, and I had better shift him before they came. I looked at my wrist-watch, and the luminous dial showed that the hour was half past nine.

Then I noticed that the bundle in the corner was sobbing. It was a horrid sound and it worried me. I had a little pocket electric torch and I flashed it on Wake's face. If he was crying, it was with dry eyes.

'What are you going to do with me?' he asked.

'That depends,' I said grimly.

'Well, I'm ready. I may be a poor creature, but I'm damned if I'm afraid of you, or anything like you.' That was a brave thing to say, for it was a lie; his teeth were chattering.

'I'm ready for a deal,' I said.

'You won't get it,' was his answer. 'Cut my throat if you mean to, but for God's sake don't insult me ... I choke when I think about you. You come to us and we welcome you, and receive you in our houses, and tell you our inmost thoughts, and all the time you're a bloody traitor. You want to sell us to Germany. You may win now, but by God! your time will come! That is my last word to you ... you swine!'

The hammer stopped beating in my head. I saw myself suddenly as a blind, preposterous fool. I strode over to Wake, and he shut his eyes as if he expected a blow. Instead I unbuckled the straps which held his legs and arms.

'Wake, old fellow,' I said, 'I'm the worst kind of idiot. I'll eat all the dirt you want. I'll give you leave to knock me black and blue, and I won't lift a hand. But not now. Now we've another job on hand. Man, we're on the same side and I never knew it. It's too bad a case for apologies, but if it's any consolation to you I feel the lowest dog in Europe at this moment.'

He was sitting up rubbing his bruised shoulders. 'What do you mean?' he asked hoarsely.

'I mean that you and I are allies. My name's not Brand. I'm a soldier - a general, if you want to know. I went to Biggleswick under orders, and I came chasing up here on the same job. Ivery's the biggest German agent in Britain and I'm after him. I've struck his communication lines, and this very night, please God, we'll get the last clue to the riddle. Do you hear? We're in this business together, and you've got to lend a hand.'

I told him briefly the story of Gresson, and how I had tracked his man here. As I talked we ate our supper, and I wish I could have watched Wake's face. He asked questions, for he wasn't convinced in a hurry. I think it was my mention of Mary Lamington that did the trick. I don't know why, but that seemed to satisfy him. But he wasn't going to give himself away.

'You may count on me,' he said, 'for this is black, blackguardly treason. But you know my politics, and I don't change them for this. I'm more against your accursed war than ever, now that I know what war involves.'

'Right-o,' I said, 'I'm a pacifist myself. You won't get any heroics about war from me. I'm all for peace, but we've got to down those devils first.'

It wasn't safe for either of us to stick in that cave, so we cleared away the marks of our occupation, and hid our packs in a deep crevice on the rock. Wake announced his intention of climbing the tower, while there was still a faint afterglow of light. 'It's broad on the top, and I can keep a watch out to sea if any light shows. I've been up it before. I found the way two years ago. No, I won't fall asleep and tumble off. I slept most of the afternoon on the top of Sgurr Vhiconnich, and I'm as wakeful as a bat now.'

I watched him shin up the face of the tower, and admired greatly the speed and neatness with which he climbed. Then I followed the crevice southward to the hollow just below the platform where I had found the footmarks. There was a big boulder there, which partly shut off the view of it from the direction of our cave. The place was perfect for my purpose, for between the boulder and the wall of the tower was a narrow gap, through which I could hear all that passed on the platform. I found a stance where I could rest in comfort and keep an eye through the crack on what happened beyond.

There was still a faint light on the platform, but soon that disappeared and black darkness settled down on the hills. It was the dark of the moon, and, as had happened the night before, a thin wrack blew over the sky, hiding the stars. The place was very still, though now and then would come the cry of a bird from the crags that beetled above me, and from the shore the pipe of a tern or oyster-catcher. An owl hooted from somewhere up on the tower. That I reckoned was Wake, so I hooted back and was answered. I unbuckled my wrist-watch and pocketed it, lest its luminous dial should betray me; and I noticed that the hour was close on eleven. I had already removed my shoes, and my jacket was buttoned at the collar so as to show no shirt. I did not think that the coming visitor would trouble to explore the crevice beyond the platform, but I wanted to be prepared for emergencies.

Then followed an hour of waiting. I felt wonderfully cheered and exhilarated, for Wake had restored my confidence in human nature. In that eerie place we were wrapped round with mystery like a fog. Some unknown figure was coming out of the sea, the emissary of that Power we had been at grips with for three years. It was as if the war had just made contact with our own shores, and never, not even when I was alone in the South German forest, had I felt so much the sport of a whimsical fate. I only wished Peter could have been with me. And so my thoughts fled to Peter in his prison camp, and I longed for another sight of my old friend as a girl longs for her lover.

Then I heard the hoot of an owl, and presently the sound of careful steps fell on my ear. I could see nothing, but I guessed it was the Portuguese Jew, for I could hear the grinding of heavily nailed boots on the gritty rock.

The figure was very quiet. It appeared to be sitting down, and then it rose and fumbled with the wall of the tower just beyond the boulder behind which I sheltered. It seemed to move a stone and to replace it. After that came silence, and then once more the hoot of an owl. There were steps on the rock staircase, the steps of a man who did not know the road well and stumbled a little. Also they were the steps of one without nails in his boots.

They reached the platform and someone spoke. It was the Portuguese Jew and he spoke in good German.

'Die vogelein schweigen im Walde,' he said.

The answer came from a clear, authoritative voice.

'Warte nur, balde ruhest du auch.'

Clearly some kind of password, for sane men don't talk about little birds in that kind of situation. It sounded to me like indifferent poetry.

Then followed a conversation in low tones, of which I only caught odd phrases. I heard two names - Chelius and what sounded like a Dutch word, Bommaerts. Then to my joy I caught Effenbein, and when uttered it seemed to be followed by a laugh. I heard too a phrase several times repeated, which seemed to me to be pure gibberish - Die Stubenvogel verstehn. It was spoken by the man from the sea. And then the word Wildvogel. The pair seemed demented about birds.

For a second an electric torch was flashed in the shelter of the rock, and I could see a tanned, bearded face looking at some papers. The light disappeared, and again the Portuguese Jew was fumbling with the stones at the base of the tower. To my joy he was close to my crack, and I could hear every word. 'You cannot come here very often,' he said, 'and it may be hard to arrange a meeting. See, therefore, the place I have made to put the Viageffutter. When I get a chance I will come here, and you will come also when you are able. Often there will be nothing, but sometimes there will be much.'

My luck was clearly in, and my exultation made me careless. A stone, on which a foot rested, slipped and though I checked myself at once, the confounded thing rolled down into the hollow, making a great clatter. I plastered myself in the embrasure of the rock and waited with a beating heart. The place was pitch dark, but they had an electric torch, and if they once flashed it on me I was gone. I heard them leave the platform and climb down into the hollow. There they stood listening, while I held my breath. Then I heard 'Nix, mein freund,' and the two went back, the naval officer's boots slipping on the gravel. They did not leave the platform together. The man from the sea bade a short farewell to the Portuguese Jew, listening, I thought, impatiently to his final message as if eager to be gone. It was a good half-hour before the latter took himself off, and I heard the sound of his nailed boots die away as he reached the heather of the moor.

I waited a little longer, and then crawled back to the cave. The owl hooted, and presently Wake descended lightly beside me; he must have known every foothold and handhold by heart to do the job in that inky blackness. I remember that he asked no question of me, but he used language rare on the lips of conscientious objectors about the men who had lately been in the crevice. We, who four hours earlier had been at death grips, now curled up on the hard floor like two tired dogs, and fell sound asleep.

I woke to find Wake in a thundering bad temper. The thing he remembered most about the night before was our scrap and the gross way I had insulted him. I didn't blame him, for if any man had taken me for a German spy I would have been out for his blood, and it was no good explaining that he had given me grounds for suspicion. He was as touchy about his blessed principles as an old maid about her age. I was feeling rather extra buckish myself and that didn't improve matters. His face was like a gargoyle as we went down to the beach to bathe, so I held my tongue. He was chewing the cud of his wounded pride.

But the salt water cleared out the dregs of his distemper. You couldn't be peevish swimming in that jolly, shining sea. We raced each other away beyond the inlet to the outer water, which a brisk morning breeze was curling. Then back to a promontory of heather, where the first beams of the sun coming over the Coolin dried our skins. He sat hunched up staring at the mountains while I prospected the rocks at the edge. Out in the Minch two destroyers were hurrying southward, and I wondered where in that waste of blue was the craft which had come here in the night watches.

I found the spoor of the man from the sea quite fresh on a patch of gravel above the tide-mark.

'There's our friend of the night,' I said.

'I believe the whole thing was a whimsy,' said Wake, his eyes on the chimneys of Sgurr Dearg. 'They were only two natives - poachers, perhaps, or tinkers.'

'They don't speak German in these parts.' 'It was Gaelic probably.'

'What do you make of this, then?' and I quoted the stuff about birds with which they had greeted each other.

Wake looked interested. 'That's Uber allen Gipfeln. Have you ever read Goethe?' 'Never a word. And what do you make of that?' I pointed to a flat rock below tide-mark covered with a tangle of seaweed. It was of a softer stone than the hard stuff in the hills and somebody had scraped off half the seaweed and a slice of the side. 'That wasn't done yesterday morning, for I had my bath here.'

Wake got up and examined the place. He nosed about in the crannies of the rocks lining the inlet, and got into the water again to explore better. When he joined me he was smiling. 'I apologize for my scepticism,' he said. 'There's been some petrol-driven craft here in the night. I can smell it, for I've a nose like a retriever. I daresay you're on the right track. Anyhow, though you seem to know a bit about German, you could scarcely invent immortal poetry.'

We took our belongings to a green crook of the burn, and made a very good breakfast. Wake had nothing in his pack but plasmon biscuits and raisins, for that, he said, was his mountaineering provender, but he was not averse to sampling my tinned stuff. He was a different-sized fellow out in the hills from the anaemic intellectual of Biggleswick. He had forgotten his beastly self-consciousness, and spoke of his hobby with a serious passion. It seemed he had scrambled about everywhere in Europe, from the Caucasus to the Pyrenees. I could see he must be good at the job, for he didn't brag of his exploits. It was the mountains that he loved, not wriggling his body up hard places. The Coolin, he said, were his favourites, for on some of them you could get two thousand feet of good rock. We got our glasses on the face of Sgurr Alasdair, and he sketched out for me various ways of getting to its grim summit. The Coolin and the Dolomites for him, for he had grown tired of the Chamonix aiguilles. I remember he described with tremendous gusto the joys of early dawn in Tyrol, when you ascended through acres of flowery meadows to a tooth of clean white limestone against a clean blue sky. He spoke, too, of the little wild hills in the Bavarian Wettersteingebirge, and of a guide he had picked up there and trained to the job.

'They called him Sebastian Buchwieser. He was the jolliest boy you ever saw, and as clever on crags as a chamois. He is probably dead by now, dead in a filthy jaeger battalion. That's you and your accursed war.'

'Well, we've got to get busy and end it in the right way,' I said. 'And you've got to help, my lad.'

He was a good draughtsman, and with his assistance I drew a rough map of the crevice where we had roosted for the night, giving its bearings carefully in relation to the burn and the sea. Then I wrote down all the details about Gresson and the Portuguese Jew, and described the latter in minute detail. I described, too, most precisely the cache where it had been arranged that the messages should be placed. That finished my stock of paper, and I left the record of the oddments overheard of the conversation for a later time. I put the thing in an old leather cigarette-case I possessed, and handed it to Wake. 'You've got to go straight off to the Kyle and not waste any time on the way. Nobody suspects you, so you can travel any road you please. When you get there you ask for Mr Andrew Amos, who has some Government job in the neighbourhood. Give him that paper from me. He'll know what to do with it all right. Tell him I'll get somehow to the Kyle before midday the day after tomorrow. I must cover my tracks a bit, so I can't come with you, and I want that thing in his hands just as fast as your legs will take you. If anyone tries to steal it from you, for God's sake eat it. You can see for yourself that it's devilish important.'

'I shall be back in England in three days,' he said. 'Any message for your other friends?'

'Forget all about me. You never saw me here. I'm still Brand, the amiable colonial studying social movements. If you meet Ivery, say you heard of me on the Clyde, deep in sedition. But if you see Miss Lamington you can tell her I'm past the Hill Difficulty. I'm coming back as soon as God will let me, and I'm going to drop right into the Biggleswick push. Only this time I'll be a little more advanced in my views ... You needn't get cross. I'm not saying anything against your principles. The main point is that we both hate dirty treason.'

He put the case in his waistcoat pocket. 'I'll go round Garsbheinn,' he said, 'and over by Camasunary. I'll be at the Kyle long before evening. I meant anyhow to sleep at Broadford tonight ... Goodbye, Brand, for I've forgotten your proper name. You're not a bad fellow, but you've landed me in melodrama for the first time in my sober existence. I have a grudge against you for mixing up the Coolin with a shilling shocker. You've spoiled their sanctity.'

'You've the wrong notion of romance,' I said. 'Why, man, last night for an hour you were in the front line - the place where the enemy forces touch our own. You were over the top - you were in No-man's-land.'

He laughed. 'That is one way to look at it'; and then he stalked off and I watched his lean figure till it was round the turn of the hill.

All that morning I smoked peacefully by the burn, and let my thoughts wander over the whole business. I had got precisely what Blenkiron wanted, a post office for the enemy. It would need careful handling, but I could see the juiciest lies passing that way to the Grosses Haupiquartier. Yet I had an ugly feeling at the back of my head that it had been all too easy, and that Ivery was not the man to be duped in this way for long. That set me thinking about the queer talk on the crevice. The poetry stuff I dismissed as the ordinary password, probably changed every time. But who were Chelius and Bommaerts, and what in the name of goodness were the Wild Birds and the Cage Birds? Twice in the past three years I had had two such riddles to solve - Scudder's scribble in his pocket-book, and Harry Bullivant's three words. I remembered how it had only been by constant chewing at them that I had got a sort of meaning, and I wondered if fate would some day expound this puzzle also.

Meantime I had to get back to London as inconspicuously as I had come. It might take some doing, for the police who had been active in Morvern might be still on the track, and it was essential that I should keep out of trouble and give no hint to Gresson and his friends that I had been so far north. However, that was for Amos to advise me on, and about noon I picked up my waterproof with its bursting pockets and set off on a long detour up the coast. All that blessed day I scarcely met a soul. I passed a distillery which seemed to have quit business, and in the evening came to a little town on the sea where I had a bed and supper in a superior kind of public-house.

Next day I struck southward along the coast, and had two experiences of interest. I had a good look at Ranna, and observed that the Tobermory was no longer there. Gresson had only waited to get his job finished; he could probably twist the old captain any way he wanted. The second was that at the door of a village smithy I saw the back of the Portuguese Jew. He was talking Gaelic this time - good Gaelic it sounded, and in that knot of idlers he would have passed for the ordinariest kind of gillie.

He did not see me, and I had no desire to give him the chance, for I had an odd feeling that the day might come when it would be good for us to meet as strangers.

That night I put up boldly in the inn at Broadford, where they fed me nobly on fresh sea-trout and I first tasted an excellent liqueur made of honey and whisky. Next morning I was early afoot, and well before midday was in sight of the narrows of the Kyle, and the two little stone clachans which face each other across the strip of sea. About two miles from the place at a turn of the road I came upon a farmer's gig, drawn up by the wayside, with the horse cropping the moorland grass. A man sat on the bank smoking, with his left arm hooked in the reins. He was an oldish man, with a short, square figure, and a woollen comforter enveloped his throat.

John Buchan

CHAPTER EIGHT

THE ADVENTURES OF A BAGMAN

'Ye're punctual to time, Mr Brand,' said the voice of Amos. 'But losh! man, what have ye done to your breeks! And your buits? Ye're no just very respectable in your appearance.'

I wasn't. The confounded rocks of the Coolin had left their mark on my shoes, which moreover had not been cleaned for a week, and the same hills had rent my jacket at the shoulders, and torn my trousers above the right knee, and stained every part of my apparel with peat and lichen.

I cast myself on the bank beside Amos and lit my pipe. 'Did you get my message?' I asked.

'Ay. It's gone on by a sure hand to the destination we ken of. Ye've managed well, Mr Brand, but I wish ye were back in London.' He sucked at his pipe, and the shaggy brows were pulled so low as to hide the wary eyes. Then he proceeded to think aloud.

'Ye canna go back by Mallaig. I don't just understand why, but they're lookin' for you down that line. It's a vexatious business when your friends, meanin' the polis, are doing their best to upset your plans and you no able to enlighten them. I could send word to the Chief Constable and get ye through to London without a stop like a load of fish from Aiberdeen, but that would be spoilin' the fine character ye've been at such

pains to construct. Na, na! Ye maun take the risk and travel by
Muirtown without ony creedentials.'

'It can't be a very big risk,' I interpolated.

'I'm no so sure. Gresson's left the Tobermory. He went by
here yesterday, on the Mallaig boat, and there was a wee
blackavised man with him that got out at the Kyle. He's there
still, stoppin' at the hotel. They ca' him Linklater and he
travels in whisky. I don't like the looks of him.'

'But Gresson does not suspect me?'

'Maybe no. But ye wouldna like him to see ye hereaways. Yon
gentry don't leave muckle to chance. Be very certain that every
man in Gresson's lot kens all about ye, and has your description down to the mole on your chin.'

'Then they've got it wrong,' I replied. 'I was speakin'
feeguratively,' said Amos. 'I was considerin' your case the feck
of yesterday, and I've brought the best I could do for ye in the
gig. I wish ye were more respectable clad, but a good topcoat
will hide defeecencies.'

From behind the gig's seat he pulled out an ancient Gladstone
bag and revealed its contents. There was a bowler of a vulgar
and antiquated style; there was a ready-made overcoat of some
dark cloth, of the kind that a clerk wears on the road to the
office; there was a pair of detachable celluloid cuffs, and there
was a linen collar and dickie. Also there was a small handcase,
such as bagmen carry on their rounds.

'That's your luggage,' said Amos with pride. 'That wee bag's
full of samples. Ye'll mind I took the precaution of measurin'
ye in Glasgow, so the things'll fit. Ye've got a new name, Mr
Brand, and I've taken a room for ye in the hotel on the
strength of it. Ye're Archibald McCaskie, and ye're travellin'
for the firm o' Todd, Sons & Brothers, of Edinburgh. Ye ken
the folk? They publish wee releegious books, that ye've bin

trying to sell for Sabbath-school prizes to the Free Kirk ministers in Skye.'

The notion amused Amos, and he relapsed into the sombre chuckle which with him did duty for a laugh.

I put my hat and waterproof in the bag and donned the bowler and the top-coat. They fitted fairly well. Likewise the cuffs and collar, though here I struck a snag, for I had lost my scarf somewhere in the Coolin, and Amos, pelican-like, had to surrender the rusty black tie which adorned his own person. It was a queer rig, and I felt like nothing on earth in it, but Amos was satisfied.

'Mr McCaskie, sir,' he said, 'ye're the very model of a publisher's traveller. Ye'd better learn a few biographical details, which ye've maybe forgotten. Ye're an Edinburgh man, but ye were some years in London, which explains the way ye speak. Ye bide at 6, Russell Street, off the Meadows, and ye're an elder in the Nethergate U.F. Kirk. Have ye ony special taste ye could lead the crack on to, if ye're engaged in conversation?'

I suggested the English classics.

'And very suitable. Ye can try poalitics, too. Ye'd better be a Free-trader but convertit by Lloyd George. That's a common case, and ye'll need to be by-ordinar common ... If I was you, I would daunder about here for a bit, and no arrive at your hotel till after dark. Then ye can have your supper and gang to bed. The Muirtown train leaves at half-seven in the morning ... Na, ye can't come with me. It wouldna do for us to be seen thegither. If I meet ye in the street I'll never let on I know ye.'

Amos climbed into the gig and jolted off home. I went down to the shore and sat among the rocks, finishing about tea-time the remains of my provisions. In the mellow gloaming I strolled into the clachan and got a boat to put me over to the inn. It proved to be a comfortable place, with a motherly old landlady who showed me to my room and promised ham and eggs and cold salmon for supper. After a good wash, which I needed, and an honest attempt to make my clothes presentable, I descended to the meal in a coffee-room lit by a single dim parafin lamp.

The food was excellent, and, as I ate, my spirits rose. In two days I should be back in London beside Blenkiron and somewhere within a day's journey of Mary. I could picture no scene now without thinking how Mary fitted into it. For her sake I held Biggleswick delectable, because I had seen her there. I wasn't sure if this was love, but it was something I had never dreamed of before, something which I now hugged the thought of. It made the whole earth rosy and golden for me, and life so well worth living that I felt like a miser towards the days to come.

I had about finished supper, when I was joined by another guest. Seen in the light of that infamous lamp, he seemed a small, alert fellow, with a bushy, black moustache, and black hair parted in the middle. He had fed already and appeared to be hungering for human society.

In three minutes he had told me that he had come down from Portree and was on his way to Leith. A minute later he had whipped out a card on which I read 'J. J. Linklater', and in the corner the name of Hatherwick Bros. His accent betrayed that he hailed from the west.

'I've been up among the distilleries,' he informed me. 'It's a poor business distillin' in these times, wi' the teetotallers yowlin' about the nation's shame and the way to lose the war. I'm a temperate man mysel', but I would think shame to spile decent folks' business. If the Government want to stop the drink, let them buy us out. They've permitted us to invest good money in the trade, and they must see that we get it back. The other way will wreck public credit. That's what I say. Supposin' some Labour Government takes the notion that soap's bad for the nation? Are they goin' to shut up Port Sunlight? Or good clothes? Or lum hats? There's no end to their daftness if they once start on that track. A lawfu' trade's a lawfu' trade, says I, and it's contrary to public policy to pit it at the mercy of wheen cranks. D'ye no agree, sir? By the way, I havena got your name?'

I told him and he rambled on.

'We're blenders and do a very high-class business, mostly foreign. The war's hit us wi' our export trade, of course, but we're no as bad as some. What's your line, Mr McCaskie?'

When he heard he was keenly interested.

'D'ye say so? Ye're from Todd's! Man, I was in the book business mysel', till I changed it for something a wee bit more lucrative. I was on the road for three years for Andrew Matheson. Ye ken the name - Paternoster Row - I've forgotten the number. I had a kind of ambition to start a book-sellin' shop of my own and to make Linklater o' Paisley a big name in the trade. But I got the offer from Hatherwick's, and I was wantin' to get married, so filthy lucre won the day. And I'm no sorry I changed. If it hadna been for this war, I would have been makin' four figures with my salary and commissions ... My pipe's out. Have you one of those rare and valuable curiosities called a spunk, Mr McCaskie?' He was a merry little grig of a man, and he babbled on, till I announced my intention of going to bed. If this was Amos's bagman, who had been seen in company with Gresson, I understood how idle may be the suspicions of a clever man. He had probably foregathered with Gresson on the Skye boat, and wearied that saturnine soul with his cackle.

I was up betimes, paid my bill, ate a breakfast of porridge and fresh haddock, and walked the few hundred yards to the station. It was a warm, thick morning, with no sun visible, and the Skye hills misty to their base. The three coaches on the little train were nearly filled when I had bought my ticket, and I selected a third-class smoking carriage which held four soldiers returning from leave.

The train was already moving when a late passenger hurried along the platform and clambered in beside me. A cheery 'Mornin', Mr McCaskie,' revealed my fellow guest at the hotel.

We jolted away from the coast up a broad glen and then on to a wide expanse of bog with big hills showing towards the north. It was a drowsy day, and in that atmosphere of shag and crowded humanity I felt my eyes closing. I had a short nap, and woke to find that Mr Linklater had changed his seat and was now beside me.

'We'll no get a Scotsman till Muirtown,' he said. 'Have ye nothing in your samples ye could give me to read?'

I had forgotten about the samples. I opened the case and found the oddest collection of little books, all in gay bindings. Some were religious, with names like Dew of Hermon and Cool Siloam; some were innocent narratives, How Tommy saved his Pennies, A Missionary Child in China, and Little Susie and her Uncle. There was a Life of David Livingstone, a child's book on sea-shells, and a richly gilt edition of the poems of one James Montgomery. I offered the selection to Mr Linklater, who grinned and chose the Missionary Child. 'It's not the reading I'm accustomed to,' he said. 'I like strong meat - Hall Caine and Jack London. By the way, how d'ye square this business of yours wi' the booksellers? When I was in Matheson's there would have been trouble if we had dealt direct wi' the public like you.'

The confounded fellow started to talk about the details of the book trade, of which I knew nothing. He wanted to know on what terms we sold 'juveniles', and what discount we gave the big wholesalers, and what class of book we put out 'on sale'. I didn't understand a word of his jargon, and I must have given myself away badly, for he asked me questions about firms of which I had never heard, and I had to make some kind of answer. I told myself that the donkey was harmless, and that his opinion of me mattered nothing, but as soon as I decently could I pretended to be absorbed in the Pilgrim's Progress, a gaudy copy of which was among the samples. It opened at the episode of Christian and Hopeful in the Enchanted Ground, and in that stuffy carriage I presently followed the example of Heedless and Too-Bold and fell sound asleep. I was awakened by the train rumbling over the points of a little moorland junction. Sunk in a pleasing lethargy, I sat with my eyes closed, and then covertly took a glance at my companion. He had abandoned the Missionary Child and was reading a little dun-coloured book, and marking passages with a pencil. His face was absorbed, and it was a new face, not the vacant, good-humoured look of the garrulous bagman, but something shrewd, purposeful, and formidable. I remained hunched up as if still sleeping, and tried to see what the book was. But my eyes, good as they are, could make out nothing of the text or title, except that I had a very strong impression that that book was not written in the English tongue.

I woke abruptly, and leaned over to him. Quick as lightning he slid his pencil up his sleeve and turned on me with a fatuous smile.

'What d'ye make o' this, Mr McCaskie? It's a wee book I picked up at a roup along with fifty others. I paid five shillings for the lot. It looks like Gairman, but in my young days they didna teach us foreign languages.'

I took the thing and turned over the pages, trying to keep any sign of intelligence out of my face. It was German right enough, a little manual of hydrography with no publisher's name on it. It had the look of the kind of textbook a Government department might issue to its officials.

I handed it back. 'It's either German or Dutch. I'm not much of a scholar, barring a little French and the Latin I got at Heriot's Hospital ... This is an awful slow train, Mr Linklater.'

The soldiers were playing nap, and the bagman proposed a game of cards. I remembered in time that I was an elder in the Nethergate U.F. Church and refused with some asperity. After that I shut my eyes again, for I wanted to think out this new phenomenon.

The fellow knew German - that was clear. He had also been seen in Gresson's company. I didn't believe he suspected me, though I suspected him profoundly. It was my business to keep strictly to my part and give him no cause to doubt me. He was clearly practising his own part on me, and I must appear to take him literally on his professions. So, presently, I woke up and engaged him in a disputatious conversation about the morality of selling strong liquors. He responded readily, and put the case for alcohol with much point and vehemence. The discussion interested the soldiers, and one of them, to show he was on Linklater's side, produced a flask and offered him a drink. I concluded by observing morosely that the bagman had been a better man when he peddled books for Alexander Matheson, and that put the closure on the business.

That train was a record. It stopped at every station, and in the afternoon it simply got tired and sat down in the middle of a moor and reflected for an hour. I stuck my head out of the window now and then, and smelt the rooty fragrance of bogs, and when we halted on a bridge I watched the trout in the pools of the brown river. Then I slept and smoked alternately, and began to get furiously hungry.

Once I woke to hear the soldiers discussing the war. There was an argument between a lance-corporal in the Camerons and a sapper private about some trivial incident on the Somme.

'I tell ye I was there,' said the Cameron. 'We were relievin' the Black Watch, and Fritz was shelling the road, and we didna get up to the line till one o'clock in the mornin'. Frae Frickout Circus to the south end o' the High Wood is every bit o' five mile.'

'Not abune three,' said the sapper dogmatically.

'Man, I've trampit it.'

John Buchan

'Same here. I took up wire every nicht for a week.'

The Cameron looked moodily round the company. 'I wish there was anither man here that kent the place. He wad bear me out. These boys are no good, for they didna join till later. I tell ye it's five mile.'

'Three,' said the sapper.

Tempers were rising, for each of the disputants felt his veracity assailed. It was too hot for a quarrel and I was so drowsy that I was heedless.

'Shut up, you fools,' I said. 'The distance is six kilometres, so you're both wrong.'

My tone was so familiar to the men that it stopped the wrangle, but it was not the tone of a publisher's traveller. Mr Linklater cocked his ears.

'What's a kilometre, Mr McCaskie?' he asked blandly.

'Multiply by five and divide by eight and you get the miles.'

I was on my guard now, and told a long story of a nephew who had been killed on the Somme, and how I had corresponded with the War Office about his case. 'Besides,' I said, 'I'm a great student o' the newspapers, and I've read all the books about the war. It's a difficult time this for us all, and if you can take a serious interest in the campaign it helps a lot. I mean working out the places on the map and reading Haig's dispatches.'

'Just so,' he said dryly, and I thought he watched me with an odd look in his eyes.

A fresh idea possessed me. This man had been in Gresson's company, he knew German, he was obviously something very different from what he professed to be. What if he were in the employ of our own Secret Service? I had appeared out of the void at the Kyle, and I had made but a poor appearance as a bagman, showing no knowledge of my own trade. I was in an area interdicted to the ordinary public; and he had good reason to keep an eye on my movements. He was going south, and so was I; clearly we must somehow part company.

'We change at Muirtown, don't we?' I asked. 'When does the train for the south leave?' He consulted a pocket timetable. 'Ten-thirty-three. There's generally four hours to wait, for we're due in at six-fifteen. But this auld hearse will be lucky if it's in by nine.'

His forecast was correct. We rumbled out of the hills into haughlands and caught a glimpse of the North Sea. Then we were hung up while a long goods train passed down the line. It was almost dark when at last we crawled into Muirtown station and disgorged our load of hot and weary soldiery.

I bade an ostentatious farewell to Linklater. 'Very pleased to have met you. I'll see you later on the Edinburgh train. I'm for a walk to stretch my legs, and a bite o' supper.' I was very determined that the ten-thirty for the south should leave without me.

My notion was to get a bed and a meal in some secluded inn, and walk out next morning and pick up a slow train down the line. Linklater had disappeared towards the guard's van to find his luggage, and the soldiers were sitting on their packs with that air of being utterly and finally lost and neglected which characterizes the British fighting-man on a journey. I gave up my ticket and, since I had come off a northern train, walked unhindered into the town.

It was market night, and the streets were crowded. Blue-jackets from the Fleet, country-folk in to shop, and every kind of military detail thronged the pavements. Fish-hawkers were crying their wares, and there was a tatterdemalion piper making the night hideous at a corner. I took a tortuous route and finally fixed on a modest-looking public-house in a back street. When I inquired for a room I could find no one in authority, but a slatternly girl informed me that there was one vacant bed, and that I could have ham and eggs in the bar. So, after hitting my head violently against a cross-beam, I stumbled down some steps and entered a frowsty little place smelling of spilt beer and stale tobacco.

The promised ham and eggs proved impossible - there were no eggs to be had in Muirtown that night - but I was given cold mutton and a pint of indifferent ale. There was nobody in the place but two farmers drinking hot whisky and water and discussing with sombre interest the rise in the price of feeding-stuffs. I ate my supper, and was just preparing to find the whereabouts of my bedroom when through the street door there entered a dozen soldiers.

In a second the quiet place became a babel. The men were strictly sober; but they were in that temper of friendliness which demands a libation of some kind. One was prepared to stand treat; he was the leader of the lot, and it was to celebrate the end of his leave that he was entertaining his pals. From where I sat I could not see him, but his voice was dominant. 'What's your fancy, jock? Beer for you, Andra? A pint and a dram for me. This is better than vongblong and vongrooge, Davie. Man, when I'm sittin' in those estamints, as they ca' them, I often long for a guid Scots public.'

The voice was familiar. I shifted my seat to get a view of the speaker, and then I hastily drew back. It was the Scots Fusilier I had clipped on the jaw in defending Gresson after the Glasgow meeting.

But by a strange fatality he had caught sight of me.

'Whae's that i' the corner?' he cried, leaving the bar to stare at me. Now it is a queer thing, but if you have once fought with a man, though only for a few seconds, you remember his face, and the scrap in Glasgow had been under a lamp. The jock recognized me well enough.

'By God!' he cried, 'if this is no a bit o' luck! Boys, here's the man I feucht wi' in Glesca. Ye mind I telled ye about it. He laid me oot, and it's my turn to do the same wi' him. I had a notion I was gaun to mak' a nicht o't. There's naebody can hit Geordie Hamilton without Geordie gettin' his ain back some day. Get up, man, for I'm gaun to knock the heid off ye.'

I duly got up, and with the best composure I could muster looked him in the face.

'You're mistaken, my friend. I never clapped eyes on you before, and I never was in Glasgow in my life.'

'That's a damned lee,' said the Fusilier. 'Ye're the man, and if ye're no, ye're like enough him to need a hidin'!'

'Confound your nonsense!' I said. 'I've no quarrel with you, and I've better things to do than be scrapping with a stranger in a public-house.'

'Have ye sae? Well, I'll learn ye better. I'm gaun to hit ye, and then ye'll hae to fecht whether ye want it or no. Tam, haud my jacket, and see that my drink's no skailed.'

This was an infernal nuisance, for a row here would bring in the police, and my dubious position would be laid bare. I thought of putting up a fight, for I was certain I could lay out the jock a second time, but the worst of that was that I did not know where the thing would end. I might have to fight the lot of them, and that meant a noble public shindy. I did my best to speak my opponent fair. I said we were all good friends and offered to stand drinks for the party. But the Fusilier's blood was up and he was spoiling for a row, ably abetted by his comrades. He had his tunic off now and was stamping in front of me with doubled fists. I did the best thing I could think of in the circumstances. My seat was close to the steps which led to the other part of the inn. I grabbed my hat, darted up them, and before they realized what I was doing had bolted the door behind me. I could hear pandemonium break loose in the bar.

I slipped down a dark passage to another which ran at right angles to it, and which seemed to connect the street door of the inn itself with the back premises. I could hear voices in the little hall, and that stopped me short. One of them was Linklater's, but he was not talking as Linklater had talked. He was speaking educated English. I heard another with a Scots accent, which I took to be the landlord's, and a third which sounded like some superior sort of constable's, very prompt and official. I heard one phrase, too, from Linklater - 'He calls himself McCaskie.' Then they stopped, for the turmoil from the bar had reached the front door. The Fusilier and his friends were looking for me by the other entrance.

The attention of the men in the hall was distracted, and that gave me a chance. There was nothing for it but the back door. I slipped through it into a courtyard and almost tumbled over a tub of water. I planted the thing so that anyone coming that way would fall over it. A door led me into an empty stable, and from that into a lane. It was all absurdly easy, but as I started down the lane I heard a mighty row and the sound of angry voices. Someone had gone into the tub and I hoped it was Linklater. I had taken a liking to the Fusilier jock.

There was the beginning of a moon somewhere, but that lane was very dark. I ran to the left, for on the right it looked like a cul-de-sac. This brought me into a quiet road of two-storied cottages which showed at one end the lights of a street. So I took the other way, for I wasn't going to have the whole population of Muirtown on the hue-and-cry after me. I came into a country lane, and I also came into the van of the pursuit, which must have taken a short cut. They shouted when they saw me, but I had a small start, and legged it down that road in the belief that I was making for open country.

That was where I was wrong. The road took me round to the other side of the town, and just when I was beginning to think

I had a fair chance I saw before me the lights of a signal-box and a little to the left of it the lights of the station. In half an hour's time the Edinburgh train would be leaving, but I had made that impossible. Behind me I could hear the pursuers, giving tongue like hound puppies, for they had attracted some pretty drunken gentlemen to their party. I was badly puzzled where to turn, when I noticed outside the station a long line of blurred lights, which could only mean a train with the carriage blinds down. It had an engine attached and seemed to be waiting for the addition of a couple of trucks to start. It was a wild chance, but the only one I saw. I scrambled across a piece of waste ground, climbed an embankment and found myself on the metals. I ducked under the couplings and got on the far side of the train, away from the enemy.

Then simultaneously two things happened. I heard the yells of my pursuers a dozen yards off, and the train jolted into motion. I jumped on the footboard, and looked into an open window. The compartment was packed with troops, six a side and two men sitting on the floor, and the door was locked. I dived headforemost through the window and landed on the neck of a weary warrior who had just dropped off to sleep.

While I was falling I made up my mind on my conduct. I must be intoxicated, for I knew the infinite sympathy of the British soldier towards those thus overtaken. They pulled me to my feet, and the man I had descended on rubbed his skull and blasphemously demanded explanations.

'Gen'lmen,' I hiccoughed, 'I 'pologize. I was late for this bl-blighted train and I mus' be in E'inburgh 'morrow or I'll get the sack. I 'pologize. If I've hurt my friend's head, I'll kiss it and make it well.'

At this there was a great laugh. 'Ye'd better accept, Pete,' said one. 'It's the first time anybody ever offered to kiss your ugly heid.'

A man asked me who I was, and I appeared to be searching for a card-case.

'Losht,' I groaned. 'Losht, and so's my wee bag and I've bashed my po' hat. I'm an awful sight, gen'lmen - an awful warning to be in time for trains. I'm John Johnstone, managing clerk to Messrs Watters, Brown & Elph'stone, 923 Charl'tte Street, E'inburgh. I've been up north seein' my mamma.'

'Ye should be in France,' said one man.

'Wish't I was, but they wouldn't let me. "Mr Johnstone," they said, "ye're no dam good. Ye've varicose veins and a bad heart," they said. So I says, "Good mornin', gen'lmen. Don't blame me if the country's ru'ned". That's what I said.'

I had by this time occupied the only remaining space left on the floor. With the philosophy of their race the men had accepted my presence, and were turning again to their own talk. The train had got up speed, and as I judged it to be a special of some kind I looked for few stoppings. Moreover it was not a corridor carriage, but one of the old-fashioned kind, so I was safe for a time from the unwelcome attention of conductors. I stretched my legs below the seat, rested my head against the knees of a brawny gunner, and settled down to make the best of it.

My reflections were not pleasant. I had got down too far below the surface, and had the naked feeling you get in a dream when you think you have gone to the theatre in your nightgown. I had had three names in two days, and as many characters. I felt as if I had no home or position anywhere, and was only a stray dog with everybody's hand and foot against me. It was an ugly sensation, and it was not redeemed by any acute fear or any knowledge of being mixed up in some desperate drama. I knew I could easily go on to Edinburgh, and when the police made trouble, as they would, a wire to Scotland Yard would settle matters in a couple of hours. There wasn't a suspicion of bodily danger to restore my dignity. The worst that could happen would be that Ivery would hear of my being befriended by the authorities, and the part I had settled to play would be impossible. He would certainly hear. I had the greatest respect for his intelligence service.

Yet that was bad enough. So far I had done well. I had put Gresson off the scent. I had found out what Bullivant wanted to know, and I had only to return unostentatiously to London to have won out on the game. I told myself all that, but it didn't cheer my spirits. I was feeling mean and hunted and very cold about the feet.

But I have a tough knuckle of obstinacy in me which makes me unwilling to give up a thing till I am fairly choked off it. The chances were badly against me. The Scottish police were actively interested in my movements and would be ready to welcome me at my journey's end. I had ruined my hat, and my clothes, as Amos had observed, were not respectable. I had got rid of a four-days' beard the night before, but had cut myself in the process, and what with my weather-beaten face and tangled hair looked liker a tinker than a decent bagman. I thought with longing of my portmanteau in the Pentland Hotel, Edinburgh, and the neat blue serge suit and the clean linen that reposed in it. It was no case for a subtle game, for I held no cards. Still I was determined not to chuck in my hand till I was forced to. If the train stopped anywhere I would get out, and trust to my own wits and the standing luck of the British Army for the rest.

The chance came just after dawn, when we halted at a little junction. I got up yawning and tried to open the door, till I remembered it was locked. Thereupon I stuck my legs out of the window on the side away from the platform, and was immediately seized upon by a sleepy Seaforth who thought I contemplated suicide.

'Let me go,' I said. 'I'll be back in a jiffy.'

'Let him gang, jock,' said another voice. 'Ye ken what a man's like when he's been on the bash. The cauld air'll sober him.'

I was released, and after some gymnastics dropped on the metals and made my way round the rear of the train. As I clambered on the platform it began to move, and a face looked out of one of the back carriages. It was Linklater and he recognized me. He tried to get out, but the door was promptly slammed by an indignant porter. I heard him protest, and he kept his head out till the train went round the curve. That cooked my goose all right. He would wire to the police from the next station. Meantime in that clean, bare, chilly place there was only one traveller. He was a slim young man, with a kit-bag and a gun-case. His clothes were beautiful, a green Homburg hat, a smart green tweed overcoat, and boots as brightly polished as a horse chestnut. I caught his profile as he gave up his ticket and to my amazement I recognized it.

The station-master looked askance at me as I presented myself, dilapidated and dishevelled, to the official gaze. I tried to speak in a tone of authority.

'Who is the man who has just gone out?'

'Whaur's your ticket?'

'I had no time to get one at Muirtown, and as you see I have left my luggage behind me. Take it out of that pound and I'll come back for the change. I want to know if that was Sir Archibald Roylance.'

He looked suspiciously at the note. 'I think that's the name. He's a captain up at the Fleein' School. What was ye wantin' with him?'

I charged through the booking-office and found my man about to enter a big grey motor-car.

'Archie,' I cried and beat him on the shoulders.

He turned round sharply. 'What the devil -! Who are you?' And then recognition crept into his face and he gave a joyous

shout. 'My holy aunt! The General disguised as Charlie
Chaplin! Can I drive you anywhere, sir?'

John Buchan

CHAPTER NINE

I TAKE THE WINGS OF A DOVE

'Drive me somewhere to breakfast, Archie,' I said, 'for I'm perishing hungry.'

He and I got into the tonneau, and the driver swung us out of the station road up a long incline of hill. Sir Archie had been one of my subalterns in the old Lennox Highlanders, and had left us before the Somme to join the Flying Corps. I had heard that he had got his wings and had done well before Arras, and was now training pilots at home. He had been a light-hearted youth, who had endured a good deal of rough-tonguing from me for his sins of omission. But it was the casual class of lad I was looking for now.

I saw him steal amused glances at my appearance.

'Been seein' a bit of life, sir?' he inquired respectfully.

'I'm being hunted by the police,' I said.

'Dirty dogs! But don't worry, sir; we'll get you off all right. I've been in the same fix myself. You can lie snug in my little log hut, for that old image Gibbons won't blab. Or, tell you what, I've got an aunt who lives near here and she's a bit of a sportsman. You can hide in her moated grange till the bobbies get tired.'

I think it was Archie's calm acceptance of my position as natural and becoming that restored my good temper. He was far too well bred to ask what crime I had committed, and I didn't propose to enlighten him much. But as we swung up the moorland road I let him know that I was serving the Government, but that it was necessary that I should appear to be unauthenticated and that therefore I must dodge the police. He whistled his appreciation.

'Gad, that's a deep game. Sort of camouflage? Speaking from my experience it is easy to overdo that kind of stunt. When I was at Misieux the French started out to camouflage the caravans where they keep their pigeons, and they did it so damned well that the poor little birds couldn't hit 'em off, and spent the night out.'

We entered the white gates of a big aerodrome, skirted a forest of tents and huts, and drew up at a shanty on the far confines of the place. The hour was half past four, and the world was still asleep. Archie nodded towards one of the hangars, from the mouth of which projected the propeller end of an aeroplane.

'I'm by way of flyin' that bus down to Farnton tomorrow,' he remarked. 'It's the new Shark-Gladas. Got a mouth like a tree.'

An idea flashed into my mind.

'You're going this morning,' I said.

'How did you know?' he exclaimed. 'I'm due to go today, but the grouse up in Caithness wanted shootin' so badly that I decided to wangle another day's leave. They can't expect a man to start for the south of England when he's just off a frowsy journey.'

'All the same you're going to be a stout fellow and start in two hours' time. And you're going to take me with you.'

He stared blankly, and then burst into a roar of laughter. 'You're the man to go tiger-shootin' with. But what price my commandant? He's not a bad chap, but a trifle shaggy about the fetlocks. He won't appreciate the joke.'

'He needn't know. He mustn't know. This is an affair between you and me till it's finished. I promise you I'll make it all square with the Flying Corps. Get me down to Farnton before evening, and you'll have done a good piece of work for the country.'

'Right-o! Let's have a tub and a bit of breakfast, and then I'm your man. I'll tell them to get the bus ready.'

In Archie's bedroom I washed and shaved and borrowed a green tweed cap and a brand-new Aquascutum. The latter covered the deficiencies of my raiment, and when I command-eered a pair of gloves I felt almost respectable. Gibbons, who seemed to be a jack-of-all-trades, cooked us some bacon and an omelette, and as he ate Archie yarned. In the battalion his conversation had been mostly of race-meetings and the forsaken delights of town, but now he had forgotten all that, and, like every good airman I have ever known, wallowed enthusiastically in 'shop'. I have a deep respect for the Flying Corps, but it is apt to change its jargon every month, and its conversation is hard for the layman to follow. He was desperately keen about the war, which he saw wholly from the viewpoint of the air. Arras to him was over before the infantry crossed the top, and the tough bit of the Somme was October, not September. He calculated that the big air-fighting had not come along yet, and all he hoped for was to be allowed out to France to have his share in it. Like all good airmen, too, he was very modest about himself. 'I've done a bit of steeple-chasin' and huntin' and I've good hands for a horse, so I can handle a bus fairly well. It's all a matter of hands, you know. There ain't half the risk of the infantry down below you, and a million times the fun. jolly glad I changed, sir.'

We talked of Peter, and he put him about top. Voss, he

thought, was the only Boche that could compare with him, for he hadn't made up his mind about Lensch. The Frenchman Guynemer he ranked high, but in a different way. I remember he had no respect for Richthofen and his celebrated circus.

At six sharp we were ready to go. A couple of mechanics had got out the machine, and Archie put on his coat and gloves and climbed into the pilot's seat, while I squeezed in behind in the observer's place. The aerodrome was waking up, but I saw no officers about. We were scarcely seated when Gibbons called our attention to a motor-car on the road, and presently we heard a shout and saw men waving in our direction.

'Better get off, my lad,' I said. 'These look like my friends.'

The engine started and the mechanics stood clear. As we taxied over the turf I looked back and saw several figures running in our direction. The next second we had left the bumpy earth for the smooth highroad of the air.

I had flown several dozen times before, generally over the enemy lines when I wanted to see for myself how the land lay. Then we had flown low, and been nicely dusted by the Hun Archies, not to speak of an occasional machine-gun. But never till that hour had I realized the joy of a straight flight in a swift plane in perfect weather. Archie didn't lose time. Soon the hangars behind looked like a child's toys, and the world ran away from us till it seemed like a great golden bowl spilling over with the quintessence of light. The air was cold and my hands numbed, but I never felt them. As we throbbed and tore southward, sometimes bumping in eddies, sometimes swimming evenly in a stream of motionless ether, my head and heart grew as light as a boy's. I forgot all about the vexations of my job and saw only its joyful comedy. I didn't think that anything on earth could worry me again. Far to the left was a wedge of silver and beside it a cluster of toy houses. That must be Edinburgh, where reposed my portmanteau, and where a most efficient police force was now inquiring for me. At the thought I laughed so loud that Archie must have heard me. He turned round, saw my grinning face, and grinned back. Then he signalled to me to strap myself in. I obeyed, and he proceeded to practise 'stunts' - the loop, the spinning nose-dive, and others I didn't know the names of. It was glorious fun, and he handled his machine as a good rider coaxes a nervous horse over a stiff hurdle. He had that extra something in his blood that makes the great pilot.

Presently the chessboard of green and brown had changed to a deep purple with faint silvery lines like veins in a rock. We were crossing the Border hills, the place where I had legged it for weary days when I was mixed up in the Black Stone business. What a marvellous element was this air, which took one far above the fatigues of humanity! Archie had done well to change. Peter had been the wise man. I felt a tremendous pity for my old friend hobbling about a German prison-yard, when he had once flown a hawk. I reflected that I had wasted my life hitherto. And then I remembered that all this glory had only one use in war and that was to help the muddy British infantryman to down his Hun opponent. He was the fellow, after all, that decided battles, and the thought comforted me.

A great exhilaration is often the precursor of disaster, and mine was to have a sudden downfall. It was getting on for noon and we were well into England - I guessed from the rivers we had passed that we were somewhere in the north of Yorkshire - when the machine began to make odd sounds, and we bumped in perfectly calm patches of air. We dived and then climbed, but the confounded thing kept sputtering. Archie passed back a slip of paper on which he had scribbled: 'Engine conked. Must land at Micklegill. Very sorry.' So we dropped to a lower elevation where we could see clearly the houses and roads and the long swelling ridges of a moorland country. I could never have found my way about, but Archie's practised eye knew every landmark. We were trundling along very slowly now, and even I was soon able to pick up the hangars of a big aerodrome.

We made Micklegill, but only by the skin of our teeth. We

were so low that the smoky chimneys of the city of Bradfield seven miles to the east were half hidden by a ridge of down. Archie achieved a clever descent in the lee of a belt of firs, and got out full of imprecations against the Gladas engine. 'I'll go up to the camp and report,' he said, 'and send mechanics down to tinker this darned gramophone. You'd better go for a walk, sir. I don't want to answer questions about you till we're ready to start. I reckon it'll be an hour's job.' The cheerfulness I had acquired in the upper air still filled me. I sat down in a ditch, as merry as a sand-boy, and lit a pipe. I was possessed by a boyish spirit of casual adventure, and waited on the next turn of fortune's wheel with only a pleasant amusement.

That turn was not long in coming. Archie appeared very breathless.

'Look here, sir, there's the deuce of a row up there. They've been wirin' about you all over the country, and they know you're with me. They've got the police, and they'll have you in five minutes if you don't leg it. I lied like billy-o and said I had never heard of you, but they're comin' to see for themselves. For God's sake get off ... You'd better keep in cover down that hollow and round the back of these trees. I'll stay here and try to brazen it out. I'll get strafed to blazes anyhow ... I hope you'll get me out of the scrape, sir.'

'Don't you worry, my lad,' I said. 'I'll make it all square when I get back to town. I'll make for Bradfield, for this place is a bit conspicuous. Goodbye, Archie. You're a good chap and I'll see you don't suffer.'

I started off down the hollow of the moor, trying to make speed atone for lack of strategy, for it was hard to know how much my pursuers commanded from that higher ground. They must have seen me, for I heard whistles blown and men's cries. I struck a road, crossed it, and passed a ridge from which I had a view of Bradfield six miles off. And as I ran I began to reflect that this kind of chase could not last long. They were bound to round me up in the next half-hour unless I could puzzle them. But in that bare green place there was no cover, and it looked as if my chances were pretty much those of a hare coursed by a good greyhound on a naked moor.

Suddenly from just in front of me came a familiar sound. It was the roar of guns - the slam of field-batteries and the boom of small howitzers. I wondered if I had gone off my head. As I plodded on the rattle of machine-guns was added, and over the ridge before me I saw the dust and fumes of bursting shells. I concluded that I was not mad, and that therefore the Germans must have landed. I crawled up the last slope, quite forgetting the pursuit behind me.

And then I'm blessed if I did not look down on a veritable battle.

There were two sets of trenches with barbed wire and all the fixings, one set filled with troops and the other empty. On these latter shells were bursting, but there was no sign of life in them. In the other lines there seemed the better part of two brigades, and the first trench was stiff with bayonets. My first thought was that Home Forces had gone dotty, for this kind of show could have no sort of training value. And then I saw other things - cameras and camera-men on platforms on the flanks, and men with megaphones behind them on wooden scaffoldings. One of the megaphones was going full blast all the time. I saw the meaning of the performance at last. Some movie-merchant had got a graft with the Government, and troops had been turned out to make a war film. It occurred to me that if I were mixed up in that push I might get the cover I was looking for. I scurried down the hill to the nearest camera-man.

As I ran, the first wave of troops went over the top. They did it uncommon well, for they entered into the spirit of the thing, and went over with grim faces and that slow, purposeful lope that I had seen in my own fellows at Arras. Smoke grenades burst among them, and now and then some resourceful mountebank would roll over. Altogether it was about the best show I have ever seen. The cameras clicked, the guns banged, a background of boy scouts applauded, and the dust rose in billows to the sky.

But all the same something was wrong. I could imagine that this kind of business took a good deal of planning from the point of view of the movie-merchant, for his purpose was not the same as that of the officer in command. You know how a photographer finicks about and is dissatisfied with a pose that seems all right to his sitter. I should have thought the spectacle enough to get any cinema audience off their feet, but the man on the scaffolding near me judged differently. He made his megaphone boom like the swan-song of a dying buffalo. He wanted to change something and didn't know how to do it. He hopped on one leg; he took the megaphone from his mouth to curse; he waved it like a banner and yelled at some opposite number on the other flank. And then his patience forsook him and he skipped down the ladder, dropping his megaphone, past the camera-men, on to the battlefield.

That was his undoing. He got in the way of the second wave and was swallowed up like a leaf in a torrent. For a moment I saw a red face and a loud-checked suit, and the rest was silence. He was carried on over the hill, or rolled into an enemy trench, but anyhow he was lost to my ken.

I bagged his megaphone and hopped up the steps to the platform. At last I saw a chance of first-class cover, for with Archie's coat and cap I made a very good appearance as a movie-merchant. Two waves had gone over the top, and the cinema-men, working like beavers, had filmed the lot. But there was still a fair amount of troops to play with, and I determined to tangle up that outfit so that the fellows who were after me would have better things to think about.

My advantage was that I knew how to command men. I could see that my opposite number with the megaphone was helpless, for the mistake which had swept my man into a shell-hole had reduced him to impotence. The troops seemed to be mainly in charge of N.C.O.s (I could imagine that the officers would try to shirk this business), and an N.C.O. is the most literal creature on earth. So with my megaphone I proceeded to change the battle order.

I brought up the third wave to the front trenches. In about three minutes the men had recognized the professional touch and were moving smartly to my orders. They thought it was part of the show, and the obedient cameras clicked at everything that came into their orbit. My aim was to deploy the troops on too narrow a front so that they were bound to fan outward, and I had to be quick about it, for I didn't know when the hapless movie-merchant might be retrieved from the battle-field and dispute my authority.

It takes a long time to straighten a thing out, but it does not take long to tangle it, especially when the thing is so delicate a machine as disciplined troops. In about eight minutes I had produced chaos. The flanks spread out, in spite of all the shepherding of the N.C.O.s, and the fringe engulfed the photographers. The cameras on their little platforms went down like ninepins. It was solemn to see the startled face of a photographer, taken unawares, supplicating the purposeful infantry, before he was swept off his feet into speechlessness.

It was no place for me to linger in, so I chucked away the megaphone and got mixed up with the tail of the third wave. I was swept on and came to anchor in the enemy trenches, where I found, as I expected, my profane and breathless predecessor, the movie-merchant. I had nothing to say to him, so I stuck to the trench till it ended against the slope of the hill.

On that flank, delirious with excitement, stood a knot of boy scouts. My business was to get to Bradfield as quick as my legs would take me, and as inconspicuously as the gods would permit. Unhappily I was far too great an object of interest to that nursery of heroes. Every boy scout is an amateur detective and hungry for knowledge. I was followed by several, who plied me with questions, and were told that I was off to

Bradfield to hurry up part of the cinema outfit. It sounded lame enough, for that cinema outfit was already past praying for.

We reached the road and against a stone wall stood several bicycles. I selected one and prepared to mount.

'That's Mr Emmott's machine,' said one boy sharply. 'He told me to keep an eye on it.'

'I must borrow it, sonny,' I said. 'Mr Emmott's my very good friend and won't object.'

From the place where we stood I overlooked the back of the battle-field and could see an anxious congress of officers. I could see others, too, whose appearance I did not like. They had not been there when I operated on the megaphone. They must have come downhill from the aerodrome and in all likelihood were the pursuers I had avoided. The exhilaration which I had won in the air and which had carried me into the tomfoolery of the past half-hour was ebbing. I had the hunted feeling once more, and grew middle-aged and cautious. I had a baddish record for the day, what with getting Archie into a scrape and busting up an official cinema show - neither consistent with the duties of a brigadier-general. Besides, I had still to get to London.

I had not gone two hundred yards down the road when a boy scout, pedalling furiously, came up abreast me.

'Colonel Edgeworth wants to see you,' he panted. 'You're to come back at once.'

'Tell him I can't wait now,' I said. 'I'll pay my respects to him in an hour.'

'He said you were to come at once,' said the faithful messenger. 'He's in an awful temper with you, and he's got bobbies with him.'

I put on pace and left the boy behind. I reckoned I had the better part of two miles' start and could beat anything except petrol. But my enemies were bound to have cars, so I had better get off the road as soon as possible. I coasted down a long hill to a bridge which spanned a small discoloured stream that flowed in a wooded glen. There was nobody for the moment on the hill behind me, so I slipped into the covert, shoved the bicycle under the bridge, and hid Archie's aquascutum in a bramble thicket. I was now in my own disreputable tweeds and I hoped that the shedding of my most conspicuous garment would puzzle my pursuers if they should catch up with me.

But this I was determined they should not do. I made good going down that stream and out into a lane which led from the downs to the market-gardens round the city. I thanked Heaven I had got rid of the aquascutum, for the August afternoon was warm and my pace was not leisurely. When I was in secluded ground I ran, and when anyone was in sight I walked smartly.

As I went I reflected that Bradfield would see the end of my adventures. The police knew that I was there and would watch the stations and hunt me down if I lingered in the place. I knew no one there and had no chance of getting an effective disguise. Indeed I very soon began to wonder if I should get even as far as the streets. For at the moment when I had got a lift on the back of a fishmonger's cart and was screened by its flapping canvas, two figures passed on motor-bicycles, and one of them was the inquisitive boy scout. The main road from the aerodrome was probably now being patrolled by motor-cars. It looked as if there would be a degrading arrest in one of the suburbs.

The fish-cart, helped by half a crown to the driver, took me past the outlying small-villadom, between long lines of workmen's houses, to narrow cobbled lanes and the purlieus of great factories. As soon as I saw the streets well crowded I got out and walked. In my old clothes I must have appeared like some second-class bookie or seedy horse-coper. The only respectable thing I had about me was my gold watch. I looked at the time and found it half past five.

I wanted food and was casting about for an eating-house when I heard the purr of a motor-cycle and across the road saw the intelligent boy scout. He saw me, too, and put on the brake with a sharpness which caused him to skid and all but come to grief under the wheels of a wool-wagon. That gave me time to efface myself by darting up a side street. I had an unpleasant sense that I was about to be trapped, for in a place I knew nothing of I had not a chance to use my wits.

I remember trying feverishly to think, and I suppose that my preoccupation made me careless. I was now in a veritable slum, and when I put my hand to my vest pocket I found that my watch had gone. That put the top stone on my depression. The reaction from the wild burnout of the forenoon had left me very cold about the feet. I was getting into the under-world again and there was no chance of a second Archie Roylance turning up to rescue me. I remember yet the sour smell of the factories and the mist of smoke in the evening air. It is a smell I have never met since without a sort of dulling of spirit.

Presently I came out into a market-place. Whistles were blowing, and there was a great hurrying of people back from the mills. The crowd gave me a momentary sense of security, and I was just about to inquire my way to the railway station when someone jostled my arm.

A rough-looking fellow in mechanic's clothes was beside me.

'Mate,' he whispered. 'I've got summat o' yours here.' And to my amazement he slipped my watch into my hand.

'It was took by mistake. We're friends o' yours. You're right enough if you do what I tell you. There's a peeler over there got his eye on you. Follow me and I'll get you off.'

I didn't much like the man's looks, but I had no choice, and

John Buchan

anyhow he had given me back my watch. He sidled into an alley between tall houses and I sidled after him. Then he took to his heels, and led me a twisting course through smelly courts into a tanyard and then by a narrow lane to the back-quarters of a factory. Twice we doubled back, and once we climbed a wall and followed the bank of a blue-black stream with a filthy scum on it. Then we got into a very mean quarter of the town, and emerged in a dingy garden, strewn with tin cans and broken flowerpots. By a back door we entered one of the cottages and my guide very carefully locked it behind him.

He lit the gas and drew the blinds in a small parlour and looked at me long and quizzically. He spoke now in an educated voice.

'I ask no questions,' he said, 'but it's my business to put my services at your disposal. You carry the passport.'

I stared at him, and he pulled out his watch and showed a white-and-purple cross inside the lid.

'I don't defend all the people we employ,' he said, grinning. 'Men's morals are not always as good as their patriotism. One of them pinched your watch, and when he saw what was inside it he reported to me. We soon picked up your trail, and observed you were in a bit of trouble. As I say, I ask no questions. What can we do for you?'

'I want to get to London without any questions asked. They're looking for me in my present rig, so I've got to change it.'

'That's easy enough,' he said. 'Make yourself comfortable for a little and I'll fix you up. The night train goes at eleven-thirty. ... You'll find cigars in the cupboard and there's this week's Critic on that table. It's got a good article on Conrad, if you care for such things.'

I helped myself to a cigar and spent a profitable half-hour reading about the vices of the British Government. Then my host returned and bade me ascend to his bedroom. 'You're Private Henry Tomkins of the 12th Gloucesters, and you'll find your clothes ready for you. I'll send on your present togs if you give me an address.'

I did as I was bid, and presently emerged in the uniform of a British private, complete down to the shapeless boots and the dropsical puttees. Then my friend took me in hand and finished the transformation. He started on my hair with scissors and arranged a lock which, when well oiled, curled over my forehead. My hands were hard and rough and only needed some grubbiness and hacking about the nails to pass muster. With my cap on the side of my head, a pack on my back, a service rifle in my hands, and my pockets bursting with penny picture papers, I was the very model of the British soldier returning from leave. I had also a packet of Woodbine cigarettes and a hunch of bread-and-cheese for the journey. And I had a railway warrant made out in my name for London.

Then my friend gave me supper - bread and cold meat and a bottle of Bass, which I wolfed savagely, for I had had nothing since breakfast. He was a curious fellow, as discreet as a tombstone, very ready to speak about general subjects, but never once coming near the intimate business which had linked him and me and Heaven knew how many others by means of a little purple-and-white cross in a watch-case. I remember we talked about the topics that used to be popular at Biggleswick - the big political things that begin with capital letters. He took Amos's view of the soundness of the British working-man, but he said something which made me think. He was convinced that there was a tremendous lot of German spy work about, and that most of the practitioners were innocent. 'The ordinary Briton doesn't run to treason, but he's not very bright. A clever man in that kind of game can make better use of a fool than a rogue.'

As he saw me off he gave me a piece of advice. 'Get out of these clothes as soon as you reach London. Private Tomkins

John Buchan

will frank you out of Bradfield, but it mightn't be a healthy alias in the metropolis.'

At eleven-thirty I was safe in the train, talking the jargon of the returning soldier with half a dozen of my own type in a smoky third-class carriage. I had been lucky in my escape, for at the station entrance and on the platform I had noticed several men with the unmistakable look of plainclothes police. Also - though this may have been my fancy - I thought I caught in the crowd a glimpse of the bagman who had called himself Linklater.

CHAPTER TEN

THE ADVANTAGES OF AN AIR RAID

The train was abominably late. It was due at eight-twenty-seven, but it was nearly ten when we reached St Pancras. I had resolved to go straight to my rooms in Westminster, buying on the way a cap and waterproof to conceal my uniform should anyone be near my door on my arrival. Then I would ring up Blenkiron and tell him all my adventures. I breakfasted at a coffee-stall, left my pack and rifle in the cloak-room, and walked out into the clear sunny morning.

I was feeling very pleased with myself. Looking back on my madcap journey, I seemed to have had an amazing run of luck and to be entitled to a little credit too. I told myself that persistence always pays and that nobody is beaten till he is dead. All Blenkiron's instructions had been faithfully carried out. I had found Ivery's post office. I had laid the lines of our own special communications with the enemy, and so far as I could see I had left no clue behind me. Ivery and Gresson took me for a well-meaning nincompoop. It was true that I had aroused profound suspicion in the breasts of the Scottish police. But that mattered nothing, for Cornelius Brand, the suspect, would presently disappear, and there was nothing against that rising soldier, Brigadier-General Richard Hannay, who would soon be on his way to France. After all this piece of service had not been so very unpleasant. I laughed when I remembered my grim forebodings in Gloucestershire. Bullivant had said it would be damnably risky in the long run,

John Buchan

but here was the end and I had never been in danger of anything worse than making a fool of myself.

I remember that, as I made my way through Bloomsbury, I was not thinking so much of my triumphant report to Blenkiron as of my speedy return to the Front. Soon I would be with my beloved brigade again. I had missed Messines and the first part of Third Ypres, but the battle was still going on, and I had yet a chance. I might get a division, for there had been talk of that before I left. I knew the Army Commander thought a lot of me. But on the whole I hoped I would be left with the brigade. After all I was an amateur soldier, and I wasn't certain of my powers with a bigger command.

In Charing Cross Road I thought of Mary, and the brigade seemed suddenly less attractive. I hoped the war wouldn't last much longer, though with Russia heading straight for the devil I didn't know how it was going to stop very soon. I was determined to see Mary before I left, and I had a good excuse, for I had taken my orders from her. The prospect entranced me, and I was mooning along in a happy dream, when I collided violently with in agitated citizen.

Then I realized that something very odd was happening.

There was a dull sound like the popping of the corks of flat soda-water bottles. There was a humming, too, from very far up in the skies. People in the street were either staring at the heavens or running wildly for shelter. A motor-bus in front of me emptied its contents in a twinkling; a taxi pulled up with a jar and the driver and fare dived into a second-hand bookshop. It took me a moment or two to realize the meaning of it all, and I had scarcely done this when I got a very practical proof. A hundred yards away a bomb fell on a street island, shivering every window-pane in a wide radius, and sending splinters of stone flying about my head. I did what I had done a hundred times before at the Front, and dropped flat on my face.

The man who says he doesn't mind being bombed or shelled is

either a liar or a maniac. This London air raid seemed to me a singularly unpleasant business. I think it was the sight of the decent civilized life around one and the orderly streets, for what was perfectly natural in a rubble-heap like Ypres or Arras seemed an outrage here. I remember once being in billets in a Flanders village where I had the Maire's house and sat in a room upholstered in cut velvet, with wax flowers on the mantelpiece and oil paintings of three generations on the walls. The Boche took it into his head to shell the place with a long-range naval gun, and I simply loathed it. It was horrible to have dust and splinters blown into that snug, homely room, whereas if I had been in a ruined barn I wouldn't have given the thing two thoughts. In the same way bombs dropping in central London seemed a grotesque indecency. I hated to see plump citizens with wild eyes, and nursemaids with scared children, and miserable women scuttling like rabbits in a warren.

The drone grew louder, and, looking up, I could see the enemy planes flying in a beautiful formation, very leisurely as it seemed, with all London at their mercy. Another bomb fell to the right, and presently bits of our own shrapnel were clattering viciously around me. I thought it about time to take cover, and ran shamelessly for the best place I could see, which was a Tube station. Five minutes before the street had been crowded; now I left behind me a desert dotted with one bus and three empty taxicabs.

I found the Tube entrance filled with excited humanity. One stout lady had fainted, and a nurse had become hysterical, but on the whole people were behaving well. Oddly enough they did not seem inclined to go down the stairs to the complete security of underground; but preferred rather to collect where they could still get a glimpse of the upper world, as if they were torn between fear of their lives and interest in the spectacle. That crowd gave me a good deal of respect for my country-men. But several were badly rattled, and one man a little way off, whose back was turned, kept twitching his shoulders as if he had the colic.

I watched him curiously, and a movement of the crowd brought his face into profile. Then I gasped with amazement, for I saw that it was Ivery.

And yet it was not Ivery. There were the familiar nondescript features, the blandness, the plumpness, but all, so to speak, in ruins. The man was in a blind funk. His features seemed to be dislimning before my eyes. He was growing sharper, finer, in a way younger, a man without grip on himself, a shapeless creature in process of transformation. He was being reduced to his rudiments. Under the spell of panic he was becoming a new man.

And the crazy thing was that I knew the new man better than the old.

My hands were jammed close to my sides by the crowd; I could scarcely turn my head, and it was not the occasion for one's neighbours to observe one's expression. If it had been, mine must have been a study. My mind was far away from air raids, back in the hot summer weather Of 1914. I saw a row of villas perched on a headland above the sea. In the garden of one of them two men were playing tennis, while I was crouching behind an adjacent bush. One of these was a plump young man who wore a coloured scarf round his waist and babbled of golf handicaps ... I saw him again in the villa dining-room, wearing a dinner-jacket, and lisping a little. ... I sat opposite him at bridge, I beheld him collared by two of Macgillivray's men, when his comrade had rushed for the thirty-nine steps that led to the sea ... I saw, too, the sitting-room of my old flat in Portland Place and heard little Scudder's quick, anxious voice talking about the three men he feared most on earth, one of whom lisped in his speech. I had thought that all three had long ago been laid under the turf ...

He was not looking my way, and I could devour his face in safety. There was no shadow of doubt. I had always put him down as the most amazing actor on earth, for had he not played the part of the First Sea Lord and deluded that officer's daily colleagues? But he could do far more than any human actor, for he could take on a new personality and with it a new appearance, and live steadily in the character as if he had been born in it ... My mind was a blank, and I could only make blind gropings at conclusions ... How had he escaped the death of a spy and a murderer, for I had last seen him in the hands of justice? ... Of course he had known me from the first day in Biggleswick ... I had thought to play with him, and he had played most cunningly and damnably with me. In that sweating sardine-tin of refugees I shivered in the bitterness of my chagrin.

And then I found his face turned to mine, and I knew that he recognized me. more, I knew that he knew that I had recognized him - not as Ivery, but as that other man. There came into his eyes a curious look of comprehension, which for a moment overcame his funk.

I had sense enough to see that that put the final lid on it. There was still something doing if he believed that I was blind, but if he once thought that I knew the truth he would be through our meshes and disappear like a fog.

My first thought was to get at him and collar him and summon everybody to help me by denouncing him for what he was. Then I saw that that was impossible. I was a private soldier in a borrowed uniform, and he could easily turn the story against me. I must use surer weapons. I must get to Bullivant and Macgillivray and set their big machine to work. Above all I must get to Blenkiron.

I started to squeeze out of that push, for air raids now seemed far too trivial to give a thought to. Moreover the guns had stopped, but so sheeplike is human nature that the crowd still hung together, and it took me a good fifteen minutes to edge my way to the open air. I found that the trouble was over, and the street had resumed its usual appearance. Buses and taxis were running, and voluble knots of people were recounting their experiences. I started off for Blenkiron's bookshop, as the nearest harbour of refuge.

But in Piccadilly Circus I was stopped by a military policeman. He asked my name and battalion, and I gave him them, while his suspicious eye ran over my figure. I had no pack or rifle, and the crush in the Tube station had not improved my appearance. I explained that I was going back to France that evening, and he asked for my warrant. I fancy my preoccupation made me nervous and I lied badly. I said I had left it with my kit in the house of my married sister, but I fumbled in giving the address. I could see that the fellow did not believe a word of it.

Just then up came an A.P.M. He was a pompous dug-out, very splendid in his red tabs and probably bucked up at having just been under fire. Anyhow he was out to walk in the strict path of duty.

'Tomkins!' he said. 'Tomkins! We've got some fellow of that name on our records. Bring him along, Wilson.'

'But, sir,' I said, 'I must - I simply must meet my friend. It's urgent business, and I assure you I'm all right. If you don't believe me, I'll take a taxi and we'll go down to Scotland Yard and I'll stand by what they say.'

His brow grew dark with wrath. 'What infernal nonsense is this? Scotland Yard! What the devil has Scotland Yard to do with it? You're an imposter. I can see it in your face. I'll have your depot rung up, and you'll be in jail in a couple of hours. I know a deserter when I see him. Bring him along, Wilson. You know what to do if he tries to bolt.'

I had a momentary thought of breaking away, but decided that the odds were too much against me. Fuming with impatience, I followed the A.P.M. to his office on the first floor in a side street. The precious minutes were slipping past; Ivery, now thoroughly warned, was making good his escape; and I, the sole repository of a deadly secret, was tramping in this absurd procession.

The A.P.M. issued his orders. He gave instructions that my depot should be rung up, and he bade Wilson remove me to what he called the guard-room. He sat down at his desk, and busied himself with a mass of buff dockets.

In desperation I renewed my appeal. 'I implore you to telephone to Mr Macgillivray at Scotland Yard. It's a matter of life and death, Sir. You're taking a very big responsibility if you don't.'

I had hopelessly offended his brittle dignity. 'Any more of your insolence and I'll have you put in irons. I'll attend to you soon enough for your comfort. Get out of this till I send for you.'

As I looked at his foolish, irritable face I realized that I was fairly UP against it. Short of assault and battery on everybody I was bound to submit. I saluted respectfully and was marched away.

The hours I spent in that bare anteroom are like a nightmare in my recollection. A sergeant was busy at a desk with more buff dockets and an orderly waited on a stool by a telephone. I looked at my watch and observed that it was one o'clock. Soon the slamming of a door announced that the A.P.M. had gone to lunch. I tried conversation with the fat sergeant, but he very soon shut me up. So I sat hunched up on the wooden form and chewed the cud of my vexation.

I thought with bitterness of the satisfaction which had filled me in the morning. I had fancied myself the devil of a fine fellow, and I had been no more than a mountebank. The adventures of the past days seemed merely childish. I had been telling lies and cutting capers over half Britain, thinking I was playing a deep game, and I had only been behaving like a schoolboy. On such occasions a man is rarely just to himself, and the intensity of my self-abasement would have satisfied my worst enemy. It didn't console me that the futility of it all was not my blame. I was looking for excuses. It was the facts that cried out against me, and on the facts I had been an idiotic failure.

For of course Ivery had played with me, played with me since the first day at Biggleswick. He had applauded my speeches and flattered me, and advised me to go to the Clyde, laughing at me all the time. Gresson, too, had known. Now I saw it all. He had tried to drown me between Colonsay and Mull. It was Gresson who had set the police on me in Morvern. The bagman Linklater had been one of Gresson's creatures. The only meagre consolation was that the gang had thought me dangerous enough to attempt to murder me, and that they knew nothing about my doings in Skye. Of that I was positive. They had marked me down, but for several days I had slipped clean out of their ken.

As I went over all the incidents, I asked if everything was yet lost. I had failed to hoodwink Ivery, but I had found out his post office, and if he only believed I hadn't recognized him for the miscreant of the Black Stone he would go on in his old ways and play into Blenkiron's hands. Yes, but I had seen him in undress, so to speak, and he knew that I had so seen him. The only thing now was to collar him before he left the country, for there was ample evidence to hang him on. The law must stretch out its long arm and collect him and Gresson and the Portuguese Jew, try them by court martial, and put them decently underground. But he had now had more than an hour's warning, and I was entangled with red-tape in this damned A.P.M.'s office. The thought drove me frantic, and I got up and paced the floor. I saw the orderly with rather a scared face making ready to press the bell, and I noticed that the fat sergeant had gone to lunch.

'Say, mate,' I said, 'don't you feel inclined to do a poor fellow a good turn? I know I'm for it all right, and I'll take my medicine like a lamb. But I want badly to put a telephone call through.'

'It ain't allowed,' was the answer. 'I'd get 'ell from the old man.'

'But he's gone out,' I urged. 'I don't want you to do anything wrong, mate, I leave you to do the talkin' if you'll only send my message. I'm flush of money, and I don't mind handin' you a quid for the job.'

He was a pinched little man with a weak chin, and he obviously wavered.

"Oo d'ye want to talk to?' he asked.

'Scotland Yard,' I said, 'the home of the police. Lord bless you, there can't be no harm in that. Ye've only got to ring up Scotland Yard - I'll give you the number - and give the message to Mr Macgillivray. He's the head bummer of all the bobbies.'

'That sounds a bit of all right,' he said. 'The old man 'e won't be back for 'alf an hour, nor the sergeant neither. Let's see your quid though.'

I laid a pound note on the form beside me. 'It's yours, mate, if you get through to Scotland Yard and speak the piece I'm goin' to give you.'

He went over to the instrument. 'What d'you want to say to the bloke with the long name?' 'Say that Richard Hannay is detained at the A.P.M.'s office in Claxton Street. Say he's got important news - say urgent and secret news - and ask Mr Macgillivray to do something about it at once.' 'But 'Annay ain't the name you gave.'

'Lord bless you, no. Did you never hear of a man borrowin' another name? Anyhow that's the one I want you to give.'

'But if this Mac man comes round 'ere, they'll know 'e's bin rung up, and I'll 'ave the old man down on me.'

It took ten minutes and a second pound note to get him past this hurdle. By and by he screwed up courage and rang up the number. I listened with some nervousness while he gave my message - he had to repeat it twice - and waited eagerly on the next words.

'No, sir,' I heard him say, "e don't want you to come round 'ere. E thinks as 'ow - I mean to say, 'e wants -'

I took a long stride and twitched the receiver from him.

'Macgillivray,' I said, 'is that you? Richard Hannay! For the love of God come round here this instant and deliver me from the clutches of a tomfool A.P.M. I've got the most deadly news. There's not a second to waste. For God's sake come quick!' Then I added: 'Just tell your fellows to gather Ivery in at once. You know his lairs.'

I hung up the receiver and faced a pale and indignant orderly. 'It's all right,' I said. 'I promise you that you won't get into any trouble on my account. And there's your two quid.'

The door in the next room opened and shut. The A.P.M. had returned from lunch ...

Ten minutes later the door opened again. I heard Macgillivray's voice, and it was not pitched in dulcet tones. He had run up against minor officialdom and was making hay with it.

I was my own master once more, so I forsook the company of the orderly. I found a most rattled officer trying to save a few rags of his dignity and the formidable figure of Macgillivray instructing him in manners.

'Glad to see you, Dick,' he said. 'This is General Hannay, sir. It may comfort you to know that your folly may have made just the difference between your country's victory and defeat. I shall have a word to say to your superiors.'

It was hardly fair. I had to put in a word for the old fellow, whose red tabs seemed suddenly to have grown dingy.

'It was my blame wearing this kit. We'll call it a misunderstanding and forget it. But I would suggest that civility is not wasted even on a poor devil of a defaulting private soldier.'

Once in Macgillivray's car, I poured out my tale. 'Tell me it's a nightmare,' I cried. 'Tell me that the three men we collected on the Ruff were shot long ago.'

'Two,' he replied, 'but one escaped. Heaven knows how he managed it, but he disappeared clean out of the world.'

'The plump one who lisped in his speech?'

Macgillivray nodded.

'Well, we're in for it this time. Have you issued instructions?'

'Yes. With luck we shall have our hands on him within an hour. We've our net round all his haunts.'

'But two hours' start! It's a big handicap, for you're dealing with a genius.'

'Yet I think we can manage it. Where are you bound for?'

I told him my rooms in Westminster and then to my old flat in Park Lane. 'The day of disguises is past. In half an hour I'll be Richard Hannay. It'll be a comfort to get into uniform again. Then I'll look up Blenkiron.'

He grinned. 'I gather you've had a riotous time. We've had a good many anxious messages from the north about a certain Mr Brand. I couldn't discourage our men, for I fancied it might have spoiled your game. I heard that last night they had lost touch with you in Bradfield, so I rather expected to see you here today. Efficient body of men the Scottish police.'

John Buchan

'Especially when they have various enthusiastic amateur helpers.'

'So?' he said. 'Yes, of course. They would have. But I hope presently to congratulate you on the success of your mission.'

'I'll bet you a pony you don't,' I said.

'I never bet on a professional subject. Why this pessimism?'

'Only that I know our gentleman better than you. I've been twice up against him. He's the kind of wicked that don't cease from troubling till they're stone-dead. And even then I'd want to see the body cremated and take the ashes into mid-ocean and scatter them. I've got a feeling that he's the biggest thing you or I will ever tackle.'

CHAPTER ELEVEN

THE VALLEY OF HUMILIATION

I collected some baggage and a pile of newly arrived letters from my rooms in Westminster and took a taxi to my Park Lane flat. Usually I had gone back to that old place with a great feeling of comfort, like a boy from school who ranges about his room at home and examines his treasures. I used to like to see my hunting trophies on the wall and to sink into my own armchairs But now I had no pleasure in the thing. I had a bath, and changed into uniform, and that made me feel in better fighting trim. But I suffered from a heavy conviction of abject failure, and had no share in Macgillivray's optimism. The awe with which the Black Stone gang had filled me three years before had revived a thousandfold. Personal humiliation was the least part of my trouble. What worried me was the sense of being up against something inhumanly formidable and wise and strong. I believed I was willing to own defeat and chuck up the game.

Among the unopened letters was one from Peter, a very bulky one which I sat down to read at leisure. It was a curious epistle, far the longest he had ever written me, and its size made me understand his loneliness. He was still at his German prison-camp, but expecting every day to go to Switzerland. He said he could get back to England or South Africa, if he wanted, for they were clear that he could never be a combatant again; but he thought he had better stay in Switzerland, for he would be unhappy in England with all his friends fighting. As usual he

John Buchan

made no complaints, and seemed to be very grateful for his small mercies. There was a doctor who was kind to him, and some good fellows among the prisoners.

But Peter's letter was made up chiefly of reflection. He had always been a bit of a philosopher, and now, in his isolation, he had taken to thinkin hard, and poured out the results to me on pages of thin paper in his clumsy handwriting. I could read between the lines that he was having a stiff fight with himself. He was trying to keep his courage going in face of the bitterest trial he could be called on to face - a crippled old age. He had always known a good deal about the Bible, and that and the Pilgrim's Progress were his chief aids in reflection. Both he took quite literally, as if they were newspaper reports of actual recent events.

He mentioned that after much consideration he had reached the conclusion that the three greatest men he had ever heard of or met were Mr Valiant-for-Truth, the Apostle Paul, and a certain Billy Strang who had been with him in Mashonaland in '92. Billy I knew all about; he had been Peter's hero and leader till a lion got him in the Blaauwberg. Peter preferred Valiant-for-Truth to Mr Greatheart, I think, because of his superior truculence, for, being very gentle himself, he loved a bold speaker. After that he dropped into a vein of self-examination. He regretted that he fell far short of any of the three. He thought that he might with luck resemble Mr Standfast, for like him he had not much trouble in keeping wakeful, and was also as 'poor as a howler', and didn't care for women. He only hoped that he could imitate him in making a good end.

Then followed some remarks of Peter's on courage, which came to me in that London room as if spoken by his living voice. I have never known anyone so brave, so brave by instinct, or anyone who hated so much to be told so. It was almost the only thing that could make him angry. All his life he had been facing death, and to take risks seemed to him as natural as to get up in the morning and eat his breakfast. But he had started out to consider the very thing which before he had taken for granted, and here is an extract from his conclusions. I paraphrase him, for he was not grammatical.

It's easy enough to be brave if you're feeling well and have food inside you. And it's not so difficult even if you're short of a meal and seedy, for that makes you inclined to gamble. I mean by being brave playing the game by the right rules without letting it worry you that you may very likely get knocked on the head. It's the wisest way to save your skin. It doesn't do to think about death if you're facing a charging lion or trying to bluff a lot of savages. If you think about it you'll get it; if you don't, the odds are you won't. That kind of courage is only good nerves and experience ... Most courage is experience. Most people are a little scared at new things...

You want a bigger heart to face danger which you go out to look for, and which doesn't come to you in the ordinary way of business. Still, that's Pretty much the same thing - good nerves and good health, and a natural liking for rows. You see, Dick, in all that game there's a lot Of fun. There's excitement and the fun of using your wits and skill, and you know that the bad bits can't last long. When Arcoll sent me to Makapan's kraal I didn't altogether fancy the job, but at the worst it was three parts sport, and I got so excited that I never thought of the risk till it was over ...

But the big courage is the cold-blooded kind, the kind that never lets go even when you're feeling empty inside, and your blood's thin, and there's no kind of fun or profit to be had, and the trouble's not over in an hour or two but lasts for months and years. One of the men here was speaking about that kind, and he called it 'Fortitude'. I reckon fortitude's the biggest thing a man can have - just to go on enduring when there's no guts or heart left in you. Billy had it when he trekked solitary from Garungoze to the Limpopo with fever and a broken arm just to show the Portugooses that he wouldn't be downed by them. But the head man at the job was the Apostle Paul ...

Peter was writing for his own comfort, for fortitude was all that was left to him now. But his words came pretty straight to me, and I read them again and again, for I needed the lesson. Here was I losing heart just because I had failed in the first round and my pride had taken a knock. I felt honestly ashamed of myself, and that made me a far happier man. There could be no question of dropping the business, whatever its difficulties. I had a queer religious feeling that Ivery and I had our fortunes intertwined, and that no will of mine could keep us apart. I had faced him before the war and won; I had faced him again and lost; the third time or the twentieth time we would reach a final decision. The whole business had hitherto appeared to me a trifle unreal, at any rate my own connection with it. I had been docilely obeying orders, but my real self had been standing aside and watching my doings with a certain aloofness. But that hour in the Tube station had brought me into the serum, and I saw the affair not as Bullivant's or even Blenkiron's, but as my own. Before I had been itching to get back to the Front; now I wanted to get on to Ivery's trail, though it should take me through the nether pit. Peter was right; fortitude was the thing a man must possess if he would save his soul.

The hours passed, and, as I expected, there came no word from Macgillivray. I had some dinner sent up to me at seven o'clock, and about eight I was thinking of looking up Blenkiron. just then came a telephone call asking me to go round to Sir Walter Bullivant's house in Queen Anne's Gate.

Ten minutes later I was ringing the bell, and the door was opened to me by the same impassive butler who had admitted me on that famous night three years before. Nothing had changed in the pleasant green-panelled hall; the alcove was the same as when I had watched from it the departure of the man who now called himself Ivery; the telephone book lay in the very place from which I had snatched it in order to ring up the First Sea Lord. And in the back room, where that night five anxious officials had conferred, I found Sir Walter and Blenkiron.

Both looked worried, the American feverishly so. He walked up and down the hearthrug, sucking an unlit black cigar.

'Say, Dick,' he said, this is a bad business. It wasn't no fault of yours. You did fine. It was us - me and Sir Walter and Mr Macgillivray that were the quitters.'

'Any news?' I asked.

'So far the cover's drawn blank,' Sir Walter replied. 'It was the devil's own work that our friend looked your way today. You're pretty certain he saw that you recognized him?'

'Absolutely. As sure as that he knew I recognized him in your hall three years ago when he was swaggering as Lord Alloa.'

'No,' said Blenkiron dolefully, that little flicker of recognition is just the one thing you can't be wrong about. Land alive! I wish Mr Macgillivray would come.'

The bell rang, and the door opened, but it was not Macgillivray. It was a young girl in a white ball-gown, with a cluster of blue cornflowers at her breast. The sight of her fetched Sir Walter out of his chair so suddenly that he upset his coffee cup. 'Mary, my dear, how did you manage it? I didn't expect you till the late train.' 'I was in London, you see, and they telephoned on your telegram. I'm staying with Aunt Doria, and I cut her theatre party. She thinks I'm at the Shandwick's dance, so I needn't go home till morning ... Good evening, General Hannay. You got over the Hill Difficulty.'

'The next stage is the Valley of Humiliation,' I answered.

'So it would appear,' she said gravely, and sat very quietly on the edge of Sir Walter's chair with her small, cool hand upon his.

I had been picturing her in my recollection as very young and glimmering, a dancing, exquisite child. But now I revised that picture. The crystal freshness of morning was still there, but I saw how deep the waters were. It was the clean fineness and strength of her that entranced me. I didn't even think of her as pretty, any more than a man thinks of the good looks of the friend he worships.

We waited, hardly speaking a word, till Macgillivray came. The first sight of his face told his story.

'Gone?' asked Blenkiron sharply. The man's lethargic calm seemed to have wholly deserted him.

'Gone,' repeated the newcomer. 'We have just tracked him down. Oh, he managed it cleverly. Never a sign of disturbance in any of his lairs. His dinner ordered at Biggleswick and several people invited to stay with him for the weekend - one a member of the Government. Two meetings at which he was to speak arranged for next week. Early this afternoon he flew over to France as a passenger in one of the new planes. He had been mixed up with the Air Board people for months - of course as another man with another face. Miss Lamington discovered that just too late. The bus went out of its course and came down in Normandy. By this time our man's in Paris or beyond it.'

Sir Walter took off his big tortoiseshell spectacles and laid them carefully on the table.

'Roll up the map of Europe,' he said. 'This is our Austerlitz. Mary, my dear, I am feeling very old.'

Macgillivray had the sharpened face of a bitterly disappointed man. Blenkiron had got very red, and I could see that he was blaspheming violently under his breath. Mary's eyes were quiet and solemn. She kept on patting Sir Walter's hand. The sense of some great impending disaster hung heavily on me, and to break the spell I asked for details.

'Tell me just the extent of the damage,' I asked. 'Our neat plan for deceiving the Boche has failed. That is bad. A dangerous spy has got beyond our power. That's worse. Tell me, is there still a worst? What's the limit of mischief he can do?' Sir Walter had risen and joined Blenkiron on the hearthrug. His brows were furrowed and his mouth hard as if he were suffering Pain.

'There is no limit,' he said. 'None that I can see, except the long-suffering of God. You know the man as Ivery, and you knew him as that other whom you believed to have been shot one summer morning and decently buried. You feared the second - at least if you didn't, I did - most mortally. You realized that we feared Ivery, and you knew enough about him to see his fiendish cleverness. Well, you have the two men combined in one man. Ivery was the best brain Macgillivray and I ever encountered, the most cunning and patient and long-sighted. Combine him with the other, the chameleon who can blend himself with his environment, and has as many personalities as there are types and traits on the earth. What kind of enemy is that to have to fight?'

'I admit it's a steep proposition. But after all how much ill can he do? There are pretty strict limits to the activity of even the cleverest spy.'

'I agree. But this man is not a spy who buys a few wretched subordinates and steals a dozen private letters. He's a genius who has been living as part of our English life. There's nothing he hasn't seen. He's been on terms of intimacy with all kinds of politicians. We know that. He did it as Ivery. They rather liked him, for he was clever and flattered them, and they told him things. But God knows what he saw and heard in his other personalities. For all I know he may have breakfasted at Downing Street with letters of introduction from President Wilson, or visited the Grand Fleet as a distinguished neutral. Then think of the women; how they talk. We're the leakiest society on earth, and we safeguard ourselves by keeping dangerous people out of it. We trust to our outer barrage. But anyone who has really slipped inside has a million chances.

And this, remember, is one man in ten millions, a man whose brain never sleeps for a moment, who is quick to seize the slightest hint, who can piece a plan together out of a dozen bits of gossip. It's like - it's as if the Chief of the Intelligence Department were suddenly to desert to the enemy ... The ordinary spy knows only bits of unconnected facts. This man knows our life and our way of thinking and everything about us.'

'Well, but a treatise on English life in time of war won't do much good to the Boche.'

Sir Walter shook his head. 'Don't you realize the explosive stuff that is lying about? Ivery knows enough to make the next German peace offensive really deadly - not the blundering thing which it has been up to now, but something which gets our weak spots on the raw. He knows enough to wreck our campaign in the field. And the awful thing is that we don't know just what he knows or what he is aiming for. This war's a packet of surprises. Both sides are struggling for the margin, the little fraction of advantage, and between evenly matched enemies it's just the extra atom of foreknowledge that tells.' 'Then we've got to push off and get after him,' I said cheerfully.

'But what are you going to do?' asked Macgillivray. 'If it were merely a question of destroying an organization it might be managed, for an organization presents a big front. But it's a question of destroying this one man, and his front is a razor edge. How are you going to find him? It's like looking for a needle in a haystack, and such a needle! A needle which can become a piece of straw or a tin-tack when it chooses!'

'All the same we've got to do it,' I said, remembering old Peter's lesson on fortitude, though I can't say I was feeling very stout-hearted.

Sir Walter flung himself wearily into an arm-chair. 'I wish I could be an optimist,' he said, 'but it looks as if we must own defeat. I've been at this work for twenty years, and, though I've been often beaten, I've always held certain cards in the game. Now I'm hanged if I've any. It looks like a knock-out, Hannay. It's no good deluding ourselves. We're men enough to look facts in the face and tell ourselves the truth. I don't see any ray of light in the business. We've missed our shot by a hairsbreadth and that's the same as missing by miles.'

I remember he looked at Mary as if for confirmation, but she did not smile or nod. Her face was very grave and her eyes looked steadily at him. Then they moved and met mine, and they seemed to give me my marching orders.

'Sir Walter,' I said, 'three years ago you and I sat in this very room. We thought we were done to the world, as we think now. We had just that one miserable little clue to hang on to - a dozen words scribbled in a notebook by a dead man. You thought I was mad when I asked for Scudder's book, but we put our backs into the job and in twenty-four hours we had won out. Remember that then we were fighting against time. Now we have a reasonable amount of leisure. Then we had nothing but a sentence of gibberish. Now we have a great body of knowledge, for Blenkiron has been brooding over Ivery like an old hen, and he knows his ways of working and his breed of confederate. You've got something to work on now. Do you mean to tell me that, when the stakes are so big, you're going to chuck in your hand?'

Macgillivray raised his head. 'We know a good deal about Ivery, but Ivery's dead. We know nothing of the man who was gloriously resurrected this evening in Normandy.'

'Oh, yes we do. There are many faces to the man, but only one mind, and you know plenty about that mind.'

'I wonder,' said Sir Walter. 'How can you know a mind which has no characteristics except that it is wholly and supremely competent? Mere mental powers won't give us a clue. We want to know the character which is behind all the personalities.

John Buchan

Above all we want to know its foibles. If we had only a hint of some weakness we might make a plan.'

'Well, let's set down all we know,' I cried, for the more I argued the keener I grew. I told them in some detail the story of the night in the Coolin and what I had heard there.

'There's the two names Chelius and Bommaerts. The man spoke them in the same breath as Effenbein, so they must be associated with Ivery's gang. You've got to get the whole Secret Service of the Allies busy to fit a meaning to these two words. Surely to goodness you'll find something! Remember those names don't belong to the Ivery part, but to the big game behind all the different disguises ... Then there's the talk about the Wild Birds and the Cage Birds. I haven't a guess at what it means. But it refers to some infernal gang, and among your piles of records there must be some clue. You set the intelligence of two hemispheres busy on the job. You've got all the machinery, and it's my experience that if even one solitary man keeps chewing on at a problem he discovers something.'

My enthusiasm was beginning to strike sparks from Macgillivray. He was looking thoughtful now, instead of despondent.

'There might be something in that,' he said, 'but it's a far-out chance.'

'Of course it's a far-out chance, and that's all we're ever going to get from Ivery. But we've taken a bad chance before and won ... Then you've all that you know about Ivery here. Go through his dossier with a small-tooth comb and I'll bet you find something to work on. Blenkiron, you're a man with a cool head. You admit we've a sporting chance.'

'Sure, Dick. He's fixed things so that the lines are across the track, but we'll clear somehow. So far as John S. Blenkiron is concerned he's got just one thing to do in this world, and that's to follow the yellow dog and have him neatly and cleanly tidied up. I've got a stack of personal affronts to settle. I was easy fruit and he hasn't been very respectful. You can count me in, Dick.'

'Then we're agreed,' I cried. 'Well, gentlemen, it's up to you to arrange the first stage. You've some pretty solid staff work to put in before you get on the trail.'

'And you?' Sir Walter asked.

'I'm going back to my brigade. I want a rest and a change. Besides, the first stage is office work, and I'm no use for that. But I'll be waiting to be summoned, and I'll come like a shot as soon as you hoick me out. I've got a presentiment about this thing. I know there'll be a finish and that I'll be in at it, and I think it will be a desperate, bloody business too.'

I found Mary's eyes fixed upon me, and in them I read the same thought. She had not spoken a word, but had sat on the edge of a chair, swinging a foot idly, one hand playing with an ivory fan. She had given me my old orders and I looked to her for confirmation of the new.

'Miss Lamington, you are the wisest of the lot of us. What do you say?'

She smiled - that shy, companionable smile which I had been picturing to myself through all the wanderings of the past month.

'I think you are right. We've a long way to go yet, for the Valley of Humiliation comes only half-way in the Pilgrim's Progress. The next stage was Vanity Fair. I might be of some use there, don't you think?'

I remember the way she laughed and flung back her head like a gallant boy.

'The mistake we've all been making,' she said, 'is that our

John Buchan

methods are too terre-a-terre. We've a poet to deal with, a great poet, and we must fling our imaginations forward to catch up with him. His strength is his unexpectedness, you know, and we won't beat him by plodding only. I believe the wildest course is the wisest, for it's the most likely to intersect his ... Who's the poet among us?'

'Peter,' I said. 'But he's pinned down with a game leg in Germany. All the same we must rope him in.'

By this time we had all cheered up, for it is wonderful what a tonic there is in a prospect of action. The butler brought in tea, which it was Bullivant's habit to drink after dinner. To me it seemed fantastic to watch a slip of a girl pouring it out for two grizzled and distinguished servants of the State and one battered soldier - as decorous a family party as you would ask to see - and to reflect that all four were engaged in an enterprise where men's lives must be reckoned at less than thistledown.

After that we went upstairs to a noble Georgian drawing-room and Mary played to us. I don't care two straws for music from an instrument - unless it be the pipes or a regimental band - but I dearly love the human voice. But she would not sing, for singing to her, I fancy, was something that did not come at will, but flowed only like a bird's note when the mood favoured. I did not want it either. I was content to let 'Cherry Ripe' be the one song linked with her in my memory.

It was Macgillivray who brought us back to business.

'I wish to Heaven there was one habit of mind we could definitely attach to him and to no one else.' (At this moment 'He' had only one meaning for us.)

'You can't do nothing with his mind,' Blenkiron drawled. 'You can't loose the bands of Orion, as the Bible says, or hold Leviathan with a hook. I reckoned I could and made a mighty close study of his de-vices. But the darned cuss wouldn't stay put. I thought I had tied him down to the double bluff, and he went and played the triple bluff on me. There's nothing doing that line.'

A memory of Peter recurred to me.

'What about the "blind spot"?' I asked, and I told them old Peter's pet theory. 'Every man that God made has his weak spot somewhere, some flaw in his character which leaves a dull patch in his brain. We've got to find that out, and I think I've made a beginning.' Macgillivray in a sharp voice asked my meaning.

'He's in a funk ... of something. Oh, I don't mean he's a coward. A man in his trade wants the nerve of a buffalo. He could give us all points in courage. What I mean is that he's not clean white all through. There are yellow streaks somewhere in him ... I've given a good deal of thought to this courage business, for I haven't got a great deal of it myself. Not like Peter, I mean. I've got heaps of soft places in me. I'm afraid of being drowned for one thing, or of getting my eyes shot out. Ivery's afraid of bombs - at any rate he's afraid of bombs in a big city. I once read a book which talked about a thing called agoraphobia. Perhaps it's that ... Now if we know that weak spot it helps us in our work. There are some places he won't go to, and there are some things he can't do - not well, anyway. I reckon that's useful.'

'Ye-es,' said Macgillivray. 'Perhaps it's not what you'd call a burning and a shining light.'

'There's another chink in his armour,' I went on. 'There's one person in the world he can never practise his transformations on, and that's me. I shall always know him again, though he appeared as Sir Douglas Haig. I can't explain why, but I've got a feel in my bones about it. I didn't recognize him before, for I thought he was dead, and the nerve in my brain which should have been looking for him wasn't working. But I'm on my guard now, and that nerve's functioning at full power.

John Buchan

Whenever and wherever and howsoever we meet again on the face of the earth, it will be "Dr Livingstone, I presume" between him and me.'

'That is better,' said Macgillivray. 'If we have any luck, Hannay, it won't be long till we pull you out of His Majesty's Forces.'

Mary got up from the piano and resumed her old perch on the arm of Sir Walter's chair.

'There's another blind spot which you haven't mentioned.' It was a cool evening, but I noticed that her cheeks had suddenly flushed.

'Last week Mr Ivery asked me to marry him,' she said.

PART II

CHAPTER TWELVE

I BECOME A COMBATANT ONCE MORE

I returned to France on 13 September, and took over my old brigade on the 19th of the same month. We were shoved in at the Polygon Wood on the 26th, and after four days got so badly mauled that we were brought out to refit. On 7 October, very much to my surprise, I was given command of a division and was on the fringes of the Ypres fighting during the first days of November. From that front we were hurried down to Cambrai in support, but came in only for the last backwash of that singular battle. We held a bit of the St Quentin sector till just before Christmas, when we had a spell of rest in billets, which endured, so far as I was concerned, till the beginning of January, when I was sent off on the errand which I shall presently relate.

That is a brief summary of my military record in the latter part of 1917. I am not going to enlarge on the fighting. Except for the days of the Polygon Wood it was neither very severe nor very distinguished, and you will find it in the history books. What I have to tell of here is my own personal quest, for all the time I was living with my mind turned two ways. In the morasses of the Haanebeek flats, in the slimy support lines at Zonnebeke, in the tortured uplands about Flesquieres, and in many other odd places I kept worrying at my private conundrum. At night I would lie awake thinking of it, and many a

John Buchan

toss I took into shell-holes and many a time I stepped off the duckboards, because my eyes were on a different landscape. Nobody ever chewed a few wretched clues into such a pulp as I did during those bleak months in Flanders and Picardy.

For I had an instinct that the thing was desperately grave, graver even than the battle before me. Russia had gone headlong to the devil, Italy had taken it between the eyes and was still dizzy, and our own prospects were none too bright. The Boche was getting uppish and with some cause, and I foresaw a rocky time ahead till America could line up with us in the field. It was the chance for the Wild Birds, and I used to wake in a sweat to think what devilry Ivery might be engineering. I believe I did my proper job reasonably well, but I put in my most savage thinking over the other. I remember how I used to go over every hour of every day from that June night in the Cotswolds till my last meeting with Bullivant in London, trying to find a new bearing. I should probably have got brain-fever, if I hadn't had to spend most of my days and nights fighting a stiffish battle with a very watchful Hun. That kept my mind balanced, and I dare say it gave an edge to it; for during those months I was lucky enough to hit on a better scent than Bullivant and Macgillivray and Blenkiron, pulling a thousand wires in their London offices.

I will set down in order of time the various incidents in this private quest of mine. The first was my meeting with Geordie Hamilton. It happened just after I rejoined the brigade, when I went down to have a look at our Scots Fusilier battalion. The old brigade had been roughly handled on 31st July, and had had to get heavy drafts to come anywhere near strength. The Fusiliers especially were almost a new lot, formed by joining our remnants to the remains of a battalion in another division and bringing about a dozen officers from the training unit at home. I inspected the men and my eyes caught sight of a familiar face. I asked his name and the colonel got it from the sergeant-major. It was Lance-Corporal George Hamilton.

Now I wanted a new batman, and I resolved then and there to

have my old antagonist. That afternoon he reported to me at brigade headquarters. As I looked at that solid bandy-legged figure, standing as stiff to attention as a tobacconist's sign, his ugly face hewn out of brown oak, his honest, sullen mouth, and his blue eyes staring into vacancy, I knew I had got the man I wanted.

'Hamilton,' I said, 'you and I have met before.'

'Sirr?' came the mystified answer.

'Look at me, man, and tell me if you don't recognize me.'

He moved his eyes a fraction, in a respectful glance.

'Sirr, I don't mind of you.'

'Well, I'll refresh your memory. Do you remember the hall in Newmilns Street and the meeting there? You had a fight with a man outside, and got knocked down.'

He made no answer, but his colour deepened.

'And a fortnight later in a public-house in Muirtown you saw the same man, and gave him the chase of his life.'

I could see his mouth set, for visions of the penalties laid down by the King's Regulations for striking an officer must have crossed his mind. But he never budged.

'Look me in the face, man,' I said. 'Do you remember me now?'

He did as he was bid.

'Sirr, I mind of you.' 'Have you nothing more to say?'

He cleared his throat. 'Sirr, I did not ken I was hittin' an officer.' 'Of course you didn't. You did perfectly right, and if the war was over and we were both free men, I would give you a chance of knocking me down here and now. That's got to wait. When you saw me last I was serving my country, though you didn't know it. We're serving together now, and you must get your revenge out of the Boche. I'm going to make you my servant, for you and I have a pretty close bond between us. What do you say to that?'

This time he looked me full in the face. His troubled eye appraised me and was satisfied. 'I'm proud to be servant to ye, sirr,' he said. Then out of his chest came a strangled chuckle, and he forgot his discipline. 'Losh, but ye're the great lad!' He recovered himself promptly, saluted, and marched off.

The second episode befell during our brief rest after the Polygon Wood, when I had ridden down the line one afternoon to see a friend in the Heavy Artillery. I was returning in the drizzle of evening, clanking along the greasy path between the sad poplars, when I struck a Labour company repairing the ravages of a Boche strafe that morning. I wasn't very certain of my road and asked one of the workers. He straightened himself and saluted, and I saw beneath a disreputable cap the features of the man who had been with me in the Coolin crevice.

I spoke a word to his sergeant, who fell him out, and he walked a bit of the way with me.

'Great Scot, Wake, what brought you here?' I asked.

'Same thing as brought you. This rotten war.'

I had dismounted and was walking beside him, and I noticed that his lean face had lost its pallor and that his eyes were less hot than they used to be.

'You seem to thrive on it,' I said, for I did not know what to say. A sudden shyness possessed me. Wake must have gone through some violent cyclones of feeling before it came to this. He saw what I was thinking and laughed in his sharp, ironical way.

'Don't flatter yourself you've made a convert. I think as I always thought. But I came to the conclusion that since the fates had made me a Government servant I might as well do my work somewhere less cushioned than a chair in the Home Office ... Oh, no, it wasn't a matter of principle. One kind of work's as good as another, and I'm a better clerk than a navvy. With me it was self-indulgence: I wanted fresh air and exercise.'

I looked at him - mud to the waist, and his hands all blistered and cut with unaccustomed labour. I could realize what his associates must mean to him, and how he would relish the rough tonguing of non-coms.

'You're a confounded humbug,' I said. 'Why on earth didn't you go into an O.T.C. and come out with a commission? They're easy enough to get.'

'You mistake my case,' he said bitterly. 'I experienced no sudden conviction about the justice of the war. I stand where I always stood. I'm a non-combatant, and I wanted a change of civilian work ... No, it wasn't any idiotic tribunal sent me here. I came of my own free will, and I'm really rather enjoying myself.'

'It's a rough job for a man like you,' I said. 'Not so rough as the fellows get in the trenches. I watched a battalion marching back today and they looked like ghosts who had been years in muddy graves. White faces and dazed eyes and leaden feet. Mine's a cushy job. I like it best when the weather's foul. It cheats me into thinking I'm doing my duty.'

I nodded towards a recent shell-hole. 'Much of that sort of thing?'

'Now and then. We had a good dusting this morning. I can't say I liked it at the time, but I like to look back on it. A sort of

John Buchan

moral anodyne.'

'I wonder what on earth the rest of your lot make of you?'

'They don't make anything. I'm not remarkable for my bonhomie. They think I'm a prig - which I am. It doesn't amuse me to talk about beer and women or listen to a gramophone or grouse about my last meal. But I'm quite content, thank you. Sometimes I get a seat in a corner of a Y.M.C.A. hut, and I've a book or two. My chief affliction is the padre. He was up at Keble in my time, and, as one of my colleagues puts it, wants to be "too bloody helpful". ... What are you doing, Hannay? I see you're some kind of general. They're pretty thick on the ground here.'

'I'm a sort of general. Soldiering in the Salient isn't the softest of jobs, but I don't believe it's as tough as yours is for you. D'you know, Wake, I wish I had you in my brigade. Trained or untrained, you're a dashed stout-hearted fellow.'

He laughed with a trifle less acidity than usual. 'Almost thou persuadest me to be combatant. No, thank you. I haven't the courage, and besides there's my jolly old principles. All the same I'd like to be near you. You're a good chap, and I've had the honour to assist in your education ... I must be getting back, or the sergeant will think I've bolted.'

We shook hands, and the last I saw of him was a figure saluting stiffly in the wet twilight.

The third incident was trivial enough, though momentous in its results. just before I got the division I had a bout of malaria. We were in support in the Salient, in very uncomfortable trenches behind Wieltje, and I spent three days on my back in a dug-out. Outside was a blizzard of rain, and the water now and then came down the stairs through the gas curtain and stood in pools at my bed foot. It wasn't the merriest place to convalesce in, but I was as hard as nails at the time and by the third day I was beginning to sit up and be bored.

I read all my English papers twice and a big stack of German ones which I used to have sent up by a friend in the G.H.Q. Intelligence, who knew I liked to follow what the Boche was saying. As I dozed and ruminated in the way a man does after fever, I was struck by the tremendous display of one advertisement in the English press. It was a thing called 'Gussiter's Deep-breathing System,' which, according to its promoter, was a cure for every ill, mental, moral, or physical, that man can suffer. Politicians, generals, admirals, and music-hall artists all testified to the new life it had opened up for them. I remember wondering what these sportsmen got for their testimonies, and thinking I would write a spoof letter myself to old Gussiter.

Then I picked up the German papers, and suddenly my eye caught an advertisement of the same kind in the Frankfurter Zeitung. It was not Gussiter this time, but one Weissmann, but his game was identical - 'deep breathing'. The Hun style was different from the English - all about the Goddess of Health, and the Nymphs of the Mountains, and two quotations from Schiller. But the principle was the same.

That made me ponder a little, and I went carefully through the whole batch. I found the advertisement in the Frankfurter and in one or two rather obscure Volkstimmes and Volkszeitungs. I found it too in Der Grosse Krieg, the official German propagandist picture-paper. They were the same all but one, and that one had a bold variation, for it contained four of the sentences used in the ordinary English advertisement.

This struck me as fishy, and I started to write a letter to Macgillivray pointing out what seemed to be a case of trading with the enemy, and advising him to get on to Mr Gussiter's financial backing. I thought he might find a Hun syndicate behind him. And then I had another notion, which made me rewrite my letter.

I went through the papers again. The English ones which contained the advertisement were all good, solid, bellicose organs; the kind of thing no censorship would object to leaving the country. I had before me a small sheaf of pacifist prints, and they had not the advertisement. That might be for reasons of circulation, or it might not. The German papers were either Radical or Socialist publications, just the opposite of the English lot, except the Grosse Krieg. Now we have a free press, and Germany has, strictly speaking, none. All her journalistic indiscretions are calculated. Therefore the Boche has no objection to his rags getting to enemy countries. He wants it. He likes to see them quoted in columns headed 'Through German Glasses', and made the text of articles showing what a good democrat he is becoming.

As I puzzled over the subject, certain conclusions began to form in my mind. The four identical sentences seemed to hint that 'Deep Breathing' had Boche affiliations. Here was a chance of communicating with the enemy which would defy the argus-eyed gentlemen who examine the mails. What was to hinder Mr A at one end writing an advertisement with a good cipher in it, and the paper containing it getting into Germany by Holland in three days? Herr B at the other end replied in the Frankfurter, and a few days later shrewd editors and acute Intelligence officers - and Mr A - were reading it in London, though only Mr A knew what it really meant.

It struck me as a bright idea, the sort of simple thing that doesn't occur to clever people, and very rarely to the Boche. I wished I was not in the middle of a battle, for I would have had a try at investigating the cipher myself. I wrote a long letter to Macgillivray putting my case, and then went to sleep. When I awoke I reflected that it was a pretty thin argument, and would have stopped the letter, if it hadn't gone off early by a ration party.

After that things began very slowly to happen. The first was when Hamilton, having gone to Boulogne to fetch some mess-stores, returned with the startling news that he had seen Gresson. He had not heard his name, but described him dramatically to me as the wee red-headed devil that kicked Ecky Brockie's knee yon time in Glesca, sirr,' I recognized the description.

Gresson, it appeared, was joy-riding. He was with a party of Labour delegates who had been met by two officers and carried off in chars-a-bancs. Hamilton reported from inquiries among his friends that this kind of visitor came weekly. I thought it a very sensible notion on the Government's part, but I wondered how Gresson had been selected. I had hoped that Macgillivray had weeks ago made a long arm and quodded him. Perhaps they had too little evidence to hang him, but he was the blackest sort of suspect and should have been interned.

A week later I had occasion to be at G.H.Q. on business connected with my new division. My friends in the Intelligence allowed me to use the direct line to London, and I called up Macgillivray. For ten minutes I had an exciting talk, for I had had no news from that quarter since I left England. I heard that the Portuguese Jew had escaped - had vanished from his native heather when they went to get him. They had identified him as a German professor of Celtic languages, who had held a chair in a Welsh college - a dangerous fellow, for he was an upright, high-minded, raging fanatic. Against Gresson they had no evidence at all, but he was kept under strict observation. When I asked about his crossing to France, Macgillivray replied that that was part of their scheme. I inquired if the visit had given them any clues, but I never got an answer, for the line had to be cleared at that moment for the War Office. I hunted up the man who had charge of these Labour visits, and made friends with him. Gresson, he said, had been a quiet, well-mannered, and most appreciative guest. He had wept tears on Vimy Ridge, and - strictly against orders - had made a speech to some troops he met on the Arras road about how British Labour was remembering the Army in its prayers and sweating blood to make guns. On the last day he had had a misadventure, for he got very sick on the road - some kidney trouble that couldn't stand the jolting of the car - and had to be left at a village and picked up by the party on its way back. They found him better, but still shaky. I cross-examined the particular officer in charge about that halt, and learned that Gresson had been left alone in a peasant's cottage, for he said he only needed to lie down. The place was the hamlet of Eaucourt Sainte-Anne.

For several weeks that name stuck in my head. It had a pleasant, quaint sound, and I wondered how Gresson had spent his hours there. I hunted it up on the map, and promised myself to have a look at it the next time we came out to rest. And then I forgot about it till I heard the name mentioned again.

On 23rd October I had the bad luck, during a tour of my first-line trenches, to stop a small shell-fragment with my head. It was a close, misty day and I had taken off my tin hat to wipe my brow when the thing happened. I got a long, shallow scalp wound which meant nothing but bled a lot, and, as we were not in for any big move, the M.O. sent me back to a clearing station to have it seen to. I was three days in the place and, being perfectly well, had leisure to look about me and reflect, so that I recall that time as a queer, restful interlude in the infernal racket of war. I remember yet how on my last night there a gale made the lamps swing and flicker, and turned the grey-green canvas walls into a mass of mottled shadows. The floor canvas was muddy from the tramping of many feet bringing in the constant dribble of casualties from the line. In my tent there was no one very bad at the time, except a boy with his shoulder half-blown off by a whizz-bang, who lay in a drugged sleep at the far end. The majority were influenza, bronchitis, and trench-fever - waiting to be moved to the base, or convalescent and about to return to their units.

A small group of us dined off tinned chicken, stewed fruit, and radon cheese round the smoky stove, where two screens manufactured from packing cases gave some protection against the draughts which swept like young tornadoes down the tent. One man had been reading a book called the Ghost Stories of an Antiquary, and the talk turned on the unexplainable things that happen to everybody once or twice in a lifetime. I contributed a yarn about the men who went to look for

Kruger's treasure in the bushveld and got scared by a green wildebeeste. It is a good yarn and I'll write it down some day. A tall Highlander, who kept his slippered feet on the top of the stove, and whose costume consisted of a kilt, a British warm, a grey hospital dressing-gown, and four pairs of socks, told the story of the Camerons at First Ypres, and of the Lowland subaltern who knew no Gaelic and suddenly found himself encouraging his men with some ancient Highland rigmarole. The poor chap had a racking bronchial cough, which suggested that his country might well use him on some warmer battle-ground than Flanders. He seemed a bit of a scholar and explained the Cameron business in a lot of long words.

I remember how the talk meandered on as talk does when men are idle and thinking about the next day. I didn't pay much attention, for I was reflecting on a change I meant to make in one of my battalion commands, when a fresh voice broke in. It belonged to a Canadian captain from Winnipeg, a very silent fellow who smoked shag tobacco.

'There's a lot of ghosts in this darned country,' he said.

Then he started to tell about what happened to him when his division was last back in rest billets. He had a staff job and put up with the divisional command at an old French chateau. They had only a little bit of the house; the rest was shut up, but the passages were so tortuous that it was difficult to keep from wandering into the unoccupied part. One night, he said, he woke with a mighty thirst, and, since he wasn't going to get cholera by drinking the local water in his bedroom, he started out for the room they messed in to try to pick up a whisky-and-soda. He couldn't find it, though he knew the road like his own name. He admitted he might have taken a wrong turning, but he didn't think so. Anyway he landed in a passage which he had never seen before, and, since he had no candle, he tried to retrace his steps. Again he went wrong, and groped on till he saw a faint light which he thought must be the room of the G.S.O., a good fellow and a friend of his. So he barged in, and found a big, dim salon with two figures in it and a lamp burning between them, and a queer, unpleasant smell about. He took a step forward, and then he saw that the figures had no faces. That fairly loosened his joints with fear, and he gave a cry. One of the two ran towards him, the lamp went out, and the sickly scent caught suddenly at his throat. After that he knew nothing till he awoke in his own bed next morning with a splitting headache. He said he got the General's permission and went over all the unoccupied part of the house, but he couldn't find the room. Dust lay thick on everything, and there was no sign of recent human presence.

I give the story as he told it in his drawling voice. 'I reckon that was the genuine article in ghosts. You don't believe me and conclude I was drunk? I wasn't. There isn't any drink concocted yet that could lay me out like that. I just struck a crack in the old universe and pushed my head outside. It may happen to you boys any day.'

The Highlander began to argue with him, and I lost interest in the talk. But one phrase brought me to attention. 'I'll give you the name of the darned place, and next time you're around you can do a bit of prospecting for yourself. It's called the Chateau of Eaucourt Sainte-Anne, about seven kilometres from Douvecourt. If I was purchasing real estate in this country I guess I'd give that location a miss.'

After that I had a grim month, what with the finish of Third Ypres and the hustles to Cambrai. By the middle of December we had shaken down a bit, but the line my division held was not of our choosing, and we had to keep a wary eye on the Boche doings. It was a weary job, and I had no time to think of anything but the military kind of intelligence - fixing the units against us from prisoners' stories, organizing small raids, and keeping the Royal Flying Corps busy. I was keen about the last, and I made several trips myself over the lines with Archie Roylance, who had got his heart's desire and by good luck belonged to the squadron just behind me. I said as little as possible about this, for G.H.Q. did not encourage divisional generals to practise such methods, though there was one famous army commander who made a hobby of them. It was on one of these trips that an incident occurred which brought my spell of waiting on the bigger game to an end.

One dull December day, just after luncheon, Archie and I set out to reconnoitre. You know the way that fogs in Picardy seem suddenly to reek out of the ground and envelop the slopes like a shawl. That was our luck this time. We had crossed the lines, flying very high, and received the usual salute of Hun Archies. After a mile or two the ground seemed to climb up to us, though we hadn't descended, and presently we were in the heart of a cold, clinging mist. We dived for several thousand feet, but the confounded thing grew thicker and no sort of landmark could be found anywhere. I thought if we went on at this rate we should hit a tree or a church steeple and be easy fruit for the enemy.

The same thought must have been in Archie's mind, for he climbed again. We got into a mortally cold zone, but the air was no clearer. Thereupon he decided to head for home, and passed me word to work out a compass course on the map. That was easier said than done, but I had a rough notion of the rate we had travelled since we had crossed the lines and I knew our original direction, so I did the best I could. On we went for a bit, and then I began to get doubtful. So did Archie. We dropped low down, but we could hear none of the row that's always going on for a mile on each side of the lines. The world was very eerie and deadly still, so still that Archie and I could talk through the speaking-tube.

'We've mislaid this blamed battle,'he shouted.

'I think your rotten old compass has soured on us,' I replied.

We decided that it wouldn't do to change direction, so we held on the same course. I was getting as nervous as a kitten, chiefly owing to the silence. It's not what you expect in the middle of a battle-field ... I looked at the compass carefully and saw that it was really crocked. Archie must have damaged it on a former flight and forgotten to have it changed.

He had a very scared face when I pointed this out.

'Great God!' he croaked - for he had a fearsome cold - 'we're either about Calais or near Paris or miles the wrong side of the Boche line. What the devil are we to do?'

And then to put the lid on it his engine went wrong. It was the same performance as on the Yorkshire moors, and seemed to be a speciality of the Shark-Gladas type. But this time the end came quick. We dived steeply, and I could see by Archie's grip on the stick that he was going to have his work cut out to save our necks. Save them he did, but not by much for we jolted down on the edge of a ploughed field with a series of bumps that shook the teeth in my head. It was the same dense, dripping fog, and we crawled out of the old bus and bolted for cover like two ferreted rabbits.

Our refuge was the lee of a small copse.

'It's my opinion,' said Archie solemnly, 'that we're somewhere about La Cateau. Tim Wilbraham got left there in the Retreat, and it took him nine months to make the Dutch frontier. It's a giddy prospect, sir.'

I sallied out to reconnoitre. At the other side of the wood was a highway, and the fog so blanketed sound that I could not hear a man on it till I saw his face. The first one I saw made me lie flat in the covert ... For he was a German soldier, field-grey, forage cap, red band and all, and he had a pick on his shoulder.

A second's reflection showed me that this was not final proof. He might be one of our prisoners. But it was no place to take chances. I went back to Archie, and the pair of us crossed the ploughed field and struck the road farther on. There we saw a farmer's cart with a woman and child in it. They looked French, but melancholy, just what you would expect from the inhabitants of a countryside in enemy occupation.

Then we came to the park wall of a great house, and saw dimly the outlines of a cottage. Here sooner or later we would get proof of our whereabouts, so we lay and shivered among the poplars of the roadside. No one seemed abroad that afternoon. For a quarter of an hour it was as quiet as the grave. Then came a sound of whistling, and muffled steps.

'That's an Englishman,' said Archie joyfully. 'No Boche could make such a beastly noise.'

He was right. The form of an Army Service Corps private emerged from the mist, his cap on the back of his head, his hands in his pockets, and his walk the walk of a free man. I never saw a welcomer sight than that jam-merchant.

We stood up and greeted him. 'What's this place?' I shouted.

He raised a grubby hand to his forelock. 'Ockott Saint Anny, sir,' he said. 'Beg pardon, sir, but you ain't hurt, sir?'

Ten minutes later I was having tea in the mess of an M.T. workshop while Archie had gone to the nearest Signals to telephone for a car and give instructions about his precious bus. It was almost dark, but I gulped my tea and hastened out into the thick dusk. For I wanted to have a look at the Chateau.

I found a big entrance with high stone pillars, but the iron gates were locked and looked as if they had not been opened in the memory of man. Knowing the way of such places, I hunted for the side entrance and found a muddy road which led to the back of the house. The front was evidently towards a kind of park; at the back was a nest of outbuildings and a section of moat which looked very deep and black in the winter twilight. This was crossed by a stone bridge with a door at the end of it.

Clearly the Chateau was not being used for billets. There was

John Buchan

no sign of the British soldier; there was no sign of anything human. I crept through the fog as noiselessly as if I trod on velvet, and I hadn't even the company of my own footsteps. I remembered the Canadian's ghost story, and concluded I would be imagining the same sort of thing if I lived in such a place.

The door was bolted and padlocked. I turned along the side of the moat, hoping to reach the house front, which was probably modern and boasted a civilized entrance. There must be somebody in the place, for one chimney was smoking. Presently the moat petered out, and gave place to a cobbled causeway, but a wall, running at right angles with the house, blocked my way. I had half a mind to go back and hammer at the door, but I reflected that major-generals don't pay visits to deserted chateaux at night without a reasonable errand. I should look a fool in the eyes of some old concierge. The daylight was almost gone, and I didn't wish to go groping about the house with a candle.

But I wanted to see what was beyond the wall - one of those whims that beset the soberest men. I rolled a dissolute water-butt to the foot of it, and gingerly balanced myself on its rotten staves. This gave me a grip on the flat brick top, and I pulled myself up.

I looked down on a little courtyard with another wall beyond it, which shut off any view of the park. On the right was the Chateau, on the left more outbuildings; the whole place was not more than twenty yards each way. I was just about to retire by the road I had come, for in spite of my fur coat it was uncommon chilly on that perch, when I heard a key turn in the door in the Chateau wall beneath me.

A lantern made a blur of light in the misty darkness. I saw that the bearer was a woman, an oldish woman, round-shouldered like most French peasants. In one hand she carried a leather bag, and she moved so silently that she must have worn rubber boots. The light was held level with her head and illumined her face. It was the evillest thing I have ever beheld, for a horrible scar had puckered the skin of the forehead and drawn up the eyebrows so that it looked like some diabolical Chinese mask.

Slowly she padded across the yard, carrying the bag as gingerly as if it had been an infant. She stopped at the door of one of the outhouses and set down the lantern and her burden on the ground. From her apron she drew something which looked like a gas-mask, and put it over her head. She also put on a pair of long gauntlets. Then she unlocked the door, picked up the lantern and went in. I heard the key turn behind her.

Crouching on that wall, I felt a very ugly tremor run down my spine. I had a glimpse of what the Canadian's ghost might have been. That hag, hooded like some venomous snake, was too much for my stomach. I dropped off the wall and ran - yes, ran till I reached the highroad and saw the cheery headlights of a transport wagon, and heard the honest speech of the British soldier. That restored me to my senses, and made me feel every kind of a fool.

As I drove back to the line with Archie, I was black ashamed of my funk. I told myself that I had seen only an old country-woman going to feed her hens. I convinced my reason, but I did not convince the whole of me. An insensate dread of the place hung around me, and I could only retrieve my self-respect by resolving to return and explore every nook of it.

CHAPTER THIRTEEN

THE ADVENTURE OF THE PICARDY CHATEAU

I looked up Eaucourt Sainte-Anne on the map, and the more I studied its position the less I liked it. It was the knot from which sprang all the main routes to our Picardy front. If the Boche ever broke us, it was the place for which old Hindenburg would make. At all hours troops and transport trains were moving through that insignificant hamlet. Eminent generals and their staffs passed daily within sight of the Chateau. It was a convenient halting-place for battalions coming back to rest. Supposing, I argued, our enemies wanted a key-spot for some assault upon the morale or the discipline or health of the British Army, they couldn't find a better than Eaucourt Sainte-Anne. It was the ideal centre of espionage. But when I guardedly sounded my friends of the Intelligence they didn't seem to be worrying about it. From them I got a chit to the local French authorities, and, as soon as we came out of the line, towards the end of December, I made straight for the country town of Douvecourt. By a bit of luck our divisional quarters were almost next door. I interviewed a tremendous swell in a black uniform and black kid gloves, who received me affably and put his archives and registers at my disposal. By this time I talked French fairly well, having a natural turn for languages, but half the rapid speech of the sous-prifet was lost on me. By and by he left me with the papers and a clerk, and I proceeded to grub up the history of the Chateau.

It had belonged since long before Agincourt to the noble house of the D'Eaucourts, now represented by an ancient Marquise who dwelt at Biarritz. She had never lived in the place, which a dozen years before had been falling to ruins, when a rich American leased it and partially restored it. He had soon got sick of it - his daughter had married a blackguard French cavalry officer with whom he quarrelled, said the clerk - and since then there had been several tenants. I wondered why a house so unattractive should have let so readily, but the clerk explained that the cause was the partridge-shooting. It was about the best in France, and in 1912 had shown the record bag.

The list of the tenants was before me. There was a second American, an Englishman called Halford, a Paris Jew-banker, and an Egyptian prince. But the space for 1913 was blank, and I asked the clerk about it. He told me that it had been taken by a woollen manufacturer from Lille, but he had never shot the partridges, though he had spent occasional nights in the house. He had a five years' lease, and was still paying rent to the Marquise. I asked the name, but the clerk had forgotten. 'It will be written there,' he said.

'But, no,' I said. 'Somebody must have been asleep over this register. There's nothing after 1912.'

He examined the page and blinked his eyes. 'Someone indeed must have slept. No doubt it was young Louis who is now with the guns in Champagne. But the name will be on the Commissary's list. It is, as I remember, a sort of Flemish.'

He hobbled off and returned in five minutes.

'Bommaerts,' he said, 'Jacques Bommaerts. A young man with no wife but with money - Dieu de Dieu, what oceans of it!'

That clerk got twenty-five francs, and he was cheap at the price. I went back to my division with a sense of awe on me. It was a marvellous fate that had brought me by odd routes to this out-of-the-way corner. First, the accident of Hamilton's seeing Gresson; then the night in the Clearing Station; last the mishap of Archie's plane getting lost in the fog. I had three grounds of suspicion - Gresson's sudden illness, the Canadian's ghost, and that horrid old woman in the dusk. And now I had one tremendous fact. The place was leased by a man called Bommaerts, and that was one of the two names I had heard whispered in that far-away cleft in the Coolin by the stranger from the sea.

A sensible man would have gone off to the contre-espionage people and told them his story. I couldn't do this; I felt that it was my own private find and I was going to do the prospecting myself. Every moment of leisure I had I was puzzling over the thing. I rode round by the Chateau one frosty morning and examined all the entrances. The main one was the grand avenue with the locked gates. That led straight to the front of the house where the terrace was - or you might call it the back, for the main door was on the other side. Anyhow the drive came up to the edge of the terrace and then split into two, one branch going to the stables by way of the outbuildings where I had seen the old woman, the other circling round the house, skirting the moat, and joining the back road just before the bridge. If I had gone to the right instead of the left that first evening with Archie, I should have circumnavigated the place without any trouble.

Seen in the fresh morning light the house looked commonplace enough. Part of it was as old as Noah, but most was newish and jerry-built, the kind of flat-chested, thin French Chateau, all front and no depth, and full of draughts and smoky chimneys. I might have gone in and ransacked the place, but I knew I should find nothing. It was borne in on me that it was only when evening fell that that house was interesting and that I must come, like Nicodemus, by night. Besides I had a private account to settle with my conscience. I had funked the place in the foggy twilight, and it does not do to let a matter like that slide. A man's courage is like a horse that refuses a fence; you have got to take him by the head and cram him at it again. If you don't, he will funk worse next time. I hadn't enough courage to be able to take chances with it, though I was afraid of many things, the thing I feared most mortally was being afraid.

I did not get a chance till Christmas Eve. The day before there had been a fall of snow, but the frost set in and the afternoon ended in a green sunset with the earth crisp and crackling like a shark's skin. I dined early, and took with me Geordie Hamilton, who added to his many accomplishments that of driving a car. He was the only man in the B.E.F. who guessed anything of the game I was after, and I knew that he was as discreet as a tombstone. I put on my oldest trench cap, slacks, and a pair of scaife-soled boots, that I used to change into in the evening. I had a useful little electric torch, which lived in my pocket, and from which a cord led to a small bulb of light that worked with a switch and could be hung on my belt. That left my arms free in case of emergencies. Likewise I strapped on my pistol.

There was little traffic in the hamlet of Eaucourt Sainte-Anne that night. Few cars were on the road, and the M.T. detachment, judging from the din, seemed to be busy on a private spree. It was about nine o'clock when we turned into the side road, and at the entrance to it I saw a solid figure in khaki mounting guard beside two bicycles. Something in the man's gesture, as he saluted, struck me as familiar, but I had no time to hunt for casual memories. I left the car just short of the bridge, and took the road which would bring me to the terraced front of the house.

Once I turned the corner of the Chateau and saw the long ghostly facade white in the moonlight, I felt less confident. The eeriness of the place smote me. In that still, snowy world it loomed up immense and mysterious with its rows of shuttered windows, each with that air which empty houses have of concealing some wild story. I longed to have old Peter with me, for he was the man for this kind of escapade. I had heard that he had been removed to Switzerland and I pictured him now in some mountain village where the snow lay deep. I would have given anything to have had Peter with a whole leg by my side.

I stepped on the terrace and listened. There was not a sound in the world, not even the distant rumble of a cart. The pile towered above me like a mausoleum, and I reflected that it must take some nerve to burgle an empty house. It would be good enough fun to break into a bustling dwelling and pinch the plate when the folk were at dinner, but to burgle emptiness and silence meant a fight with the terrors in a man's soul. It was worse in my case, for I wasn't cheered with prospects of loot. I wanted to get inside chiefly to soothe my conscience.

I hadn't much doubt I would find a way, for three years of war and the frequent presence of untidy headquarters' staffs have loosened the joints of most Picardy houses. There's generally a window that doesn't latch or a door that doesn't bar. But I tried window after window on the terrace without result. The heavy green sun-shutters were down over each, and when I broke the hinges of one there was a long bar within to hold it firm. I was beginning to think of shinning up a rain-pipe and trying the second floor, when a shutter I had laid hold on swung back in my hand. It had been left unfastened, and, kicking the snow from my boots, I entered a room.

A gleam of moonlight followed me and I saw I was in a big salon with a polished wood floor and dark lumps of furniture swathed in sheets. I clicked the bulb at my belt, and the little circle of light showed a place which had not been dwelt in for years. At the far end was another door, and as I tiptoed towards it something caught my eye on the parquet. It was a piece of fresh snow like that which clumps on the heel of a boot. I had not brought it there. Some other visitor had passed this way, and not long before me.

Very gently I opened the door and slipped in. In front of me was a pile of furniture which made a kind of screen, and behind that I halted and listened. There was somebody in the room. I heard the sound of human breathing and soft movements; the man, whoever he was, was at the far end from me, and though there was a dim glow of Moon through a broken shutter I could see nothing of what he was after. I was beginning to enjoy myself now. I knew of his presence and he did not know of mine, and that is the sport of stalking.

An unwary movement of my hand caused the screen to creak. Instantly the movements ceased and there was utter silence. I held my breath, and after a second or two the tiny sounds began again. I had a feeling, though my eyes could not assure me, that the man before me was at work, and was using a very small shaded torch. There was just the faintest moving shimmer on the wall beyond, though that might come from the crack of moonlight. Apparently he was reassured, for his movements became more distinct. There was a jar as if a table had been pushed back. Once more there was silence, and I heard only the intake of breath. I have very quick ears, and to me it sounded as if the man was rattled. The breathing was quick and anxious.

Suddenly it changed and became the ghost of a whistle - the kind of sound one makes with the lips and teeth without ever letting the tune break out clear. We all do it when we are preoccupied with something - shaving, or writing letters, or reading the newspaper. But I did not think my man was preoccupied. He was whistling to quiet fluttering nerves.

Then I caught the air. It was 'Cherry Ripe'.

In a moment, from being hugely at my ease, I became the nervous one. I had been playing peep-bo with the unseen, and the tables were turned. My heart beat against my ribs like a hammer. I shuffled my feet, and again there fell the tense silence.

'Mary,' I said - and the word seemed to explode like a bomb in the stillness -'Mary! It's me - Dick Hannay.'

There was no answer but a sob and the sound of a timid step.

I took four paces into the darkness and caught in my arms a trembling girl ...

Often in the last months I had pictured the kind of scene which would be the culminating point of my life. When our work was over and war had been forgotten, somewhere - perhaps in a green Cotswold meadow or in a room of an old manor - I would talk with Mary. By that time we should know each other well and I would have lost my shyness. I would try to tell her that I loved her, but whenever I thought of what I should say my heart sank, for I knew I would make a fool of myself. You can't live my kind of life for forty years wholly among men and be of any use at pretty speeches to women. I knew I should stutter and blunder, and I used despairingly to invent impossible situations where I might make my love plain to her without words by some piece of melodramatic sacrifice.

But the kind Fates had saved me the trouble. Without a syllable save Christian names stammered in that eerie darkness we had come to complete understanding. The fairies had been at work unseen, and the thoughts of each of us had been moving towards the other, till love had germinated like a seed in the dark. As I held her in my arms I stroked her hair and murmured things which seemed to spring out of some ancestral memory. Certainly my tongue had never used them before, nor my mind imagined them ... By and by she slipped her arms round my neck and with a half sob strained towards me. She was still trembling.

'Dick,' she said, and to hear that name on her lips was the sweetest thing I had ever known. 'Dick, is it really you? Tell me I'm not dreaming.'

'It's me, sure enough, Mary dear. And now I have found you I will never let you go again. But, my precious child, how on earth did you get here?'

She disengaged herself and let her little electric torch wander over my rough habiliments.

'You look a tremendous warrior, Dick. I have never seen you like this before. I was in Doubting Castle and very much afraid of Giant Despair, till you came.'

'I think I call it the Interpreter's House,' I said.

'It's the house of somebody we both know,' she went on. 'He calls himself Bommaerts here. That was one of the two names, you remember. I have seen him since in Paris. Oh, it is a long story and you shall hear it all soon. I knew he came here sometimes, so I came here too. I have been nursing for the last fortnight at the Douvecourt Hospital only four miles away.'

'But what brought you alone at night?'

'Madness, I think. Vanity, too. You see I had found out a good deal, and I wanted to find out the one vital thing which had puzzled Mr Blenkiron. I told myself it was foolish, but I couldn't keep away. And then my courage broke down, and before you came I would have screamed at the sound of a mouse. If I hadn't whistled I would have cried.'

'But why alone and at this hour?'

'I couldn't get off in the day. And it was safest to come alone. You see he is in love with me, and when he heard I was coming to Douvecourt forgot his caution and proposed to meet me here. He said he was going on a long journey and wanted to say goodbye. If he had found me alone - well, he would have said goodbye. If there had been anyone with me, he would have suspected, and he mustn't suspect me. Mr Blenkiron says that would be fatal to his great plan. He believes I am like my aunts, and that I think him an apostle of peace working by his own methods against the stupidity and wickedness of all the Governments. He talks more bitterly about Germany than about England. He had told me how he had to disguise himself and play many parts on his mission, and of course I have applauded him. Oh, I have had a difficult autumn.'

'Mary,' I cried, 'tell me you hate him.'

'No,' she said quietly. 'I do not hate him. I am keeping that for later. I fear him desperately. Some day when we have broken him utterly I will hate him, and drive all likeness of him out of my memory like an unclean thing. But till then I won't waste energy on hate. We want to hoard every atom of our strength for the work of beating him.'

She had won back her composure, and I turned on my light to look at her. She was in nurses' outdoor uniform, and I thought her eyes seemed tired. The priceless gift that had suddenly come to me had driven out all recollection of my own errand. I thought of Ivery only as a would-be lover of Mary, and forgot the manufacturer from Lille who had rented his house for the partridge-shooting. 'And you, Dick,' she asked; 'is it part of a general's duties to pay visits at night to empty houses?'

'I came to look for traces of M. Bommaerts. I, too, got on his track from another angle, but that story must wait.'

'You observe that he has been here today?'

She pointed to some cigarette ash spilled on the table edge, and a space on its surface cleared from dust. 'In a place like this the dust would settle again in a few hours, and that is quite clean. I should say he has been here just after luncheon.'

'Great Scott!' I cried, 'what a close shave! I'm in the mood at this moment to shoot him at sight. You say you saw him in Paris and knew his lair. Surely you had a good enough case to have him collared.'

She shook her head. 'Mr Blenkiron - he's in Paris too - wouldn't hear of it. He hasn't just figured the thing out yet, he says. We've identified one of your names, but we're still in doubt about Chelius.'

'Ah, Chelius! Yes, I see. We must get the whole business

complete before we strike. Has old Blenkiron had any luck?'

'Your guess about the "Deep-breathing" advertisement was very clever, Dick. It was true, and it may give us Chelius. I must leave Mr Blenkiron to tell you how. But the trouble is this. We know something of the doings of someone who may be Chelius, but we can't link them with Ivery. We know that Ivery is Bommaerts, and our hope is to link Bommaerts with Chelius. That's why I came here. I was trying to burgle this escritoire in an amateur way. It's a bad piece of fake Empire and deserves smashing.'

I could see that Mary was eager to get my mind back to business, and with some difficulty I clambered down from the exultant heights. The intoxication of the thing was on me - the winter night, the circle of light in that dreary room, the sudden coming together of two souls from the ends of the earth, the realization of my wildest hopes, the gilding and glorifying of all the future. But she had always twice as much wisdom as me, and we were in the midst of a campaign which had no use for day-dreaming. I turned my attention to the desk.

It was a flat table with drawers, and at the back a half-circle of more drawers with a central cupboard. I tilted it up and most of the drawers slid out, empty of anything but dust. I forced two open with my knife and they held empty cigar boxes. Only the cupboard remained, and that appeared to be locked. I wedged a key from my pocket into its keyhole, but the thing would not budge.

'It's no good,' I said. 'He wouldn't leave anything he valued in a place like this. That sort of fellow doesn't take risks. If he wanted to hide something there are a hundred holes in this Chateau which would puzzle the best detective.'

'Can't you open it?' she asked. 'I've a fancy about that table. He was sitting here this afternoon and he may be coming back.'

John Buchan

I solved the problem by turning up the escritoire and putting my knee through the cupboard door. Out of it tumbled a little dark-green attache case.

'This is getting solemn,' said Mary. 'Is it locked?'

It was, but I took my knife and cut the lock out and spilled the contents on the table. There were some papers, a newspaper or two, and a small bag tied with black cord. The last I opened, while Mary looked over my shoulder. It contained a fine yellowish powder.

'Stand back,' I said harshly. 'For God's sake, stand back and don't breathe.'

With trembling hands I tied up the bag again, rolled it in a newspaper, and stuffed it into my pocket. For I remembered a day near Peronne when a Boche plane had come over in the night and had dropped little bags like this. Happily they were all collected, and the men who found them were wise and took them off to the nearest laboratory. They proved to be full of anthrax germs ...

I remembered how Eaucourt Sainte-Anne stood at the junction of a dozen roads where all day long troops passed to and from the lines. From such a vantage ground an enemy could wreck the health of an army ...

I remembered the woman I had seen in the courtyard of this house in the foggy dusk, and I knew now why she had worn a gas-mask.

This discovery gave me a horrid shock. I was brought down with a crash from my high sentiment to something earthly and devilish. I was fairly well used to Boche filthiness, but this seemed too grim a piece of the utterly damnable. I wanted to have Ivery by the throat and force the stuff into his body, and watch him decay slowly into the horror he had contrived for honest men.

'Let's get out of this infernal place,' I said.

But Mary was not listening. She had picked up one of the newspapers and was gloating over it. I looked and saw that it was open at an advertisement of Weissmann's 'Deep-breathing' system.

'Oh, look, Dick,' she cried breathlessly.

The column of type had little dots made by a red pencil below certain words.

'It's it,' she whispered, 'it's the cipher - I'm almost sure it's the cipher!'

'Well, he'd be likely to know it if anyone did.'

'But don't you see it's the cipher which Chelius uses - the man in Switzerland? Oh, I can't explain now, for it's very long, but I think - I think - I have found out what we have all been wanting. Chelius ...'

'Whisht!' I said. 'What's that?'

There was a queer sound from the out-of-doors as if a sudden wind had risen in the still night.

'It's only a car on the main road,' said Mary.

'How did you get in?' I asked.

'By the broken window in the next room. I cycled out here one morning, and walked round the place and found the broken catch.'

'Perhaps it is left open on purpose. That may be the way M. Bommaerts visits his country home ... Let's get off, Mary, for this place has a curse on it. It deserves fire from heaven.'

I slipped the contents of the attache case into my pockets. 'I'm going to drive you back,' I said. 'I've got a car out there.'

'Then you must take my bicycle and my servant too. He's an old friend of yours - one Andrew Amos.'

'Now how on earth did Andrew get over here?'

'He's one of us,' said Mary, laughing at my surprise. 'A most useful member of our party, at present disguised as an infirmier in Lady Manorwater's Hospital at Douvecourt. He is learning French, and ...'

'Hush!' I whispered. 'There's someone in the next room.'

I swept her behind a stack of furniture, with my eyes glued on a crack of light below the door. The handle turned and the shadows raced before a big electric lamp of the kind they have in stables. I could not see the bearer, but I guessed it was the old woman.

There was a man behind her. A brisk step sounded on the parquet, and a figure brushed past her. It wore the horizon-blue of a French officer, very smart, with those French riding-boots that show the shape of the leg, and a handsome fur-lined pelisse. I would have called him a young man, not more than thirty-five. The face was brown and clean-shaven, the eyes bright and masterful ... Yet he did not deceive me. I had not boasted idly to Sir Walter when I said that there was one man alive who could never again be mistaken by me.

I had my hand on my pistol, as I motioned Mary farther back into the shadows. For a second I was about to shoot. I had a perfect mark and could have put a bullet through his brain with utter certitude. I think if I had been alone I might have fired. Perhaps not. Anyhow now I could not do it. It seemed like potting at a sitting rabbit. I was obliged, though he was my worst enemy, to give him a chance, while all the while my sober senses kept calling me a fool.

I stepped into the light.

'Hullo, Mr Ivery,' I said. 'This is an odd place to meet again!'

In his amazement he fell back a step, while his hungry eyes took in my face. There was no mistake about the recognition. I saw something I had seen once before in him, and that was fear. Out went the light and he sprang for the door.

I fired in the dark, but the shot must have been too high. In the same instant I heard him slip on the smooth parquet and the tinkle of glass as the broken window swung open. Hastily I reflected that his car must be at the moat end of the terrace, and that therefore to reach it he must pass outside this very room. Seizing the damaged escritoire, I used it as a ram, and charged the window nearest me. The panes and shutters went with a crash, for I had driven the thing out of its rotten frame. The next second I was on the moonlit snow.

I got a shot at him as he went over the terrace, and again I went wide. I never was at my best with a pistol. Still I reckoned I had got him, for the car which was waiting below must come back by the moat to reach the highroad. But I had forgotten the great closed park gates. Somehow or other they must have been opened, for as soon as the car started it headed straight for the grand avenue. I tried a couple of long-range shots after it, and one must have damaged either Ivery or his chauffeur, for there came back a cry of pain.

I turned in deep chagrin to find Mary beside me. She was bubbling with laughter.

'Were you ever a cinema actor, Dick? The last two minutes have been a really high-class performance. "Featuring Mary Lamington." How does the jargon go?'

'I could have got him when he first entered,' I said ruefully.

'I know,' she said in a graver tone. 'Only of course you

couldn't ... Besides, Mr Blenkiron doesn't want it - yet.'

She put her hand on my arm. 'Don't worry about it. It wasn't written it should happen that way. It would have been too easy. We have a long road to travel yet before we clip the wings of the Wild Birds.'

'Look,' I cried. 'The fire from heaven!'

Red tongues of flame were shooting up from the out-buildings at the farther end, the place where I had first seen the woman. Some agreed plan must have been acted on, and Ivery was destroying all traces of his infamous yellow powder. Even now the concierge with her odds and ends of belongings would be slipping out to some refuge in the village.

In the still dry night the flames rose, for the place must have been made ready for a rapid burning. As I hurried Mary round the moat I could see that part of the main building had caught fire. The hamlet was awakened, and before we reached the corner of the highroad sleepy British soldiers were hurrying towards the scene, and the Town Major was mustering the fire brigade. I knew that Ivery had laid his plans well, and that they hadn't a chance - that long before dawn the Chateau of Eaucourt Sainte-Anne would be a heap of ashes and that in a day or two the lawyers of the aged Marquise at Biarritz would be wrangling with the insurance company.

At the corner stood Amos beside two bicycles, solid as a graven image. He recognized me with a gap-toothed grin.

'It's a cauld night, General, but the home fires keep burnin'. I havena seen such a cheery lowe since Dickson's mill at Gawly.'

We packed, bicycles and all, into my car with Amos wedged in the narrow seat beside Hamilton. Recognizing a fellow countryman, he gave thanks for the lift in the broadest Doric. 'For,' said he, 'I'm not what you would call a practised hand wi' a velocipede, and my feet are dinnled wi' standin' in the snaw.'

As for me, the miles to Douvecourt passed as in a blissful moment of time. I wrapped Mary in a fur rug, and after that we did not speak a word. I had come suddenly into a great possession and was dazed with the joy of it.

CHAPTER FOURTEEN

MR BLENKIRON DISCOURSES ON LOVE AND WAR

Three days later I got my orders to report at Paris for special service. They came none too soon, for I chafed at each hour's delay. Every thought in my head was directed to the game which we were playing against Ivery. He was the big enemy, compared to whom the ordinary Boche in the trenches was innocent and friendly. I had almost lost interest in my division, for I knew that for me the real battle-front was not in Picardy, and that my job was not so easy as holding a length of line. Also I longed to be at the same work as Mary.

I remember waking up in billets the morning after the night at the Chateau with the feeling that I had become extraordinarily rich. I felt very humble, too, and very kindly towards all the world - even to the Boche, though I can't say I had ever hated him very wildly. You find hate more among journalists and politicians at home than among fighting men. I wanted to be quiet and alone to think, and since that was impossible I went about my work in a happy abstraction. I tried not to look ahead, but only to live in the present, remembering that a war was on, and that there was desperate and dangerous business before me, and that my hopes hung on a slender thread. Yet for all that I had sometimes to let my fancies go free, and revel in delicious dreams.

But there was one thought that always brought me back to hard ground, and that was Ivery. I do not think I hated anybody in the world but him. It was his relation to Mary that stung me. He had the insolence with all his toad-like past to make love to that clean and radiant girl. I felt that he and I stood as mortal antagonists, and the thought pleased me, for it helped me to put some honest detestation into my job. Also I was going to win. Twice I had failed, but the third time I should succeed. It had been like ranging shots for a gun - first short, second over, and I vowed that the third should be dead on the mark.

I was summoned to G.H.Q., where I had half an hour's talk with the greatest British commander. I can see yet his patient, kindly face and that steady eye which no vicissitude of fortune could perturb. He took the biggest view, for he was statesman as well as soldier, and knew that the whole world was one battle-field and every man and woman among the combatant nations was in the battle-line. So contradictory is human nature, that talk made me wish for a moment to stay where I was. I wanted to go on serving under that man. I realized suddenly how much I loved my work, and when I got back to my quarters that night and saw my men swinging in from a route march I could have howled like a dog at leaving them. Though I say it who shouldn't, there wasn't a better division in the Army.

One morning a few days later I picked up Mary in Amiens. I always liked the place, for after the dirt of the Somme it was a comfort to go there for a bath and a square meal, and it had the noblest church that the hand of man ever built for God. It was a clear morning when we started from the boulevard beside the railway station; and the air smelt of washed streets and fresh coffee, and women were going marketing and the little trams ran clanking by, just as in any other city far from the sound of guns. There was very little khaki or horizon-blue about, and I remember thinking how completely Amiens had got out of the war-zone. Two months later it was a different story.

To the end I shall count that day as one of the happiest in my life. Spring was in the air, though the trees and fields had still their winter colouring. A thousand good fresh scents came out of the earth, and the larks were busy over the new furrows. I remember that we ran up a little glen, where a stream spread into pools among sallows, and the roadside trees were heavy with mistletoe. On the tableland beyond the Somme valley the sun shone like April. At Beauvais we lunched badly in an inn - badly as to food, but there was an excellent Burgundy at two francs a bottle. Then we slipped down through little flat-chested townships to the Seine, and in the late afternoon passed through St Germains forest. The wide green spaces among the trees set my fancy dwelling on that divine English countryside where Mary and I would one day make our home. She had been in high spirits all the journey, but when I spoke of the Cotswolds her face grew grave.

'Don't let us speak of it, Dick,' she said. 'It's too happy a thing and I feel as if it would wither if we touched it. I don't let myself think of peace and home, for it makes me too homesick ... I think we shall get there some day, you and I ... but it's a long road to the Delectable Mountains, and Faithful, you know, has to die first ... There is a price to be paid.'

The words sobered me.

'Who is our Faithful?' I asked.

'I don't know. But he was the best of the Pilgrims.'

Then, as if a veil had lifted, her mood changed, and when we came through the suburbs of Paris and swung down the Champs Elysees she was in a holiday humour. The lights were twinkling in the blue January dusk, and the warm breath of the city came to greet us. I knew little of the place, for I had visited it once only on a four days' Paris leave, but it had seemed to me then the most habitable of cities, and now, coming from the battle-field with Mary by my side, it was like the happy ending of a dream.

I left her at her cousin's house near the Rue St Honore, and deposited myself, according to instructions, at the Hotel Louis Quinze. There I wallowed in a hot bath, and got into the civilian clothes which had been sent on from London. They made me feel that I had taken leave of my division for good and all this time. Blenkiron had a private room, where we were to dine; and a more wonderful litter of books and cigar boxes I have never seen, for he hadn't a notion of tidiness. I could hear him grunting at his toilet in the adjacent bedroom, and I noticed that the table was laid for three. I went downstairs to get a paper, and on the way ran into Launcelot Wake.

He was no longer a private in a Labour Battalion. Evening clothes showed beneath his overcoat. 'Hullo, Wake, are you in this push too?'

'I suppose so,' he said, and his manner was not cordial. 'Anyhow I was ordered down here. My business is to do as I am told.'

'Coming to dine?' I asked.

'No. I'm dining with some friends at the Crillon.'

Then he looked me in the face, and his eyes were hot as I first remembered them. 'I hear I've to congratulate you, Hannay,' and he held out a limp hand.

I never felt more antagonism in a human being.

'You don't like it?' I said, for I guessed what he meant.

'How on earth can I like it?' he cried angrily. 'Good Lord, man, you'll murder her soul. You an ordinary, stupid, success-ful fellow and she - she's the most precious thing God ever made. You can never understand a fraction of her preciousness, but you'll clip her wings all right. She can never fly now ...'

He poured out this hysterical stuff to me at the foot of the staircase within hearing of an elderly French widow with a poodle. I had no impulse to be angry, for I was far too happy.

'Don't, Wake,' I said. 'We're all too close together to quarrel. I'm not fit to black Mary's shoes. You can't put me too low or her too high. But I've at least the sense to know it. You couldn't want me to be humbler than I felt.'

He shrugged his shoulders, as he went out to the street. 'Your infernal magnanimity would break any man's temper.'

I went upstairs to find Blenkiron, washed and shaven, admiring a pair of bright patent-leather shoes.

'Why, Dick, I've been wearying bad to see you. I was nervous you would be blown to glory, for I've been reading awful things about your battles in the noospapers. The war correspondents worry me so I can't take breakfast.'

He mixed cocktails and clinked his glass on mine. 'Here's to the young lady. I was trying to write her a pretty little sonnet, but the darned rhymes wouldn't fit. I've gotten a heap of things to say to you when we've finished dinner.'

Mary came in, her cheeks bright from the weather, and Blenkiron promptly fell abashed. But she had a way to meet his shyness, for, when he began an embarrassed speech of good wishes, she put her arms round his neck and kissed him. Oddly enough, that set him completely at his ease.

It was pleasant to eat off linen and china again, pleasant to see old Blenkiron's benignant face and the way he tucked into his food, but it was delicious for me to sit at a meal with Mary across the table. It made me feel that she was really mine, and not a pixie that would vanish at a word. To Blenkiron she bore herself like an affectionate but mischievous daughter, while the desperately refined manners that afflicted him whenever women were concerned mellowed into something like his everyday self. They did most of the talking, and I remember he fetched from some mysterious hiding-place a great box of chocolates, which you could no longer buy in Paris, and the two ate them like spoiled children. I didn't want to talk, for it was pure happiness for me to look on. I loved to watch her, when the servants had gone, with her elbows on the table like a schoolboy, her crisp gold hair a little rumpled, cracking walnuts with gusto, like some child who has been allowed down from the nursery for dessert and means to make the most of it.

With his first cigar Blenkiron got to business.

'You want to know about the staff-work we've been busy on at home. Well, it's finished now, thanks to you, Dick. We weren't getting on very fast till you took to peroosing the press on your sick-bed and dropped us that hint about the "Deep-breathing" ads.'

'Then there was something in it?' I asked.

'There was black hell in it. There wasn't any Gussiter, but there was a mighty fine little syndicate of crooks with old man Gresson at the back of them. First thing, I started out to get the cipher. It took some looking for, but there's no cipher on earth can't be got hold of somehow if you know it's there, and in this case we were helped a lot by the return messages in the German papers. It was bad stuff when we read it, and explained the darned leakages in important noos we've been up against. At first I figured to keep the thing going and turn Gussiter into a corporation with John S. Blenkiron as president. But it wouldn't do, for at the first hint of tampering with their communications the whole bunch got skeery and sent out SOS signals. So we tenderly plucked the flowers.'

'Gresson, too?' I asked.

He nodded. 'I guess your seafaring companion's now under the sod. We had collected enough evidence to hang him ten times over ... But that was the least of it. For your little old cipher, Dick, gave us a line on Ivery.'

I asked how, and Blenkiron told me the story. He had about a dozen cross-bearings proving that the organization of the 'Deep-breathing' game had its headquarters in Switzerland. He suspected Ivery from the first, but the man had vanished out of his ken, so he started working from the other end, and instead of trying to deduce the Swiss business from Ivery he tried to deduce Ivery from the Swiss business. He went to Berne and made a conspicuous public fool of himself for several weeks. He called himself an agent of the American propaganda there, and took some advertising space in the press and put in spread-eagle announcements of his mission, with the result that the Swiss Government threatened to turn him out of the country if he tampered that amount with their neutrality. He also wrote a lot of rot in the Geneva newspapers, which he paid to have printed, explaining how he was a pacifist, and was going to convert Germany to peace by 'inspirational advertisement of pure-minded war aims'. All this was in keeping with his English reputation, and he wanted to make himself a bait for Ivery.

But Ivery did not rise to the fly, and though he had a dozen agents working for him on the quiet he could never hear of the name Chelius. That was, he reckoned, a very private and particular name among the Wild Birds. However, he got to know a good deal about the Swiss end of the 'Deep-breathing' business. That took some doing and cost a lot of money. His best people were a girl who posed as a mannequin in a milliner's shop in Lyons and a concierge in a big hotel at St Moritz. His most important discovery was that there was a second cipher in the return messages sent from Switzerland, different from the one that the Gussiter lot used in England. He got this cipher, but though he could read it he couldn't make anything out of it. He concluded that it was a very secret means of communication between the inner circle of the Wild Birds, and that Ivery must be at the back of it ... But he was still a long way from finding out anything that mattered.

Then the whole situation changed, for Mary got in touch with Ivery. I must say she behaved like a shameless minx, for she kept on writing to him to an address he had once given her in Paris, and suddenly she got an answer. She was in Paris herself, helping to run one of the railway canteens, and staying with her French cousins, the de Mezieres. One day he came to see her. That showed the boldness of the man, and his cleverness, for the whole secret police of France were after him and they never got within sight or sound. Yet here he was coming openly in the afternoon to have tea with an English girl. It showed another thing, which made me blaspheme. A man so resolute and single-hearted in his job must have been pretty badly in love to take a risk like that.

He came, and he called himself the Capitaine Bommaerts, with a transport job on the staff of the French G.Q.G. He was on the staff right enough too. Mary said that when she heard that name she nearly fell down. He was quite frank with her, and she with him. They are both peacemakers, ready to break the laws of any land for the sake of a great ideal. Goodness knows what stuff they talked together. Mary said she would blush to think of it till her dying day, and I gathered that on her side it was a mixture of Launcelot Wake at his most pedantic and schoolgirl silliness.

He came again, and they met often, unbeknown to the decorous Madame de Mezieres. They walked together in the Bois de Boulogne, and once, with a beating heart, she motored with him to Auteuil for luncheon. He spoke of his house in Picardy, and there were moments, I gathered, when he became the declared lover, to be rebuffed with a hoydenish shyness. Presently the pace became too hot, and after some anguished arguments with Bullivant on the long-distance telephone she went off to Douvecourt to Lady Manorwater's hospital. She went there to escape from him, but mainly, I think, to have a look - trembling in every limb, mind you - at the Chateau of Eaucourt Sainte-Anne.

I had only to think of Mary to know just what Joan of Arc

was. No man ever born could have done that kind of thing. It wasn't recklessness. It was sheer calculating courage.

Then Blenkiron took up the tale. The newspaper we found that Christmas Eve in the Chateau was of tremendous importance, for Bommaerts had pricked out in the advertisement the very special second cipher of the Wild Birds. That proved that Ivery was at the back of the Swiss business. But Blenkiron made doubly sure.

'I considered the time had come,' he said, 'to pay high for valuable noos, so I sold the enemy a very pretty de-vice. If you ever gave your mind to ciphers and illicit correspondence, Dick, you would know that the one kind of document you can't write on in invisible ink is a coated paper, the kind they use in the weeklies to print photographs of leading actresses and the stately homes of England. Anything wet that touches it corrugates the surface a little, and you can tell with a microscope if someone's been playing at it. Well, we had the good fortune to discover just how to get over that little difficulty - how to write on glazed paper with a quill so as the cutest analyst couldn't spot it, and likewise how to detect the writing. I decided to sacrifice that invention, casting my bread upon the waters and looking for a good-sized bakery in return ... I had it sold to the enemy. The job wanted delicate handling, but the tenth man from me - he was an Austrian Jew - did the deal and scooped fifty thousand dollars out of it. Then I lay low to watch how my friend would use the de-vice, and I didn't wait long.'

He took from his pocket a folded sheet of L'Illustration. Over a photogravure plate ran some words in a large sprawling hand, as if written with a brush.

'That page when I got it yesterday,' he said, 'was an unassuming picture of General Petain presenting military medals. There wasn't a scratch or a ripple on its surface. But I got busy with it, and see there!' He pointed out two names. The writing was a set of key-words we did not know, but two names stood out which I knew too well. They were 'Bommaerts' and 'Chelius'.

'My God!' I cried, 'that's uncanny. It only shows that if you chew long enough - .'

'Dick,' said Mary, 'you mustn't say that again. At the best it's an ugly metaphor, and you're making it a platitude.'

'Who is Ivery anyhow?' I asked. 'Do you know more about him than we knew in the summer? Mary, what did Bommaerts pretend to be?'

'An Englishman.' Mary spoke in the most matter-of-fact tone, as if it were a perfectly usual thing to be made love to by a spy, and that rather soothed my annoyance. 'When he asked me to marry him he proposed to take me to a country-house in Devonshire. I rather think, too, he had a place in Scotland. But of course he's a German.'

'Ye-es,' said Blenkiron slowly, 'I've got on to his record, and it isn't a pretty story. It's taken some working out, but I've got all the links tested now ... He's a Boche and a large-sized nobleman in his own state. Did you ever hear of the Graf von Schwabing?'

I shook my head.

'I think I have heard Uncle Charlie speak of him,' said Mary, wrinkling her brows. 'He used to hunt with the Pytchley.'

'That's the man. But he hasn't troubled the Pytchley for the last eight years. There was a time when he was the last thing in smartness in the German court - officer in the Guards, ancient family, rich, darned clever - all the fixings. Kaiser liked him, and it's easy to see why. I guess a man who had as many personalities as the Graf was amusing after-dinner company. Specially among the Germans, who in my experience don't excel in the lighter vein. Anyway, he was William's

John Buchan

white-headed boy, and there wasn't a mother with a daughter who wasn't out gunning for Otto von Schwabing. He was about as popular in London and Noo York - and in Paris, too. Ask Sir Walter about him, Dick. He says he had twice the brains of Kuhlmann, and better manners than the Austrian fellow he used to yarn about ... Well, one day there came an almighty court scandal, and the bottom dropped out of the Graf's World. It was a pretty beastly story, and I don't gather that SchwabIng was as deep in it as some others. But the trouble was that those others had to be shielded at all costs, and Schwabing was made the scapegoat. His name came out in the papers and he had to go .'

'What was the case called?' I asked.

Blenkiron mentioned a name, and I knew why the word SchwabIng was familiar. I had read the story long ago in Rhodesia.

'It was some smash,' Blenkiron went on. 'He was drummed out of the Guards, out of the clubs, out of the country ... Now, how would you have felt, Dick, if you had been the Graf? Your life and work and happiness crossed out, and all to save a mangy princeling. "Bitter as hell," you say. Hungering for a chance to put it across the lot that had outed you? You wouldn't rest till you had William sobbing on his knees asking your pardon, and you not thinking of granting it? That's the way you'd feel, but that wasn't the Graf's way, and what's more it isn't the German way. He went into exile hating humanity, and with a heart all poison and snakes, but itching to get back. And I'll tell you why. It's because his kind of German hasn't got any other home on this earth. Oh, yes, I know there's stacks of good old Teutons come and squat in our little country and turn into fine Americans. You can do a lot with them if you catch them young and teach them the Declaration of Independence and make them study our Sunday papers. But you can't deny there's something comic in the rough about all Germans, before you've civilized them. They're a pecooliar people, a darned pecooliar people, else they wouldn't staff all the menial and indecent occupations on the globe. But that pecooliarity, which is only skin-deep in the working Boche, is in the bone of the grandee. Your German aristocracy can't consort on terms of equality with any other Upper Ten Thousand. They swagger and bluff about the world, but they know very well that the world's sniggering at them. They're like a boss from Salt Creek Gully who's made his pile and bought a dress suit and dropped into a Newport evening party. They don't know where to put their hands or how to keep their feet still ... Your copper-bottomed English nobleman has got to keep jogging himself to treat them as equals instead of sending them down to the servants' hall. Their fine fixings are just the high light that reveals the everlasting jay. They can't be gentlemen, because they aren't sure of themselves. The world laughs at them, and they know it and it riles them like hell ... That's why when a Graf is booted out of the Fatherland, he's got to creep back somehow or be a wandering Jew for the rest of time.'

Blenkiron lit another cigar and fixed me with his steady, ruminating eye.

'For eight years the man has slaved, body and soul, for the men who degraded him. He's earned his restoration and I daresay he's got it in his pocket. If merit was rewarded he should be covered with Iron Crosses and Red Eagles ... He had a pretty good hand to start out with. He knew other countries and he was a dandy at languages. More, he had an uncommon gift for living a part. That is real genius, Dick, however much it gets up against us. Best of all he had a first-class outfit of brains. I can't say I ever struck a better, and I've come across some bright citizens in my time ... And now he's going to win out, unless we get mighty busy.'

There was a knock at the door and the solid figure of Andrew Amos revealed itself.

'It's time ye was home, Miss Mary. It chappit half-eleven as I came up the stairs. It's comin' on to rain, so I've brought

John Buchan

an umbrelly.'

'One word,' I said. 'How old is the man?'

'Just gone thirty-six,' Blenkiron replied.

I turned to Mary, who nodded. 'Younger than you, Dick,' she said wickedly as she got into her big Jaeger coat.

'I'm going to see you home,' I said. 'Not allowed. You've had quite enough of my society for one day. Andrew's on escort duty tonight.'

Blenkiron looked after her as the door closed.

'I reckon you've got the best girl in the world.' 'Ivery thinks the same,' I said grimly, for my detestation of the man who had made love to Mary fairly choked me.

'You can see why. Here's this degenerate coming out of his rotten class, all pampered and petted and satiated with the easy pleasures of life. He has seen nothing of women except the bad kind and the overfed specimens of his own country. I hate being impolite about females, but I've always considered the German variety uncommon like cows. He has had desperate years of intrigue and danger, and consorting with every kind of scallawag. Remember, he's a big man and a poet, with a brain and an imagination that takes every grade without changing gears. Suddenly he meets something that is as fresh and lovely as a spring flower, and has wits too, and the steeliest courage, and yet is all youth and gaiety. It's a new experience for him, a kind of revelation, and he's big enough to value her as she should be valued ... No, Dick, I can understand you getting cross, but I reckon it an item to the man's credit.'

'It's his blind spot all the same,' I said.

'His blind spot,' Blenkiron repeated solemnly, 'and, please God, we're going to remember that.'

Next morning in miserable sloppy weather Blenkiron carted me about Paris. We climbed five sets of stairs to a flat away up in Montmartre, where I was talked to by a fat man with spectacles and a slow voice and told various things that deeply concerned me. Then I went to a room in the Boulevard St Germain, with a little cabinet opening off it, where I was shown papers and maps and some figures on a sheet of paper that made me open my eyes. We lunched in a modest cafe tucked away behind the Palais Royal, and our companions were two Alsatians who spoke German better than a Boche and had no names - only numbers. In the afternoon I went to a low building beside the Invalides and saw many generals, including more than one whose features were familiar in two hemispheres. I told them everything about myself, and I was examined like a convict, and all particulars about my appearance and manner of speech written down in a book. That was to prepare the way for me, in case of need, among the vast army of those who work underground and know their chief but do not know each other.

The rain cleared before night, and Blenkiron and I walked back to the hotel through that lemon-coloured dusk that you get in a French winter. We passed a company of American soldiers, and Blenkiron had to stop and stare. I could see that he was stiff with pride, though he wouldn't show it.

'What d'you think of that bunch?' he asked.

'First-rate stuff,' I said.

'The men are all right,' he drawled critically. 'But some of the officer-boys are a bit puffy. They want fining down.' 'They'll get it soon enough, honest fellows. You don't keep your weight long in this war.'

'Say, Dick,' he said shyly, 'what do you truly think of our Americans? You've seen a lot of them, and I'd value your views.' His tone was that of a bashful author asking for an opinion on his first book.

John Buchan

'I'll tell you what I think. You're constructing a great middle-class army, and that's the most formidable fighting machine on earth. This kind of war doesn't want the Berserker so much as the quiet fellow with a trained mind and a lot to fight for. The American ranks are filled with all sorts, from cow-punchers to college boys, but mostly with decent lads that have good prospects in life before them and are fighting because they feel they're bound to, not because they like it. It was the same stock that pulled through your Civil War. We have a middle-class division, too - Scottish Territorials, mostly clerks and shopmen and engineers and farmers' sons. When I first struck them my only crab was that the officers weren't much better than the men. It's still true, but the men are super-excellent, and consequently so are the officers. That division gets top marks in the Boche calendar for sheer fighting devilment ... And, please God, that's what your American army's going to be. You can wash out the old idea of a regiment of scallawags commanded by dukes. That was right enough, maybe, in the days when you hurrooshed into battle waving a banner, but it don't do with high explosives and a couple of million men on each side and a battle front of five hundred miles. The hero of this war is the plain man out of the middle class, who wants to get back to his home and is going to use all the brains and grit he possesses to finish the job soon.'

'That sounds about right,' said Blenkiron reflectively. 'It pleases me some, for you've maybe guessed that I respect the British Army quite a little. Which part of it do you put top?'
'All of it's good. The French are keen judges and they give front place to the Scots and the Australians. For myself I think the backbone of the Army is the old-fashioned English county regiments that hardly ever get into the papers Though I don't know, if I had to pick, but I'd take the South Africans. There's only a brigade of them, but they're hell's delight in a battle. But then you'll say I'm prejudiced.'

'Well,' drawled Blenkiron, you're a mighty Empire anyhow. I've sojourned up and down it and I can't guess how the old-time highbrows in your little island came to put it together.

But I'll let you into a secret, Dick. I read this morning in a noospaper that there was a natural affinity between Americans and the men of the British Dominions. Take it from me, there isn't - at least not with this American. I don't understand them one little bit. When I see your lean, tall Australians with the sun at the back of their eyes, I'm looking at men from another planet. Outside you and Peter, I never got to fathom a South African. The Canadians live over the fence from us, but you mix up a Canuck with a Yank in your remarks and you'll get a bat in the eye ... But most of us Americans have gotten a grip on your Old Country. You'll find us mighty respectful to other parts of your Empire, but we say anything we damn well please about England. You see, we know her that well and like her that well, we can be free with her.

'It's like,' he concluded as we reached the hotel, 'it's like a lot of boys that are getting on in the world and are a bit jealous and stand-offish with each other. But they're all at home with the old man who used to warm them up with a hickory cane, even though sometimes in their haste they call him a stand-patter.'

That night at dinner we talked solid business - Blenkiron and I and a young French Colonel from the IIIeme Section at G.Q.G. Blenkiron, I remember, got very hurt about being called a business man by the Frenchman, who thought he was paying him a compliment.

'Cut it out,' he said. 'It is a word that's gone bad with me. There's just two kind of men, those who've gotten sense and those who haven't. A big percentage of us Americans make our living by trading, but we don't think because a man's in business or even because he's made big money that he's any natural good at every job. We've made a college professor our President, and do what he tells us like little boys, though he don't earn more than some of us pay our works' manager. You English have gotten business on the brain, and think a fellow's a dandy at handling your Government if he happens to have made a pile by some flat-catching ramp on your Stock

Exchange. It makes me tired. You're about the best business nation on earth, but for God's sake don't begin to talk about it or you'll lose your power. And don't go confusing real business with the ordinary gift of raking in the dollars. Any man with sense could make money if he wanted to, but he mayn't want. He may prefer the fun of the job and let other people do the looting. I reckon the biggest business on the globe today is the work behind your lines and the way you feed and supply and transport your army. It beats the Steel Corporation and the Standard Oil to a frazzle. But the man at the head of it all don't earn more than a thousand dollars a month ... Your nation's getting to worship Mammon, Dick. Cut it out. There's just the one difference in humanity - sense or no sense, and most likely you won't find any more sense in the man that makes a billion selling bonds than in his brother Tim that lives in a shack and sells corn-cobs. I'm not speaking out of sinful jealousy, for there was a day when I was reckoned a railroad king, and I quit with a bigger pile than kings usually retire on. But I haven't the sense of old Peter, who never even had a bank account ... And it's sense that wins in this war.'

The Colonel, who spoke good English, asked a question about a speech which some politician had made.

'There isn't all the sense I'd like to see at the top,' said Blenkiron. 'They're fine at smooth words. That wouldn't matter, but they're thinking smooth thoughts. What d'you make of the situation, Dick?' 'I think it's the worst since First Ypres,' I said. 'Everybody's cock-a-whoop, but God knows why.'

'God knows why,' Blenkiron repeated. 'I reckon it's a simple calculation, and you can't deny it any more than a mathematical law. Russia is counted out. The Boche won't get food from her for a good many months, but he can get more men, and he's got them. He's fighting only on one foot, and he's been able to bring troops and guns west so he's as strong as the Allies now on paper. And he's stronger in reality. He's got better railways behind him, and he's fighting on inside lines and can concentrate fast against any bit of our front. I'm no soldier, but that's so, Dick?'

The Frenchman smiled and shook his head. 'All the same they will not pass. They could not when they were two to one in 1914, and they will not now. If we Allies could not break through in the last year when we had many more men, how will the Germans succeed now with only equal numbers?'

Blenkiron did not look convinced. 'That's what they all say. I talked to a general last week about the coming offensive, and he said he was praying for it to hurry up, for he reckoned Fritz would get the fright of his life. It's a good spirit, maybe, but I don't think it's sound on the facts. We've got two mighty great armies of fine fighting-men, but, because we've two commands, we're bound to move ragged like a peal of bells. The Hun's got one army and forty years of stiff tradition, and, what's more, he's going all out this time. He's going to smash our front before America lines up, or perish in the attempt ... Why do you suppose all the peace racket in Germany has died down, and the very men that were talking democracy in the summer are now hot for fighting to a finish? I'll tell you. It's because old Ludendorff has promised them complete victory this spring if they spend enough men, and the Boche is a good gambler and is out to risk it. We're not up against a local attack this time. We're standing up to a great nation going bald-headed for victory or destruction. If we're broken, then America's got to fight a new campaign by herself when she's ready, and the Boche has time to make Russia his feeding-ground and diddle our blockade. That puts another five years on to the war, maybe another ten. Are we free and independent peoples going to endure that much? ... I tell you we're tossing to quit before Easter.'

He turned towards me, and I nodded assent.

'That's more or less my view,' I said. 'We ought to hold, but it'll be by our teeth and nails. For the next six months we'll be fighting without any margin.'

'But, my friends, you put it too gravely,' cried the Frenchman. 'We may lose a mile or two of ground - yes. But serious danger is not possible. They had better chances at Verdun and they failed. Why should they succeed now?'

'Because they are staking everything,' Blenkiron replied. 'It is the last desperate struggle of a wounded beast, and in these struggles sometimes the hunter perishes. Dick's right. We've got a wasting margin and every extra ounce of weight's going to tell. The battle's in the field, and it's also in every corner of every Allied land. That's why within the next two months we've got to get even with the Wild Birds.'

The French Colonel - his name was de Valliere - smiled at the name, and Blenkiron answered my unspoken question.

'I'm going to satisfy some of your curiosity, Dick, for I've put together considerable noos of the menagerie. Germany has a good army of spies outside her borders. We shoot a batch now and then, but the others go on working like beavers and they do a mighty deal of harm. They're beautifully organized, but they don't draw on such good human material as we, and I reckon they don't pay in results more than ten cents on a dollar of trouble. But there they are. They're the intelligence officers and their business is just to forward noos. They're the birds in the cage, the - what is it your friend called them?'

'Die Stubenvogel,' I said.

'Yes, but all the birds aren't caged. There's a few outside the bars and they don't collect noos. They do things. If there's anything desperate they're put on the job, and they've got power to act without waiting on instructions from home. I've investigated till my brain's tired and I haven't made out more than half a dozen whom I can say for certain are in the business. There's your pal, the Portuguese Jew, Dick. Another's a woman in Genoa, a princess of some sort married to a Greek financier. One's the editor of a pro-Ally up-country paper in the Argentine. One passes as a Baptist minister in

Colorado. One was a police spy in the Tzar's Government and is now a red-hot revolutionary in the Caucasus. And the biggest, of course, is Moxon Ivery, who in happier times was the Graf von Schwabing. There aren't above a hundred people in the world know of their existence, and these hundred call them the Wild Birds.'

'Do they work together?' I asked.

'Yes. They each get their own jobs to do, but they're apt to flock together for a big piece of devilment. There were four of them in France a year ago before the battle of the Aisne, and they pretty near rotted the French Army. That's so, Colonel?'

The soldier nodded grimly. 'They seduced our weary troops and they bought many politicians. Almost they succeeded, but not quite. The nation is sane again, and is judging and shooting the accomplices at its leisure. But the principals we have never caught.'

'You hear that, Dick,, said Blenkiron. 'You're satisfied this isn't a whimsy of a melodramatic old Yank? I'll tell you more. You know how Ivery worked the submarine business from England. Also, it was the Wild Birds that wrecked Russia. It was Ivery that paid the Bolshevists to sedooce the Army, and the Bolshevists took his money for their own purpose, thinking they were playing a deep game, when all the time he was grinning like Satan, for they were playing his. It was Ivery or some other of the bunch that doped the brigades that broke at Caporetto. If I started in to tell you the history of their doings you wouldn't go to bed, and if you did you wouldn't sleep ... There's just this to it. Every finished subtle devilry that the Boche has wrought among the Allies since August 1914 has been the work of the Wild Birds and more or less organized by Ivery. They're worth half a dozen army corps to Ludendorff. They're the mightiest poison merchants the world ever saw, and they've the nerve of hell ...'

'I don't know,' I interrupted. 'Ivery's got his soft spot. I saw

John Buchan

him in the Tube station.'

'Maybe, but he's got the kind of nerve that's wanted. And now I rather fancy he's whistling in his flock,'

Blenkiron consulted a notebook. 'Pavia - that's the Argentine man - started last month for Europe. He transhipped from a coasting steamer in the West Indies and we've temporarily lost track of him, but he's left his hunting-ground. What do you reckon that means?'

'It means,' Blenkiron continued solemnly, 'that Ivery thinks the game's nearly over. The play's working up for the big climax ... And that climax is going to be damnation for the Allies, unless we get a move on.'

'Right,' I said. 'That's what I'm here for. What's the move?'

'The Wild Birds mustn't ever go home, and the man they call Ivery or Bommaerts or Chelius has to decease. It's a cold-blooded proposition, but it's him or the world that's got to break. But before he quits this earth we're bound to get wise about some of his plans, and that means that we can't just shoot a pistol at his face. Also we've got to find him first. We reckon he's in Switzerland, but that is a state with quite a lot of diversified scenery to lose a man in ... Still I guess we'll find him. But it's the kind of business to plan out as carefully as a battle. I'm going back to Berne on my old stunt to boss the show, and I'm giving the orders. You're an obedient child, Dick, so I don't reckon on any trouble that way.'

Then Blenkiron did an ominous thing. He pulled up a little table and started to lay out Patience cards. Since his duodenum was cured he seemed to have dropped that habit, and from his resuming it I gathered that his mind was uneasy. I can see that scene as if it were yesterday - the French colonel in an armchair smoking a cigarette in a long amber holder, and Blenkiron sitting primly on the edge of a yellow silk ottoman, dealing his cards and looking guiltily towards me.

'You'll have Peter for company,' he said. 'Peter's a sad man, but he has a great heart, and he's been mighty useful to me already. They're going to move him to England very soon. The authorities are afraid of him, for he's apt to talk wild, his health having made him peevish about the British. But there's a deal of red-tape in the world, and the orders for his repatriation are slow in coming.' The speaker winked very slowly and deliberately with his left eye.

I asked if I was to be with Peter, much cheered at the prospect.

'Why, yes. You and Peter are the collateral in the deal. But the big game's not with you.'

I had a presentiment of something coming, something anxious and unpleasant.

'Is Mary in it?' I asked.

He nodded and seemed to pull himself together for an explanation.

'See here, Dick. Our main job is to get Ivery back to Allied soil where we can handle him. And there's just the one magnet that can fetch him back. You aren't going to deny that.'

I felt my face getting very red, and that ugly hammer began beating in my forehead. Two grave, patient eyes met my glare.

'I'm damned if I'll allow it!' I cried. 'I've some right to a say in the thing. I won't have Mary made a decoy. It's too infernally degrading.'

'It isn't pretty, but war isn't pretty, and nothing we do is pretty. I'd have blushed like a rose when I was young and innocent to imagine the things I've put my hand to in the last three years. But have you any other way, Dick? I'm not proud, and I'll scrap the plan if you can show me another ... Night after night I've hammered the thing out, and I can't hit on a better ... Heigh-ho, Dick, this isn't like you,' and he grinned ruefully. 'You're making yourself a fine argument in favour of celibacy - in time of war, anyhow What is it the poet sings? -

> White hands cling to the bridle rein,
> Slipping the spur from the booted heel -'

I was as angry as sin, but I felt all the time I had no case. Blenkiron stopped his game of Patience, sending the cards flying over the carpet, and straddled on the hearthrug.

'You're never going to be a piker. What's dooty, if you won't carry it to the other side of Hell? What's the use of yapping about your country if you're going to keep anything back when she calls for it? What's the good of meaning to win the war if you don't put every cent you've got on your stake? You'll make me think you're like the jacks in your English novels that chuck in their hand and say it's up to God, and call that "seeing it through" ... No, Dick, that kind of dooty don't deserve a blessing. You dursn't keep back anything if you want to save your soul. 'Besides,' he went on, 'what a girl it is! She can't scare and she can't soil. She's white-hot youth and innocence, and she'd take no more harm than clean steel from a muck-heap.'

I knew I was badly in the wrong, but my pride was all raw.

'I'm not going to agree till I've talked to Mary.'

'But Miss Mary has consented,' he said gently. 'She made the plan.'

Next day, in clear blue weather that might have been May, I drove Mary down to Fontainebleau. We lunched in the inn by the bridge and walked into the forest. I hadn't slept much, for I was tortured by what I thought was anxiety for her, but which was in truth jealousy of Ivery. I don't think that I would have minded her risking her life, for that was part of the game we were both in, but I jibbed at the notion of Ivery coming near her again. I told myself it was honourable pride, but I knew deep down in me that it was jealousy.

I asked her if she had accepted Blenkiron's plan, and she turned mischievous eyes on me.

'I knew I should have a scene with you, Dick. I told Mr Blenkiron so ... Of course I agreed. I'm not even very much afraid of it. I'm a member of the team, you know, and I must play up to my form. I can't do a man's work, so all the more reason why I should tackle the thing I can do.'

'But,' I stammered, 'it's such a ... such a degrading business for a child like you. I can't bear ... It makes me hot to think of it.'

Her reply was merry laughter. 'You're an old Ottoman, Dick. You haven't doubled Cape Turk yet, and I don't believe you're round Seraglio Point. Why, women aren't the brittle things men used to think them. They never were, and the war has made them like whipcord. Bless you, my dear, we're the tougher sex now. We've had to wait and endure, and we've been so beaten on the anvil of patience that we've lost all our megrims.'

She put her hands on my shoulders and looked me in the eyes.

'Look at me, Dick, look at your someday-to-be espoused saint. I'm nineteen years of age next August. Before the war I should have only just put my hair up. I should have been the kind of shivering debutante who blushes when she's spoken to, and oh! I should have thought such silly, silly things about life ... Well, in the last two years I've been close to it, and to death. I've nursed the dying. I've seen souls in agony and in triumph. England has allowed me to serve her as she allows her sons. Oh, I'm a robust young woman now, and indeed I think women were always robuster than men ... Dick, dear Dick, we're lovers, but we're comrades too - always comrades, and comrades trust each other.' I hadn't anything to say, except contrition, for I had my lesson. I had been slipping away in my thoughts from the gravity of our task, and Mary had brought me back to it. I remember that as we walked through the woodland we came to a place where there were no signs of war. Elsewhere there were men busy felling trees, and anti-aircraft guns, and an occasional transport wagon, but here there was only a shallow grassy vale, and in the distance, bloomed over like a plum in the evening haze, the roofs of an old dwelling-house among gardens.

Mary clung to my arm as we drank in the peace of it.

'That is what lies for us at the end of the road, Dick,' she said softly.

And then, as she looked, I felt her body shiver. She returned to the strange fancy she had had in the St Germains woods three days before.

'Somewhere it's waiting for us and we shall certainly find it ... But first we must go through the Valley of the Shadow ... And there is the sacrifice to be made ... the best of us.'

CHAPTER FIFTEEN

ST ANTON

Ten days later the porter Joseph Zimmer of Arosa, clad in the tough and shapeless trousers of his class, but sporting an old velveteen shooting-coat bequeathed to him by a former German master - speaking the guttural tongue of the Grisons, and with all his belongings in one massive rucksack, came out of the little station of St Anton and blinked in the frosty sunshine. He looked down upon the little old village beside its icebound lake, but his business was with the new village of hotels and villas which had sprung up in the last ten years south of the station. He made some halting inquiries of the station people, and a cab-driver outside finally directed him to the place he sought - the cottage of the Widow Summermatter, where resided an English intern, one Peter Pienaar.

The porter Joseph Zimmer had had a long and roundabout journey. A fortnight before he had worn the uniform of a British major-general. As such he had been the inmate of an expensive Paris hotel, till one morning, in grey tweed clothes and with a limp, he had taken the Paris-Mediterranean Express with a ticket for an officers' convalescent home at Cannes. Thereafter he had declined in the social scale. At Dijon he had been still an Englishman, but at Pontarlier he had become an American bagman of Swiss parentage, returning to wind up his father's estate. At Berne he limped excessively, and at Zurich, at a little back-street hotel, he became frankly the peasant. For he met a friend there from whom he acquired clothes with that odd rank smell, far stronger than Harris tweed, which marks the raiment of most Swiss guides and all Swiss porters. He also acquired a new name and an old aunt, who a little later received him with open arms and explained to her friends that he was her brother's son from Arosa who three winters ago had hurt his leg wood-cutting and had been discharged from the levy.

A kindly Swiss gentleman, as it chanced, had heard of the deserving Joseph and interested himself to find him employment. The said philanthropist made a hobby of the French and British prisoners returned from Germany, and had in mind an officer, a crabbed South African with a bad leg, who needed a servant. He was, it seemed, an ill-tempered old fellow who had to be billeted alone, and since he could speak German, he would be happier with a Swiss native. Joseph haggled somewhat over the wages, but on his aunt's advice he accepted the job, and, with a very complete set of papers and a store of ready-made reminiscences (it took him some time to swot up the names of the peaks and passes he had traversed) set out for St Anton, having dispatched beforehand a monstrously ill-spelt letter announcing his coming. He could barely read and write, but he was good at maps, which he had studied carefully, and he noticed with satisfaction that the valley of St Anton gave easy access to Italy.

As he journeyed south the reflections of that porter would have surprised his fellow travellers in the stuffy third-class carriage. He was thinking of a conversation he had had some days before in a cafe at Dijon with a young Englishman bound for Modane ...

We had bumped up against each other by chance in that strange flitting when all went to different places at different times, asking nothing of each other's business. Wake had greeted me rather shamefacedly and had proposed dinner together.

I am not good at receiving apologies, and Wake's embarrassed me more than they embarrassed him. 'I'm a bit of a cad sometimes,'he said. 'You know I'm a better fellow than I sounded that night, Hannay.'

I mumbled something about not talking rot - the conventional phrase. What worried me was that the man was suffering. You could see it in his eyes. But that evening I got nearer Wake than ever before, and he and I became true friends, for he laid bare his soul before me. That was his trouble, that he could lay bare his soul, for ordinary healthy folk don't analyse their feelings. Wake did, and I think it brought him relief.

'Don't think I was ever your rival. I would no more have proposed to Mary than I would have married one of her aunts. She was so sure of herself, so happy in her single-heartedness that she terrified me. My type of man is not meant for marriage, for women must be in the centre of life, and we must always be standing aside and looking on. It is a damnable thing to be left-handed.'

'The trouble about you, my dear chap,' I said, 'is that you're too hard to please.'

'That's one way of putting it. I should put it more harshly. I hate more than I love. All we humanitarians and pacifists have hatred as our mainspring. Odd, isn't it, for people who preach brotherly love? But it's the truth. We're full of hate towards everything that doesn't square in with our ideas, everything that jars on our lady-like nerves. Fellows like you are so in love with their cause that they've no time or inclination to detest what thwarts them. We've no cause - only negatives, and that means hatred, and self-torture, and a beastly jaundice of soul.'

Then I knew that Wake's fault was not spiritual pride, as I had diagnosed it at Biggleswick. The man was abased with humility.

'I see more than other people see,' he went on, 'and I feel more. That's the curse on me. You're a happy man and you get things done, because you only see one side of a case, one thing at a time. How would you like it if a thousand strings were always tugging at you, if you saw that every course meant the sacrifice of lovely and desirable things, or even the shattering of what you know to be unreplaceable? I'm the kind of stuff poets are made of, but I haven't the poet's gift, so I stagger about the world left-handed and game-legged ... Take the war. For me to fight would be worse than for another man to run away. From the bottom of my heart I believe that it needn't have happened, and that all war is a blistering iniquity. And yet belief has got very little to do with virtue. I'm not as good a man as you, Hannay, who have never thought out anything in your life. My time in the Labour battalion taught me something. I knew that with all my fine aspirations I wasn't as true a man as fellows whose talk was silly oaths and who didn't care a tinker's curse about their soul.'

I remember that I looked at him with a sudden understanding. 'I think I know you. You're the sort of chap who won't fight for his country because he can't be sure that she's altogether in the right. But he'd cheerfully die for her, right or wrong.'

His face relaxed in a slow smile. 'Queer that you should say that. I think it's pretty near the truth. Men like me aren't afraid to die, but they haven't quite the courage to live. Every man should be happy in a service like you, when he obeys orders. I couldn't get on in any service. I lack the bump of veneration. I can't swallow things merely because I'm told to. My sort are always talking about "service", but we haven't the temperament to serve. I'd give all I have to be an ordinary cog in the wheel, instead of a confounded outsider who finds fault with the machinery ... Take a great violent high-handed fellow like you. You can sink yourself till you become only a name and a number. I couldn't if I tried. I'm not sure if I want to either. I cling to the odds and ends that are my own.' 'I wish I had had you in my battalion a year ago,' I said.

'No, you don't. I'd only have been a nuisance. I've been a Fabian since Oxford, but you're a better socialist than me. I'm a rancid individualist.' 'But you must be feeling better about the war?' I asked.

'Not a bit of it. I'm still lusting for the heads of the politicians that made it and continue it. But I want to help my country. Honestly, Hannay, I love the old place. More, I think, than I love myself, and that's saying a devilish lot. Short of fighting - which would be the sin against the Holy Spirit for me - I'll do my damnedest. But you'll remember I'm not used to team work. If I'm a jealous player, beat me over the head.'

His voice was almost wistful, and I liked him enormously.

'Blenkiron will see to that,' I said. 'We're going to break you to harness, Wake, and then you'll be a happy man. You keep your mind on the game and forget about yourself. That's the cure for jibbers.'

As I journeyed to St Anton I thought a lot about that talk. He was quite right about Mary, who would never have married him. A man with such an angular soul couldn't fit into another's. And then I thought that the chief thing about Mary was just her serene certainty. Her eyes had that settled happy look that I remembered to have seen only in one other human face, and that was Peter's ... But I wondered if Peter's eyes were still the same.

I found the cottage, a little wooden thing which had been left perched on its knoll when the big hotels grew around it. It had a fence in front, but behind it was open to the hillside. At the gate stood a bent old woman with a face like a pippin. My make-up must have been good, for she accepted me before I introduced myself.

'God be thanked you are come,' she cried. 'The poor lieutenant needed a man to keep him company. He sleeps now, as he does always in the afternoon, for his leg wearies him in the night ... But he is brave, like a soldier ... Come, I will show you the house, for you two will be alone now.'

Stepping softly she led me indoors, pointing with a warning finger to the little bedroom where Peter slept. I found a kitchen with a big stove and a rough floor of planking, on which lay some badly cured skins. Off it was a sort of pantry with a bed for me. She showed me the pots and pans for cooking and the stores she had laid in, and where to find water and fuel. 'I will do the marketing daily,' she said, 'and if you need me, my dwelling is half a mile up the road beyond the new church. God be with you, young man, and be kind to that wounded one.'

When the Widow Summermatter had departed I sat down in Peter's arm-chair and took stock of the place. It was quiet and simple and homely, and through the window came the gleam of snow on the diamond hills. On the table beside the stove were Peter's cherished belongings - his buck-skin pouch and the pipe which Jannie Grobelaar had carved for him in St Helena, an aluminium field match-box I had given him, a cheap large-print Bible such as padres present to well-disposed privates, and an old battered Pilgrim's Progress with gaudy pictures. The illustration at which I opened showed Faithful going up to Heaven from the fire of Vanity Fair like a woodcock that has just been flushed. Everything in the room was exquisitely neat, and I knew that that was Peter and not the Widow Summermatter. On a peg behind the door hung his much-mended coat, and sticking out of a pocket I recognized a sheaf of my own letters. In one corner stood something which I had forgotten about - an invalid chair.

The sight of Peter's plain little oddments made me feel solemn. I wondered if his eyes would be like Mary's now, for I could not conceive what life would be for him as a cripple. Very silently I opened the bedroom door and slipped inside.

He was lying on a camp bedstead with one of those striped Swiss blankets pulled up round his ears, and he was asleep. It was the old Peter beyond doubt. He had the hunter's gift of breathing evenly through his nose, and the white scar on the deep brown of his forehead was what I had always remembered. The only change since I last saw him was that he had let his beard grow again, and it was grey.

As I looked at him the remembrance of all we had been through together flooded back upon me, and I could have cried with joy at being beside him. Women, bless their hearts! can never know what long comradeship means to men; it is something not in their lives - something that belongs only to that wild, undomesticated world which we forswear when we find our mates. Even Mary understood only a bit of it. I had just won her love, which was the greatest thing that ever came my way, but if she had entered at that moment I would scarcely have turned my head. I was back again in the old life and was not thinking of the new.

Suddenly I saw that Peter was awake and was looking at me.

'Dick,' he said in a whisper, 'Dick, my old friend.'

The blanket was tossed off, and his long, lean arms were stretched out to me. I gripped his hands, and for a little we did not speak. Then I saw how woefully he had changed. His left leg had shrunk, and from the knee down was like a pipe stem. His face, when awake, showed the lines of hard suffering and he seemed shorter by half a foot. But his eyes were still like Mary's. Indeed they seemed to be more patient and peaceful than in the days when he sat beside me on the buck-waggon and peered over the hunting-veld.

I picked him up - he was no heavier than Mary - and carried him to his chair beside the stove. Then I boiled water and made tea, as we had so often done together. 'Peter, old man,' I said, 'we're on trek again, and this is a very snug little rondavel. We've had many good yarns, but this is going to be the best. First of all, how about your health?'

'Good, I'm a strong man again, but slow like a hippo cow. I have been lonely sometimes, but that is all by now. Tell me of the big battles.'

But I was hungry for news of him and kept him to his own case. He had no complaint of his treatment except that he did not like Germans. The doctors at the hospital had been clever, he said, and had done their best for him, but nerves and sinews and small bones had been so wrecked that they could not mend his leg, and Peter had all the Boer's dislike of amputation. One doctor had been in Damaraland and talked to him of those baked sunny places and made him homesick. But he returned always to his dislike of Germans. He had seen them herding our soldiers like brute beasts, and the commandant had a face like Stumm and a chin that stuck out and wanted hitting. He made an exception for the great airman Lensch, who had downed him.

'He is a white man, that one,' he said. 'He came to see me in hospital and told me a lot of things. I think he made them treat me well. He is a big man, Dick, who would make two of me, and he has a round, merry face and pale eyes like Frickie Celliers who could put a bullet through a pauw's head at two hundred yards. He said he was sorry I was lame, for he hoped to have more fights with me. Some woman that tells fortunes had said that I would be the end of him, but he reckoned she had got the thing the wrong way on. I hope he will come through this war, for he is a good man, though a German ... But the others! They are like the fool in the Bible, fat and ugly in good fortune and proud and vicious when their luck goes. They are not a people to be happy with.'

Then he told me that to keep up his spirits he had amused himself with playing a game. He had prided himself on being a Boer, and spoken coldly of the British. He had also, I gathered, imparted many things calculated to deceive. So he left Germany with good marks, and in Switzerland had held himself aloof from the other British wounded, on the advice of Blenkiron, who had met him as soon as he crossed the frontier. I gathered it was Blenkiron who had had him sent to St Anton, and in his time there, as a disgruntled Boer, he had mixed a good deal with Germans. They had pumped him about our air service, and Peter had told them many ingenious lies and heard curious things in return.

'They are working hard, Dick,' he said. 'Never forget that. The German is a stout enemy, and when we beat him with a machine he sweats till he has invented a new one. They have great pilots, but never so many good ones as we, and I do not think in ordinary fighting they can ever beat us. But you must watch Lensch, for I fear him. He has a new machine, I hear, with great engines and a short wingspread, but the wings so cambered that he can climb fast. That will be a surprise to spring upon us. You will say that we'll soon better it. So we shall, but if it was used at a time when we were pushing hard it might make the little difference that loses battles.'

'You mean,' I said, 'that if we had a great attack ready and had driven all the Boche planes back from our front, Lensch and his circus might get over in spite of us and blow the gaff?'

'Yes,' he said solemnly. 'Or if we were attacked, and had a weak spot, Lensch might show the Germans where to get through. I do not think we are going to attack for a long time; but I am pretty sure that Germany is going to fling every man against us. That is the talk of my friends, and it is not bluff.'

That night I cooked our modest dinner, and we smoked our pipes with the stove door open and the good smell of wood-smoke in our nostrils. I told him of all my doings and of the Wild Birds and Ivery and the job we were engaged on. Blenkiron's instructions were that we two should live humbly and keep our eyes and ears open, for we were outside suspicion - the cantankerous lame Boer and his loutish servant from Arosa. Somewhere in the place was a rendezvous of our enemies, and thither came Chelius on his dark errands.

Peter nodded his head sagely, 'I think I have guessed the place. The daughter of the old woman used to pull my chair sometimes down to the village, and I have sat in cheap inns and talked to servants. There is a fresh-water pan there, it is all covered with snow now, and beside it there is a big house that they call the Pink Chalet. I do not know much about it, except that rich folk live in it, for I know the other houses and they are harmless. Also the big hotels, which are too cold and public for strangers to meet in.'

I put Peter to bed, and it was a joy to me to look after him, to give him his tonic and prepare the hot water bottle that comforted his neuralgia. His behaviour was like a docile child's, and he never lapsed from his sunny temper, though I could see how his leg gave him hell. They had tried massage for it and given it up, and there was nothing for him but to endure till nature and his tough constitution deadened the tortured nerves again. I shifted my bed out of the pantry and slept in the room with him, and when I woke in the night, as one does the first time in a strange place, I could tell by his breathing that he was wakeful and suffering.

Next day a bath chair containing a grizzled cripple and pushed by a limping peasant might have been seen descending the long hill to the village. It was clear frosty weather which makes the cheeks tingle, and I felt so full of beans that it was hard to remember my game leg. The valley was shut in on the east by a great mass of rocks and glaciers, belonging to a mountain whose top could not be seen. But on the south, above the snowy fir-woods, there was a most delicate lace-like peak with a point like a needle. I looked at it with interest, for beyond it lay the valley which led to the Staub pass, and beyond that was Italy - and Mary.

The old village of St Anton had one long, narrow street which bent at right angles to a bridge which spanned the river flowing from the lake. Thence the road climbed steeply, but at the other end of the street it ran on the level by the water's edge, lined with gimcrack boarding-houses, now shuttered to the world, and a few villas in patches of garden. At the far end, just before it plunged into a pine-wood, a promontory jutted into the lake, leaving a broad space between the road and the water. Here were the grounds of a more considerable dwelling - snow-covered laurels and rhododendrons with one or two bigger trees - and just on the water-edge stood the house itself, called the Pink Chalet.

I wheeled Peter past the entrance on the crackling snow of the highway. Seen through the gaps of the trees the front looked new, but the back part seemed to be of some age, for I could see high walls, broken by few windows, hanging over the water. The place was no more a chalet than a donjon, but I suppose the name was given in honour of a wooden gallery above the front door. The whole thing was washed in an ugly pink. There were outhouses - garage or stables among the trees - and at the entrance there were fairly recent tracks of an automobile.

On our way back we had some very bad beer in a cafe and made friends with the woman who kept it. Peter had to tell her his story, and I trotted out my aunt in Zurich, and in the end we heard her grievances. She was a true Swiss, angry at all the belligerents who had spoiled her livelihood, hating Germany most but also fearing her most. Coffee, tea, fuel, bread, even milk and cheese were hard to get and cost a ransom. It would take the land years to recover, and there would be no more tourists, for there was little money left in the world. I dropped a question about the Pink Chalet, and was told that it belonged to one Schweigler, a professor of Berne, an old man who came sometimes for a few days in the summer. It was often let, but not now. Asked if it was occupied, she remarked that some friends of the Schweiglers - rich people from Basle - had been there for the winter. 'They come and go in great cars,' she said bitterly, 'and they bring their food from the cities. They spend no money in this poor place.'

Presently Peter and I fell into a routine of life, as if we had always kept house together. In the morning he went abroad in his chair, in the afternoon I would hobble about on my own errands. We sank into the background and took its colour, and a less conspicuous pair never faced the eye of suspicion. Once a week a young Swiss officer, whose business it was to look after British wounded, paid us a hurried visit. I used to get letters from my aunt in Zurich, Sometimes with the postmark of Arosa, and now and then these letters would contain curiously worded advice or instructions from him whom my aunt called 'the kind patron'. Generally I was told to be patient. Sometimes I had word about the health of 'my little cousin across the mountains'. Once I was bidden expect a friend of the patron's, the wise doctor of whom he had often spoken, but though after that I shadowed the Pink Chalet for two days no doctor appeared.

My investigations were a barren business. I used to go down to the village in the afternoon and sit in an out-of-the-way cafe, talking slow German with peasants and hotel porters, but there was little to learn. I knew all there was to hear about the Pink Chalet, and that was nothing. A young man who ski-ed stayed for three nights and spent his days on the alps above the fir-woods. A party of four, including two women, was reported to have been there for a night - all ramifications of the rich family of Basle. I studied the house from the lake, which should have been nicely swept into ice-rinks, but from lack of visitors was a heap of blown snow. The high old walls of the back part were built straight from the water's edge. I remember I tried a short cut through the grounds to the high-road and was given 'Good afternoon' by a smiling German manservant. One way and another I gathered there were a good many serving-men about the place - too many for the infrequent guests. But beyond this I discovered nothing.

Not that I was bored, for I had always Peter to turn to. He was thinking a lot about South Africa, and the thing he liked best was to go over with me every detail of our old expeditions. They belonged to a life which he could think about without pain, whereas the war was too near and bitter for him. He liked to hobble out-of-doors after the darkness came and look at his old friends, the stars. He called them by the words they use on the veld, and the first star of morning he called the voorlooper - the little boy who inspans the oxen - a name I had not heard for twenty years. Many a great yarn we spun in the long evenings, but I always went to bed with a sore heart. The longing in his eyes was too urgent, longing not for old days or far countries, but for the health and strength which had once been his pride.

One night I told him about Mary. 'She will be a happy mysie,' he said, 'but you will need to be very clever with her, for women are queer cattle and you and I don't know their ways. They tell me English women do not cook and make clothes like our vrouws, so what will she find to do? I doubt an idle woman will be like a mealie-fed horse.'

It was no good explaining to him the kind of girl Mary was, for that was a world entirely beyond his ken. But I could see that he felt lonelier than ever at my news. So I told him of the house I meant to have in England when the war was over - an old house in a green hilly country, with fields that would carry four head of cattle to the Morgan and furrows of clear water, and orchards of plums and apples. 'And you will stay with us all the time,' I said. 'You will have your own rooms and your own boy to look after you, and you will help me to farm, and we will catch fish together, and shoot the wild ducks when they come up from the pans in the evening. I have found a better countryside than the Houtbosch, where you and I planned to have a farm. It is a blessed and happy place, England.'

He shook his head. 'You are a kind man, Dick, but your pretty mysie won't want an ugly old fellow like me hobbling about her house ... I do not think I will go back to Africa, for I should be sad there in the sun. I will find a little place in England, and some day I will visit you, old friend.'

That night his stoicism seemed for the first time to fail him. He was silent for a long time and went early to bed, where I can vouch for it he did not sleep. But he must have thought a lot in the night time, for in the morning he had got himself in hand and was as cheerful as a sandboy.

I watched his philosophy with amazement. It was far beyond

John Buchan

anything I could have compassed myself. He was so frail and so poor, for he had never had anything in the world but his bodily fitness, and he had lost that now. And remember, he had lost it after some months of glittering happiness, for in the air he had found the element for which he had been born. Sometimes he dropped a hint of those days when he lived in the clouds and invented a new kind of battle, and his voice always grew hoarse. I could see that he ached with longing for their return. And yet he never had a word of complaint. That was the ritual he had set himself, his point of honour, and he faced the future with the same kind of courage as that with which he had tackled a wild beast or Lensch himself. Only it needed a far bigger brand of fortitude.

Another thing was that he had found religion. I doubt if that is the right way to put it, for he had always had it. Men who live in the wilds know they are in the hands of God. But his old kind had been a tattered thing, more like heathen superstition, though it had always kept him humble. But now he had taken to reading the Bible and to thinking in his lonely nights, and he had got a creed of his own. I dare say it was crude enough, I am sure it was unorthodox; but if the proof of religion is that it gives a man a prop in bad days, then Peter's was the real thing. He used to ferret about in the Bible and the Pilgrim's Progress - they were both equally inspired in his eyes - and find texts which he interpreted in his own way to meet his case. He took everything quite literally. What happened three thousand years ago in Palestine might, for all he minded, have been going on next door. I used to chaff him and tell him that he was like the Kaiser, very good at fitting the Bible to his purpose, but his sincerity was so complete that he only smiled. I remember one night, when he had been thinking about his flying days, he found a passage in Thessalonians about the dead rising to meet their Lord in the air, and that cheered him a lot. Peter, I could see, had the notion that his time here wouldn't be very long, and he liked to think that when he got his release he would find once more the old rapture.

Once, when I said something about his patience, he said he

had got to try to live up to Mr Standfast. He had fixed on that character to follow, though he would have preferred Mr Valiant-for-Truth if he had thought himself good enough. He used to talk about Mr Standfast in his queer way as if he were a friend of us both, like Blenkiron ... I tell you I was humbled out of all my pride by the sight of Peter, so uncomplaining and gentle and wise. The Almighty Himself couldn't have made a prig out of him, and he never would have thought of preaching. Only once did he give me advice. I had always a liking for short cuts, and I was getting a bit restive under the long inaction. One day when I expressed my feelings on the matter, Peter upped and read from the Pilgrim's Progress: 'Some also have wished that the next way to their Father's house were here, that they might be troubled no more with either hills or mountains to go over, but the Way is the Way, and there is an end.'

All the same when we got into March and nothing happened I grew pretty anxious. Blenkiron had said we were fighting against time, and here were the weeks slipping away. His letters came occasionally, always in the shape of communications from my aunt. One told me that I would soon be out of a job, for Peter's repatriation was just about through, and he might get his movement order any day. Another spoke of my little cousin over the hills, and said that she hoped soon to be going to a place called Santa Chiara in the Val Saluzzana. I got out the map in a hurry and measured the distance from there to St Anton and pored over the two roads thither - the short one by the Staub Pass and the long one by the Marjolana. These letters made me think that things were nearing a climax, but still no instructions came. I had nothing to report in my own messages, I had discovered nothing in the Pink Chalet but idle servants, I was not even sure if the Pink Chalet were not a harmless villa, and I hadn't come within a thousand miles of finding Chelius. All my desire to imitate Peter's stoicism didn't prevent me from getting occasionally rattled and despondent.

The one thing I could do was to keep fit, for I had a notion I might soon want all my bodily strength. I had to keep up my pretence of lameness in the daytime, so I used to take my exercise at night. I would sleep in the afternoon, when Peter had his siesta, and then about ten in the evening, after putting him to bed, I would slip out-of-doors and go for a four or five hours' tramp. Wonderful were those midnight wanderings. I pushed up through the snow-laden pines to the ridges where the snow lay in great wreaths and scallops, till I stood on a crest with a frozen world at my feet and above me a host of glittering stars. Once on a night of full moon I reached the glacier at the valley head, scrambled up the moraine to where the ice began, and peered fearfully into the spectral crevasses. At such hours I had the earth to myself, for there was not a sound except the slipping of a burden of snow from the trees or the crack and rustle which reminded me that a glacier was a moving river. The war seemed very far away, and I felt the littleness of our human struggles, till I thought of Peter turning from side to side to find ease in the cottage far below me. Then I realized that the spirit of man was the greatest thing in this spacious world ... I would get back about three or four, have a bath in the water which had been warming in my absence, and creep into bed, almost ashamed of having two sound legs, when a better man a yard away had but one.

Oddly enough at these hours there seemed more life in the Pink Chalet than by day. Once, tramping across the lake long after midnight, I saw lights in the lake-front in windows which for ordinary were blank and shuttered. Several times I cut across the grounds, when the moon was dark. On one such occasion a great car with no lights swept up the drive, and I heard low voices at the door. Another time a man ran hastily past me, and entered the house by a little door on the eastern side, which I had not before noticed ... Slowly the conviction began to grow on me that we were not wrong in marking down this place, that things went on within it which it deeply concerned us to discover. But I was puzzled to think of a way. I might butt inside, but for all I knew it would be upsetting Blenkiron's plans, for he had given me no instructions about housebreaking. All this unsettled me worse than ever. I began to lie awake planning some means of entrance ... I would be a peasant from the next valley who had twisted his ankle ... I would go seeking an imaginary cousin among the servants ... I would start a fire in the place and have the doors flung open to zealous neighbours ...

And then suddenly I got instructions in a letter from Blenkiron.

It came inside a parcel of warm socks that arrived from my kind aunt. But the letter for me was not from her. It was in Blenkiron's large sprawling hand and the style of it was all his own. He told me that he had about finished his job. He had got his line on Chelius, who was the bird he expected, and that bird would soon wing its way southward across the mountains for the reason I knew of.

'We've got an almighty move on,' he wrote, 'and please God you're going to hustle some in the next week. It's going better than I ever hoped.' But something was still to be done. He had struck a countryman, one Clarence Donne, a journalist of Kansas City, whom he had taken into the business. Him he described as a 'crackerjack' and commended to my esteem. He was coming to St Anton, for there was a game afoot at the Pink Chalet, which he would give me news of. I was to meet him next evening at nine-fifteen at the little door in the east end of the house. 'For the love of Mike, Dick,' he concluded, 'be on time and do everything Clarence tells you as if he was me. It's a mighty complex affair, but you and he have sand enough to pull through. Don't worry about your little cousin. She's safe and out of the job now.'

My first feeling was one of immense relief, especially at the last words. I read the letter a dozen times to make sure I had its meaning. A flash of suspicion crossed my mind that it might be a fake, principally because there was no mention of Peter, who had figured large in the other missives. But why should Peter be mentioned when he wasn't on in this piece? The signature convinced me. Ordinarily Blenkiron signed himself in full with a fine commercial flourish. But when I was at the

John Buchan

Front he had got into the habit of making a kind of hieroglyphic of his surname to me and sticking J.S. after it in a bracket. That was how this letter was signed, and it was sure proof it was all right. I spent that day and the next in wild spirits. Peter spotted what was on, though I did not tell him for fear of making him envious. I had to be extra kind to him, for I could see that he ached to have a hand in the business. Indeed he asked shyly if I couldn't fit him in, and I had to lie about it and say it was only another of my aimless circumnavigations of the Pink Chalet.

'Try and find something where I can help,' he pleaded. 'I'm pretty strong still, though I'm lame, and I can shoot a bit.'

I declared that he would be used in time, that Blenkiron had promised he would be used, but for the life of me I couldn't see how.

At nine o'clock on the evening appointed I was on the lake opposite the house, close in under the shore, making my way to the rendezvous. It was a coal-black night, for though the air was clear the stars were shining with little light, and the moon had not yet risen. With a premonition that I might be long away from food, I had brought some slabs of chocolate, and my pistol and torch were in my pocket. It was bitter cold, but I had ceased to mind weather, and I wore my one suit and no overcoat.

The house was like a tomb for silence. There was no crack of light anywhere, and none of those smells of smoke and food which proclaim habitation. It was an eerie job scrambling up the steep bank east of the place, to where the flat of the garden started, in a darkness so great that I had to grope my way like a blind man.

I found the little door by feeling along the edge of the building. Then I stepped into an adjacent clump of laurels to wait on my companion. He was there before me.

'Say,' I heard a rich Middle West voice whisper, 'are you Joseph Zimmer? I'm not shouting any names, but I guess you are the guy I was told to meet here.'

'Mr Donne?' I whispered back.

'The same,'he replied. 'Shake.'

I gripped a gloved and mittened hand which drew me towards the door.

CHAPTER SIXTEEN

I LIE ON A HARD BED

The journalist from Kansas City was a man of action. He wasted no words in introducing himself or unfolding his plan of campaign. 'You've got to follow me, mister, and not deviate one inch from my tracks. The explaining part will come later. There's big business in this shack tonight.' He unlocked the little door with scarcely a sound, slid the crust of snow from his boots, and preceded me into a passage as black as a cellar. The door swung smoothly behind us, and after the sharp out-of-doors the air smelt stuffy as the inside of a safe.

A hand reached back to make sure that I followed. We appeared to be in a flagged passage under the main level of the house. My hobnailed boots slipped on the floor, and I steadied myself on the wall, which seemed to be of undressed stone. Mr Donne moved softly and assuredly, for he was better shod for the job than me, and his guiding hand came back constantly to make sure of my whereabouts.

I remember that I felt just as I had felt when on that August night I had explored the crevice of the Coolin - the same sense that something queer was going to happen, the same reckless-ness and contentment. Moving a foot at a time with immense care, we came to a right-hand turning. Two shallow steps led us to another passage, and then my groping hands struck a blind wall. The American was beside me, and his mouth was close to my ear.

'Got to crawl now,' he whispered. 'You lead, mister, while I shed this coat of mine. Eight feet on your stomach and then upright.'

I wriggled through a low tunnel, broad enough to take three men abreast, but not two feet high. Half-way through I felt suffocated, for I never liked holes, and I had a momentary anxiety as to what we were after in this cellar pilgrimage. Presently I smelt free air and got on to my knees.

'Right, mister?' came a whisper from behind. My companion seemed to be waiting till I was through before he followed.

'Right,' I answered, and very carefully rose to my feet.

Then something happened behind me. There was a jar and a bump as if the roof of the tunnel had subsided. I turned sharply and groped at the mouth. I stuck my leg down and found a block.

'Donne,' I said, as loud as I dared, 'are you hurt? Where are you?'

But no answer came.

Even then I thought only of an accident. Something had miscarried, and I was cut off in the cellars of an unfriendly house away from the man who knew the road and had a plan in his head. I was not so much frightened as exasperated. I turned from the tunnel-mouth and groped into the darkness before me. I might as well prospect the kind of prison into which I had blundered.

I took three steps - no more. My feet seemed suddenly to go from me and fly upward. So sudden was it that I fell heavy and dead like a log, and my head struck the floor with a crash that for a moment knocked me senseless. I was conscious of something falling on me and of an intolerable pressure on my chest. I struggled for breath, and found my arms and legs pinned and my whole body in a kind of wooden vice. I was sick with concussion, and could do nothing but gasp and choke down my nausea. The cut in the back of my head was bleeding freely and that helped to clear my wits, but I lay for a minute or two incapable of thought. I shut my eyes tight, as a man does when he is fighting with a swoon.

When I opened them there was light. It came from the left side of the room, the broad glare of a strong electric torch. I watched it stupidly, but it gave me the fillip needed to pick up the threads. I remembered the tunnel now and the Kansas journalist. Then behind the light I saw a face which pulled my flickering senses out of the mire.

I saw the heavy ulster and the cap, which I had realized, though I had not seen, outside in the dark laurels. They belonged to the journalist, Clarence Donne, the trusted emissary of Blenkiron. But I saw his face now, and it was that face which I had boasted to Bullivant I could never mistake again upon earth. I did not mistake it now, and I remember I had a faint satisfaction that I had made good my word. I had not mistaken it, for I had not had the chance to look at it till this moment. I saw with acid clearness the common denominator of all its disguises - the young man who lisped in the seaside villa, the stout philanthropist of Biggleswick, the pulpy panic-stricken creature of the Tube station, the trim French staff officer of the Picardy chateau ... I saw more, for I saw it beyond the need of disguise. I was looking at von Schwabing, the exile, who had done more for Germany than any army commander ... Mary's words came back to me - 'the most dangerous man in the world' ... I was not afraid, or broken-hearted at failure, or angry - not yet, for I was too dazed and awestruck. I looked at him as one might look at some cataclysm of nature which had destroyed a continent.

The face was smiling.

'I am happy to offer you hospitality at last,' it said.

I pulled my wits farther out of the mud to attend to him. The cross-bar on my chest pressed less hard and I breathed better. But when I tried to speak, the words would not come.

'We are old friends,' he went on. 'We have known each other quite intimately for four years, which is a long time in war. I have been interested in you, for you have a kind of crude intelligence, and you have compelled me to take you seriously. If you were cleverer you would appreciate the compliment. But you were fool enough to think you could beat me, and for that you must be punished. Oh no, don't flatter yourself you were ever dangerous. You were only troublesome and presumptuous like a mosquito one flicks off one's sleeve.'

He was leaning against the side of a heavy closed door. He lit a cigar from a little gold tinder box and regarded me with amused eyes.

'You will have time for reflection, so I propose to enlighten you a little. You are an observer of little things. So? Did you ever see a cat with a mouse? The mouse runs about and hides and manoeuvres and thinks it is playing its own game. But at any moment the cat can stretch out its paw and put an end to it. You are the mouse, my poor General - for I believe you are one of those funny amateurs that the English call Generals. At any moment during the last nine months I could have put an end to you with a nod.'

My nausea had stopped and I could understand what he said, though I had still no power to reply.

'Let me explain,' he went on. 'I watched with amusement your gambols at Biggleswick. My eyes followed you when you went to the Clyde and in your stupid twistings in Scotland. I gave you rope, because you were futile, and I had graver things to attend to. I allowed you to amuse yourself at your British Front with childish investigations and to play the fool in Paris. I have followed every step of your course in Switzerland, and I have helped your idiotic Yankee friend to plot against myself.

While you thought you were drawing your net around me, I was drawing mine around you. I assure you, it has been a charming relaxation from serious business.'

I knew the man was lying. Some part was true, for he had clearly fooled Blenkiron; but I remembered the hurried flight from Biggleswick and Eaucourt Sainte-Anne when the game was certainly against him. He had me at his mercy, and was wreaking his vanity on me. That made him smaller in my eyes, and my first awe began to pass.

'I never cherish rancour, you know,' he said. 'In my business it is silly to be angry, for it wastes energy. But I do not tolerate insolence, my dear General. And my country has the habit of doing justice on her enemies. It may interest you to know that the end is not far off. Germany has faced a jealous world in arms and she is about to be justified of her great courage. She has broken up bit by bit the clumsy organization of her opponents. Where is Russia today, the steam-roller that was to crush us? Where is the poor dupe Rumania? Where is the strength of Italy, who was once to do wonders for what she called Liberty? Broken, all of them. I have played my part in that work and now the need is past. My country with free hands is about to turn upon your armed rabble in the West and drive it into the Atlantic. Then we shall deal with the ragged remains of France and the handful of noisy Americans. By midsummer there will be peace dictated by triumphant Germany.' 'By God, there won't!' I had found my voice at last.

'By God, there will,' he said pleasantly. 'It is what you call a mathematical certainty. You will no doubt die bravely, like the savage tribes that your Empire used to conquer. But we have the greater discipline and the stronger spirit and the bigger brain. Stupidity is always punished in the end, and you are a stupid race. Do not think that your kinsmen across the Atlantic will save you. They are a commercial people and by no means sure of themselves. When they have blustered a little they will see reason and find some means of saving their faces. Their comic President will make a speech or two and write us a solemn Note, and we will reply with the serious rhetoric which he loves, and then we shall kiss and be friends. You know in your heart that it will be so.'

A great apathy seemed to settle on me. This bragging did not make me angry, and I had no longer any wish to contradict him. It may have been the result of the fall, but my mind had stopped working. I heard his voice as one listens casually to the ticking of a clock.

'I will tell you more,' he was saying. 'This is the evening of the 18th day of March. Your generals in France expect an attack, but they are not sure where it will come. Some think it may be in Champagne or on the Aisne, some at Ypres, some at St Quentin. Well, my dear General, you alone will I take into our confidence. On the morning of the 21st, three days from now, we attack the right wing of the British Army. In two days we shall be in Amiens. On the third we shall have driven a wedge as far as the sea. Then in a week or so we shall have rolled up your army from the right, and presently we shall be in Boulogne and Calais. After that Paris falls, and then Peace.'

I made no answer. The word 'Amiens' recalled Mary, and I was trying to remember the day in January when she and I had motored south from that pleasant city.

'Why do I tell you these things? Your intelligence, for you are not altogether foolish, will have supplied the answer. It is because your life is over. As your Shakespeare says, the rest is silence ... No, I am not going to kill you. That would be crude, and I hate crudities. I am going now on a little journey, and when I return in twenty-four hours' time you will be my companion. You are going to visit Germany, my dear General.'

That woke me to attention, and he noticed it, for he went on with gusto.

'You have heard of the Untergrundbahn? No? And you boast of an Intelligence service! Yet your ignorance is shared by the

John Buchan

whole of your General Staff. It is a little organization of my own. By it we can take unwilling and dangerous people inside our frontier to be dealt with as we please. Some have gone from England and many from France. Officially I believe they are recorded as "missing", but they did not go astray on any battle-field. They have been gathered from their homes or from hotels or offices or even the busy streets. I will not conceal from you that the service of our Underground Railway is a little irregular from England and France. But from Switzerland it is smooth as a trunk line. There are unwatched spots on the frontier, and we have our agents among the frontier guards, and we have no difficulty about passes. It is a pretty device, and you will soon be privileged to observe its working ... In Germany I cannot promise you comfort, but I do not think your life will be dull.'

As he spoke these words, his urbane smile changed to a grin of impish malevolence. Even through my torpor I felt the venom and I shivered. 'When I return I shall have another companion.' His voice was honeyed again. 'There is a certain pretty lady who was to be the bait to entice me into Italy. It was so? Well, I have fallen to the bait. I have arranged that she shall meet me this very night at a mountain inn on the Italian side. I have arranged, too, that she shall be alone. She is an innocent child, and I do not think that she has been more than a tool in the clumsy hands of your friends. She will come with me when I ask her, and we shall be a merry party in the Underground Express.'

My apathy vanished, and every nerve in me was alive at the words.

'You cur!' I cried. 'She loathes the sight of you. She wouldn't touch you with the end of a barge-pole.'

He flicked the ash from his cigar. 'I think you are mistaken. I am very persuasive, and I do not like to use compulsion with a woman. But, willing or not, she will come with me. I have worked hard and I am entitled to my pleasure, and I have set my heart on that little lady.'

There was something in his tone, gross, leering, assured, half contemptuous, that made my blood boil. He had fairly got me on the raw, and the hammer beat violently in my forehead. I could have wept with sheer rage, and it took all my fortitude to keep my mouth shut. But I was determined not to add to his triumph.

He looked at his watch. 'Time passes,' he said. 'I must depart to my charming assignation. I will give your remembrances to the lady. Forgive me for making no arrangements for your comfort till I return. Your constitution is so sound that it will not suffer from a day's fasting. To set your mind at rest I may tell you that escape is impossible. This mechanism has been proved too often, and if you did break loose from it my servants would deal with you. But I must speak a word of caution. If you tamper with it or struggle too much it will act in a curious way. The floor beneath you covers a shaft which runs to the lake below. Set a certain spring at work and you may find yourself shot down into the water far below the ice, where your body will rot till the spring ... That, of course, is an alternative open to you, if you do not care to wait for my return.'

He lit a fresh cigar, waved his hand, and vanished through the doorway. As it shut behind him, the sound of his footsteps instantly died away. The walls must have been as thick as a prison's.

I suppose I was what people in books call 'stunned'. The illumination during the past few minutes had been so dazzling that my brain could not master it. I remember very clearly that I did not think about the ghastly failure of our scheme, or the German plans which had been insolently unfolded to me as to one dead to the world. I saw a single picture - an inn in a snowy valley (I saw it as a small place like Peter's cottage), a solitary girl, that smiling devil who had left me, and then the unknown terror of the Underground Railway. I think my courage went for a bit, and I cried with feebleness and rage. The hammer in my forehead had stopped for it only beat when I was angry in action. Now that I lay trapped, the manhood had slipped out of my joints, and if Ivery had still been in the doorway, I think I would have whined for mercy. I would have offered him all the knowledge I had in the world if he had promised to leave Mary alone.

Happily he wasn't there, and there was no witness of my cowardice. Happily, too, it is just as difficult to be a coward for long as to be a hero. It was Blenkiron's phrase about Mary that pulled me together - 'She can't scare and she can't soil'. No, by heavens, she couldn't. I could trust my lady far better than I could trust myself. I was still sick with anxiety, but I was getting a pull on myself. I was done in, but Ivery would get no triumph out of me. Either I would go under the ice, or I would find a chance of putting a bullet through my head before I crossed the frontier. If I could do nothing else I could perish decently ... And then I laughed, and I knew I was past the worst. What made me laugh was the thought of Peter. I had been pitying him an hour ago for having only one leg, but now he was abroad in the living, breathing world with years before him, and I lay in the depths, limbless and lifeless, with my number up.

I began to muse on the cold water under the ice where I could go if I wanted. I did not think that I would take that road, for a man's chances are not gone till he is stone dead, but I was glad the way existed ... And then I looked at the wall in front of me, and, very far up, I saw a small square window.

The stars had been clouded when I entered that accursed house, but the mist must have cleared. I saw my old friend Orion, the hunter's star, looking through the bars. And that suddenly made me think.

Peter and I had watched them by night, and I knew the place of all the chief constellations in relation to the St Anton valley. I believed that I was in a room on the lake side of the Pink

Chalet: I must be, if Ivery had spoken the truth. But if so, I could not conceivably see Orion from its window ... There was no other possible conclusion, I must be in a room on the east side of the house, and Ivery had been lying. He had already lied in his boasting of how he had outwitted me in England and at the Front. He might be lying about Mary ... No, I dismissed that hope. Those words of his had rung true enough.

I thought for a minute and concluded that he had lied to terrorize me and keep me quiet; therefore this infernal contraption had probably its weak point. I reflected, too, that I was pretty strong, far stronger probably than Ivery imagined, for he had never seen me stripped. Since the place was pitch dark I could not guess how the thing worked, but I could feel the cross-bars rigid on my chest and legs and the side-bars which pinned my arms to my sides ... I drew a long breath and tried to force my elbows apart. Nothing moved, nor could I raise the bars on my legs the smallest fraction.

Again I tried, and again. The side-bar on my right seemed to be less rigid than the others. I managed to get my right hand raised above the level of my thigh, and then with a struggle I got a grip with it on the cross-bar, which gave me a small leverage. With a mighty effort I drove my right elbow and shoulder against the side-bar. It seemed to give slightly ... I summoned all my strength and tried again. There was a crack and then a splintering, the massive bar shuffled limply back, and my right arm was free to move laterally, though the cross-bar prevented me from raising it.

With some difficulty I got at my coat pocket where reposed my electric torch and my pistol. With immense labour and no little pain I pulled the former out and switched it on by drawing the catch against the cross-bar. Then I saw my prison house.

It was a little square chamber, very high, with on my left the massive door by which Ivery had departed. The dark baulks of my rack were plain, and I could roughly make out how the thing had been managed. Some spring had tilted up the flooring, and dropped the framework from its place in the right-hand wall. It was clamped, I observed, by an arrangement in the floor just in front of the door. If I could get rid of that catch it would be easy to free myself, for to a man of my strength the weight would not be impossibly heavy.

My fortitude had come back to me, and I was living only in the moment, choking down any hope of escape. My first job was to destroy the catch that clamped down the rack, and for that my only weapon was my pistol. I managed to get the little electric torch jammed in the corner of the cross-bar, where it lit up the floor towards the door. Then it was hell's own business extricating the pistol from my pocket. Wrist and fingers were always cramping, and I was in terror that I might drop it where I could not retrieve it.

I forced myself to think out calmly the question of the clamp, for a pistol bullet is a small thing, and I could not afford to miss. I reasoned it out from my knowledge of mechanics, and came to the conclusion that the centre of gravity was a certain bright spot of metal which I could just see under the cross-bars. It was bright and so must have been recently repaired, and that was another reason for thinking it important. The question was how to hit it, for I could not get the pistol in line with my eye. Let anyone try that kind of shooting, with a bent arm over a bar, when you are lying flat and looking at the mark from under the bar, and he will understand its difficulties. I had six shots in my revolver, and I must fire two or three ranging shots in any case. I must not exhaust all my cartridges, for I must have a bullet left for any servant who came to pry, and I wanted one in reserve for myself. But I did not think shots would be heard outside the room; the walls were too thick.

I held my wrist rigid above the cross-bar and fired. The bullet was an inch to the right of the piece of bright steel. Moving a fraction I fired again. I had grazed it on the left. With aching eyes glued on the mark, I tried a third time. I saw something leap apart, and suddenly the whole framework under which I lay fell loose and mobile ... I was very cool and restored the pistol to my pocket and took the torch in my hand before I moved ... Fortune had been kind, for I was free. I turned on my face, humped my back, and without much trouble crawled out from under the contraption.

I did not allow myself to think of ultimate escape, for that would only flurry me, and one step at a time was enough. I remember that I dusted my clothes, and found that the cut in the back of my head had stopped bleeding. I retrieved my hat, which had rolled into a corner when I fell ... Then I turned my attention to the next step.

The tunnel was impossible, and the only way was the door. If I had stopped to think I would have known that the chances against getting out of such a house were a thousand to one. The pistol shots had been muffled by the cavernous walls, but the place, as I knew, was full of servants and, even if I passed the immediate door, I would be collared in some passage. But I had myself so well in hand that I tackled the door as if I had been prospecting to sink a new shaft in Rhodesia.

It had no handle nor, so far as I could see, a keyhole ... But I noticed, as I turned my torch on the ground, that from the clamp which I had shattered a brass rod sunk in the floor led to one of the door-posts. Obviously the thing worked by a spring and was connected with the mechanism of the rack.

A wild thought entered my mind and brought me to my feet. I pushed the door and it swung slowly open. The bullet which freed me had released the spring which controlled it.

Then for the first time, against all my maxims of discretion, I began to hope. I took off my hat and felt my forehead burning, so that I rested it for a moment on the cool wall ... Perhaps my luck still held. With a rush came thoughts of Mary and Blenkiron and Peter and everything we had laboured for, and I was mad to win.

I had no notion of the interior of the house or where lay the main door to the outer world. My torch showed me a long passage with something like a door at the far end, but I clicked it off, for I did not dare to use it now. The place was deadly quiet. As I listened I seemed to hear a door open far away, and then silence fell again.

I groped my way down the passage till I had my hands on the far door. I hoped it might open on the hall, where I could escape by a window or a balcony, for I judged the outer door would be locked. I listened, and there came no sound from within. It was no use lingering, so very stealthily I turned the handle and opened it a crack.

It creaked and I waited with beating heart on discovery, for inside I saw the glow of light. But there was no movement, so it must be empty. I poked my head in and then followed with my body.

It was a large room, with logs burning in a stove, and the floor thick with rugs. It was lined with books, and on a table in the centre a reading-lamp was burning. Several dispatch-boxes stood on the table, and there was a little pile of papers. A man had been here a minute before, for a half-smoked cigar was burning on the edge of the inkstand.

At that moment I recovered complete use of my wits and all my self-possession. More, there returned to me some of the old devil-may-careness which before had served me well. Ivery had gone, but this was his sanctum. just as on the roofs of Erzerum I had burned to get at Stumm's papers, so now it was borne in on me that at all costs I must look at that pile.

I advanced to the table and picked up the topmost paper. It was a little typewritten blue slip with the lettering in italics, and in a corner a curious, involved stamp in red ink. On it I read:

'Die Wildvogel missen beimkehren.'

At the same moment I heard steps and the door opened on the far side, I stepped back towards the stove, and fingered the pistol in my pocket.

A man entered, a man with a scholar's stoop, an unkempt beard, and large sleepy dark eyes. At the sight of me he pulled up and his whole body grew taut. It was the Portuguese Jew, whose back I had last seen at the smithy door in Skye, and who by the mercy of God had never seen my face.

I stopped fingering my pistol, for I had an inspiration. Before he could utter a word I got in first.

'Die Vogelein schwei igem im Walde,' I said.

His face broke into a pleasant smile, and he replied:

'Warte nur, balde rubest du auch.'

'Ach,' he said in German, holding out his hand, 'you have come this way, when we thought you would go by Modane. I welcome you, for I know your exploits. You are Conradi, who did so nobly in Italy?'

I bowed. 'Yes, I am Conradi,' I said.

CHAPTER SEVENTEEN

THE COL OF THE SWALLOWS

He pointed to the slip on the table.

'You have seen the orders?'

I nodded.

'The long day's work is over. You must rejoice, for your part has been the hardest, I think. Some day you will tell me about it?'

The man's face was honest and kindly, rather like that of the engineer Gaudian, whom two years before I had met in Germany. But his eyes fascinated me, for they were the eyes of the dreamer and fanatic, who would not desist from his quest while life lasted. I thought that Ivery had chosen well in his colleague.

'My task is not done yet,' I said. 'I came here to see Chelius.'

'He will be back tomorrow evening.'

'Too late. I must see him at once. He has gone to Italy, and I must overtake him.'

'You know your duty best,' he said gravely.

'But you must help me. I must catch him at Santa Chiara, for it is a business of life and death. Is there a car to be had?'

'There is mine. But there is no chauffeur. Chelius took him.'

'I can drive myself and I know the road. But I have no pass to cross the frontier.'

'That is easily supplied,' he said, smiling.

In one bookcase there was a shelf of dummy books. He unlocked this and revealed a small cupboard, whence he took a tin dispatch-box. From some papers he selected one, which seemed to be already signed.

'Name?' he asked.

'Call me Hans Gruber of Brieg,' I said. 'I travel to pick up my master, who is in the timber trade.'

'And your return?'

'I will come back by my old road,' I said mysteriously; and if he knew what I meant it was more than I did myself.

He completed the paper and handed it to me. 'This will take you through the frontier posts. And now for the car. The servants will be in bed, for they have been preparing for a long journey, but I will myself show it you. There is enough petrol on board to take you to Rome.'

He led me through the hall, unlocked the front door, and we crossed the snowy lawn to the garage. The place was empty but for a great car, which bore the marks of having come from the muddy lowlands. To my joy I saw that it was a Daimler, a type with which I was familiar. I lit the lamps, started the engine, and ran it out on to the road.

'You will want an overcoat,' he said.

'I never wear them.'

'Food?'

'I have some chocolate. I will breakfast at Santa Chiara.'

'Well, God go with you!'

A minute later I was tearing along the lake-side towards St Anton village.

I stopped at the cottage on the hill. Peter was not yet in bed. I found him sitting by the fire, trying to read, but I saw by his face that he had been waiting anxiously on my coming.

'We're in the soup, old man,' I said as I shut the door. In a dozen sentences I told him of the night's doings, of Ivery's plan and my desperate errand.

'You wanted a share,' I cried. 'Well, everything depends on you now. I'm off after Ivery, and God knows what will happen. Meantime, you have got to get on to Blenkiron, and tell him what I've told you. He must get the news through to G.H.Q. somehow. He must trap the Wild Birds before they go. I don't know how, but he must. Tell him it's all up to him and you, for I'm out of it. I must save Mary, and if God's willing I'll settle with Ivery. But the big job is for Blenkiron - and you. Somehow he has made a bad break, and the enemy has got ahead of him. He must sweat blood to make Up. My God, Peter, it's the solemnest moment of our lives. I don't see any light, but we mustn't miss any chances. I'm leaving it all to you.'

I spoke like a man in a fever, for after what I had been through I wasn't quite sane. My coolness in the Pink Chalet had given place to a crazy restlessness. I can see Peter yet, standing in the ring of lamplight, supporting himself by a chair back, wrinkling his brows and, as he always did in moments of excitement, scratching gently the tip of his left ear. His face was happy.

'Never fear, Dick,' he said. 'It will all come right. Ons sal 'n plan maak.'

And then, still possessed with a demon of disquiet, I was on the road again, heading for the pass that led to Italy.

The mist had gone from the sky, and the stars were shining brightly. The moon, now at the end of its first quarter, was setting in a gap of the mountains, as I climbed the low col from the St Anton valley to the greater Staubthal. There was frost and the hard snow crackled under my wheels, but there was also that feel in the air which preludes storm. I wondered if I should run into snow in the high hills. The whole land was deep in peace. There was not a light in the hamlets I passed through, not a soul on the highway.

In the Staubthal I joined the main road and swung to the left up the narrowing bed of the valley. The road was in noble condition, and the car was running finely, as I mounted through forests of snowy Pines to a land where the mountains crept close together, and the highway coiled round the angles of great crags or skirted perilously some profound gorge, with only a line of wooden posts to defend it from the void. In places the snow stood in walls on either side, where the road was kept open by man's labour. In other parts it lay thin, and in the dim light one might have fancied that one was running through open meadowlands.

Slowly my head was getting clearer, and I was able to look round my problem. I banished from my mind the situation I had left behind me. Blenkiron must cope with that as best he could. It lay with him to deal with the Wild Birds, my job was with Ivery alone. Sometime in the early morning he would reach Santa Chiara, and there he would find Mary. Beyond that my imagination could forecast nothing. She would be alone - I could trust his cleverness for that; he would try to force her to come with him, or he might persuade her with

John Buchan

some lying story. Well, please God, I should come in for the tail end of the interview, and at the thought I cursed the steep gradients I was climbing, and longed for some magic to lift the Daimler beyond the summit and set it racing down the slope towards Italy.

I think it was about half-past three when I saw the lights of the frontier post. The air seemed milder than in the valleys, and there was a soft scurry of snow on my right cheek. A couple of sleepy Swiss sentries with their rifles in their hands stumbled out as I drew up.

They took my pass into the hut and gave me an anxious quarter of an hour while they examined it. The performance was repeated fifty yards on at the Italian post, where to my alarm the sentries were inclined to conversation. I played the part of the sulky servant, answering in monosyllables and pretending to immense stupidity.

'You are only just in time, friend,' said one in German. 'The weather grows bad and soon the pass will close. Ugh, it is as cold as last winter on the Tonale. You remember, Giuseppe?'

But in the end they let me move on. For a little I felt my way gingerly, for on the summit the road had many twists and the snow was confusing to the eyes. Presently came a sharp drop and I let the Daimler go. It grew colder, and I shivered a little; the snow became a wet white fog around the glowing arc of the headlights; and always the road fell, now in long curves, now in steep short dips, till I was aware of a glen opening towards the south. From long living in the wilds I have a kind of sense for landscape without the testimony of the eyes, and I knew where the ravine narrowed or widened though it was black darkness.

In spite of my restlessness I had to go slowly, for after the first rush downhill I realized that, unless I was careful, I might wreck the car and spoil everything. The surface of the road on the southern slope of the mountains was a thousand per cent worse than that on the other. I skidded and side-slipped, and once grazed the edge of the gorge. It was far more maddening than the climb up, for then it had been a straight-forward grind with the Daimler doing its utmost, whereas now I had to hold her back because of my own lack of skill. I reckon that time crawling down from the summit of the Staub as some of the weariest hours I ever spent.

Quite suddenly I ran out of the ill weather into a different climate. The sky was clear above me, and I saw that dawn was very near. The first pinewoods were beginning, and at last came a straight slope where I could let the car out. I began to recover my spirits, which had been very dashed, and to reckon the distance I had still to travel ... And then, without warning, a new world sprang up around me. Out of the blue dusk white shapes rose like ghosts, peaks and needles and domes of ice, their bases fading mistily into shadow, but the tops kindling till they glowed like jewels. I had never seen such a sight, and the wonder of it for a moment drove anxiety from my heart. More, it gave me an earnest of victory. I was in clear air once more, and surely in this diamond ether the foul things which loved the dark must be worsted ...

And then I saw, a mile ahead, the little square red-roofed building which I knew to be the inn of Santa Chiara.

It was here that misfortune met me. I had grown careless now, and looked rather at the house than the road. At one point the hillside had slipped down - it must have been recent, for the road was well kept - and I did not notice the landslide till I was on it. I slewed to the right, took too wide a curve, and before I knew the car was over the far edge. I slapped on the brakes, but to avoid turning turtle I had to leave the road altogether. I slithered down a steep bank into a meadow, where for my sins I ran into a fallen tree trunk with a jar that shook me out of my seat and nearly broke my arm. Before I examined the car I knew what had happened. The front axle was bent, and the off front wheel badly buckled.

I had not time to curse my stupidity. I clambered back to the road and set off running down it at my best speed. I was mortally stiff, for Ivery's rack was not good for the joints, but I realized it only as a drag on my pace, not as an affliction in itself. My whole mind was set on the house before me and what might be happening there.

There was a man at the door of the inn, who, when he caught sight of my figure, began to move to meet me. I saw that it was Launcelot Wake, and the sight gave me hope.

But his face frightened me. It was drawn and haggard like one who never sleeps, and his eyes were hot coals.

'Hannay,' he cried, 'for God's sake what does it mean?'

'Where is Mary?' I gasped, and I remember I clutched at a lapel of his coat.

He pulled me to the low stone wall by the roadside.

'I don't know,' he said hoarsely. 'We got your orders to come here this morning. We were at Chiavagno, where Blenkiron told us to wait. But last night Mary disappeared ... I found she had hired a carriage and come on ahead. I followed at once, and reached here an hour ago to find her gone ... The woman who keeps the place is away and there are only two old servants left. They tell me that Mary came here late, and that very early in the morning a closed car came over the Staub with a man in it. They say he asked to see the young lady, and that they talked together for some time, and that then she went off with him in the car down the valley ... I must have passed it on my way up ... There's been some black devilment that I can't follow. Who was the man? Who was the man?'

He looked as if he wanted to throttle me.

'I can tell you that,' I said. 'It was Ivery.'

He stared for a second as if he didn't understand. Then he leaped to his feet and cursed like a trooper. 'You've botched it, as I knew you would. I knew no good would come of your infernal subtleties.' And he consigned me and Blenkiron and the British army and Ivery and everybody else to the devil.

I was past being angry. 'Sit down, man,' I said, 'and listen to me.' I told him of what had happened at the Pink Chalet. He heard me out with his head in his hands. The thing was too bad for cursing.

'The Underground Railway!' he groaned. 'The thought of it drives me mad. Why are you so calm, Hannay? She's in the hands of the cleverest devil in the world, and you take it quietly. You should be a raving lunatic.'

'I would be if it were any use, but I did all my raving last night in that den of Ivery's. We've got to pull ourselves together, Wake. First of all, I trust Mary to the other side of eternity. She went with him of her own free will. I don't know why, but she must have had a reason, and be sure it was a good one, for she's far cleverer than you or me ... We've got to follow her somehow. Ivery's bound for Germany, but his route is by the Pink Chalet, for he hopes to pick me up there. He went down the valley; therefore he is going to Switzerland by the Marjolana. That is a long circuit and will take him most of the day. Why he chose that way I don't know, but there it is. We've got to get back by the Staub.'

'How did you come?' he asked.

'That's our damnable luck. I came in a first-class six-cylinder Daimler, which is now lying a wreck in a meadow a mile up the road. We've got to foot it.'

'We can't do it. It would take too long. Besides, there's the frontier to pass.'

I remembered ruefully that I might have got a return passport

John Buchan

from the Portuguese Jew, if I had thought of anything at the time beyond getting to Santa Chiara.

'Then we must make a circuit by the hillside and dodge the guards. It's no use making difficulties, Wake. We're fairly up against it, but we've got to go on trying till we drop. Otherwise I'll take your advice and go mad.'

'And supposing you get back to St Anton, you'll find the house shut up and the travellers gone hours before by the Underground Railway.'

'Very likely. But, man, there's always the glimmering of a chance. It's no good chucking in your hand till the game's out.'

'Drop your proverbial philosophy, Mr Martin Tupper, and look up there.'

He had one foot on the wall and was staring at a cleft in the snow-line across the valley. The shoulder of a high peak dropped sharply to a kind of nick and rose again in a long graceful curve of snow. All below the nick was still in deep shadow, but from the configuration of the slopes I judged that a tributary glacier ran from it to the main glacier at the river head.

'That's the Colle delle Rondini,' he said, 'the Col of the Swallows. It leads straight to the Staubthal near Grunewald. On a good day I have done it in seven hours, but it's not a pass for winter-time. It has been done of course, but not often. ... Yet, if the weather held, it might go even now, and that would bring us to St Anton by the evening. I wonder' - and he looked me over with an appraising eye -'I wonder if you're up to it.'

My stiffness had gone and I burned to set my restlessness to physical toil.

'If you can do it, I can,' I said. 'No. There you're wrong.

You're a hefty fellow, but you're no mountaineer, and the ice of the Colle delle Rondini needs knowledge. It would be insane to risk it with a novice, if there were any other way. But I'm damned if I see any, and I'm going to chance it. We can get a rope and axes in the inn. Are you game?'

'Right you are. Seven hours, you say. We've got to do it in six.'

'You will be humbler when you get on the ice,' he said grimly. 'We'd better breakfast, for the Lord knows when we shall see food again.'

We left the inn at five minutes to nine, with the sky cloudless and a stiff wind from the north-west, which we felt even in the deep-cut valley. Wake walked with a long, slow stride that tried my patience. I wanted to hustle, but he bade me keep in step. 'You take your orders from me, for I've been at this job before. Discipline in the ranks, remember.'

We crossed the river gorge by a plank bridge, and worked our way up the right bank, past the moraine, to the snout of the glacier. It was bad going, for the snow concealed the boulders, and I often floundered in holes. Wake never relaxed his stride, but now and then he stopped to sniff the air.

I observed that the weather looked good, and he differed. 'It's too clear. There'll be a full-blown gale on the Col and most likely snow in the afternoon.' He pointed to a fat yellow cloud that was beginning to bulge over the nearest peak. After that I thought he lengthened his stride.

'Lucky I had these boots resoled and nailed at Chiavagno,' was the only other remark he made till we had passed the seracs of the main glacier and turned up the lesser ice-stream from the Colle delle Rondini.

By half-past ten we were near its head, and I could see clearly the ribbon of pure ice between black crags too steep for snow to lie on, which was the means of ascent to the Col. The sky

John Buchan

had clouded over, and ugly streamers floated on the high slopes. We tied on the rope at the foot of the bergschrund, which was easy to pass because of the winter's snow. Wake led, of course, and presently we came on to the icefall.

In my time I had done a lot of scrambling on rocks and used to promise myself a season in the Alps to test myself on the big peaks. If I ever go it will be to climb the honest rock towers around Chamonix, for I won't have anything to do with snow mountains. That day on the Colle delle Rondini fairly sickened me of ice. I daresay I might have liked it if I had done it in a holiday mood, at leisure and in good spirits. But to crawl up that couloir with a sick heart and a desperate impulse to hurry was the worst sort of nightmare. The place was as steep as a wall of smooth black ice that seemed hard as granite. Wake did the step-cutting, and I admired him enormously. He did not seem to use much force, but every step was hewn cleanly the right size, and they were spaced the right distance. In this job he was the true professional. I was thankful Blenkiron was not with us, for the thing would have given a squirrel vertigo. The chips of ice slithered between my legs and I could watch them till they brought up just above the bergschrund.

The ice was in shadow and it was bitterly cold. As we crawled up I had not the exercise of using the axe to warm me, and I got very numb standing on one leg waiting for the next step. Worse still, my legs began to cramp. I was in good condition, but that time under Ivery's rack had played the mischief with my limbs. Muscles got out of place in my calves and stood in aching lumps, till I almost squealed with the pain of it. I was mortally afraid I should slip, and every time I moved I called out to Wake to warn him. He saw what was happening and got the pick of his axe fixed in the ice before I was allowed to stir. He spoke often to cheer me up, and his voice had none of its harshness. He was like some ill-tempered generals I have known, very gentle in a battle.

At the end the snow began to fall, a soft powder like the

overspill of a storm raging beyond the crest. It was just after that that Wake cried out that in five minutes we would be at the summit. He consulted his wrist-watch. 'Jolly good time, too. Only twenty-five minutes behind my best. It's not one o'clock.'

The next I knew I was lying flat on a pad of snow easing my cramped legs, while Wake shouted in my ear that we were in for something bad. I was aware of a driving blizzard, but I had no thought of anything but the blessed relief from pain. I lay for some minutes on my back with my legs stiff in the air and the toes turned inwards, while my muscles fell into their proper place.

It was certainly no spot to linger in. We looked down into a trough of driving mist, which sometimes swirled aside and showed a knuckle of black rock far below. We ate some chocolate, while Wake shouted in my ear that now we had less step-cutting. He did his best to cheer me, but he could not hide his anxiety. Our faces were frosted over like a wedding-cake and the sting of the wind was like a whiplash on our eyelids.

The first part was easy, down a slope of firm snow where steps were not needed. Then came ice again, and we had to cut into it below the fresh surface snow. This was so laborious that Wake took to the rocks on the right side of the couloir, where there was some shelter from the main force of the blast. I found it easier, for I knew something about rocks, but it was difficult enough with every handhold and foothold glazed. Presently we were driven back again to the ice, and painfully cut our way through a throat of the ravine where the sides narrowed. There the wind was terrible, for the narrows made a kind of funnel, and we descended, plastered against the wall, and scarcely able to breathe, while the tornado plucked at our bodies as if it would whisk us like wisps of grass into the abyss. After that the gorge widened and we had an easier slope, till suddenly we found ourselves perched on a great tongue of rock round which the snow blew like the froth in a whirlpool. As

John Buchan

we stopped for breath, Wake shouted in my ear that this was the Black Stone.

'The what?' I yelled.

'The Schwarzstein. The Swiss call the pass the Schwarzsteinthor. You can see it from Grunewald.'

I suppose every man has a tinge of superstition in him. To hear that name in that ferocious place gave me a sudden access of confidence. I seemed to see all my doings as part of a great predestined plan. Surely it was not for nothing that the word which had been the key of my first adventure in the long tussle should appear in this last phase. I felt new strength in my legs and more vigour in my lungs. 'A good omen,' I shouted. 'Wake, old man, we're going to win out.'

'The worst is still to come,' he said.

He was right. To get down that tongue of rock to the lower snows of the couloir was a job that fairly brought us to the end of our tether. I can feel yet the sour, bleak smell of wet rock and ice and the hard nerve pain that racked my forehead. The Kaffirs used to say that there were devils in the high berg, and this place was assuredly given over to the powers of the air who had no thought of human life. I seemed to be in the world which had endured from the eternity before man was dreamed of. There was no mercy in it, and the elements were pitting their immortal strength against two pigmies who had profaned their sanctuary. I yearned for warmth, for the glow of a fire, for a tree or blade of grass or anything which meant the sheltered homeliness of mortality. I knew then what the Greeks meant by panic, for I was scared by the apathy of nature. But the terror gave me a kind of comfort, too. Ivery and his doings seemed less formidable. Let me but get out of this cold hell and I could meet him with a new confidence.

Wake led, for he knew the road and the road wanted knowing. Otherwise he should have been last on the rope, for that is the place of the better man in a descent. I had some horrible moments following on when the rope grew taut, for I had no help from it. We zigzagged down the rock, sometimes driven to the ice of the adjacent couloirs, sometimes on the outer ridge of the Black Stone, sometimes wriggling down little cracks and over evil boiler-plates. The snow did not lie on it, but the rock crackled with thin ice or oozed ice water. Often it was only by the grace of God that I did not fall headlong, and pull Wake out of his hold to the bergschrund far below. I slipped more than once, but always by a miracle recovered myself. To make things worse, Wake was tiring. I could feel him drag on the rope, and his movements had not the precision they had had in the morning. He was the mountaineer, and I the novice. If he gave out, we should never reach the valley.

The fellow was clear grit all through. When we reached the foot of the tooth and sat huddled up with our faces away from the wind, I saw that he was on the edge of fainting. What that effort Must have cost him in the way of resolution you may guess, but he did not fail till the worst was past. His lips were colourless, and he was choking with the nausea of fatigue. I found a flask of brandy in his pocket, and a mouthful revived him.

'I'm all out,' he said. 'The road's easier now, and I can direct YOU about the rest ... You'd better leave me. I'll only be a drag. I'll come on when I feel better.'

'No, you don't, you old fool. You've got me over that infernal iceberg, and I'm going to see you home.'

I rubbed his arms and legs and made him swallow some chocolate. But when he got on his feet he was as doddery as an old man. Happily we had an easy course down a snow gradient, which we glissaded in very unorthodox style. The swift motion freshened him up a little, and he was able to put on the brake with his axe to prevent us cascading into the bergschrund. We crossed it by a snow bridge, and started out on the seracs of the Schwarzstein glacier.

I am no mountaineer - not of the snow and ice kind, anyway - but I have a big share of physical strength and I wanted it all now. For those seracs were an invention of the devil. To traverse that labyrinth in a blinding snowstorm, with a fainting companion who was too weak to jump the narrowest crevasse, and who hung on the rope like lead when there was occasion to use it, was more than I could manage. Besides, every step that brought us nearer to the valley now increased my eagerness to hurry, and wandering in that maze of clotted ice was like the nightmare when you stand on the rails with the express coming and are too weak to climb on the platform. As soon as possible I left the glacier for the hillside, and though that was laborious enough in all conscience, yet it enabled me to steer a straight course. Wake never spoke a word. When I looked at him his face was ashen under a gale which should have made his cheeks glow, and he kept his eyes half closed. He was staggering on at the very limits of his endurance ...

By and by we were on the moraine, and after splashing through a dozen little glacier streams came on a track which led up the hillside. Wake nodded feebly when I asked if this was right. Then to my joy I saw a gnarled pine.

I untied the rope and Wake dropped like a log on the ground. 'Leave me,' he groaned. 'I'm fairly done. I'll come on later.' And he shut his eyes.

My watch told me that it was after five o'clock.

'Get on my back,' I said. 'I won't part from you till I've found a cottage. You're a hero. You've brought me over those damned mountains in a blizzard, and that's what no other man in England would have done. Get up.' He obeyed, for he was too far gone to argue. I tied his wrists together with a handkerchief below my chin, for I wanted my arms to hold up his legs. The rope and axes I left in a cache beneath the pine-tree. Then I started trotting down the track for the nearest dwelling.

My strength felt inexhaustible and the quicksilver in my bones drove me forward. The snow was still falling, but the wind was dying down, and after the inferno of the pass it was like summer. The road wound over the shale of the hillside and then into what in spring must have been upland meadows. Then it ran among trees, and far below me on the right I could hear the glacier river churning in its gorge' Soon little empty huts appeared, and rough enclosed paddocks, and presently I came out on a shelf above the stream and smelt the wood-smoke of a human habitation.

I found a middle-aged peasant in the cottage, a guide by profession in summer and a woodcutter in winter.

'I have brought my Herr from Santa Chiara,' I said, 'over the Schwarzsteinthor. He is very weary and must sleep.'

I decanted Wake into a chair, and his head nodded on his chest. But his colour was better.

'You and your Herr are fools,' said the man gruffly, but not unkindly. 'He must sleep or he will have a fever. The Schwarzsteinthor in this devil's weather! Is he English?'

'Yes,' I said, 'like all madmen. But he's a good Herr, and a brave mountaineer.'

We stripped Wake of his Red Cross uniform, now a collection of sopping rags, and got him between blankets with a huge earthenware bottle of hot water at his feet. The woodcutter's wife boiled milk, and this, with a little brandy added, we made him drink. I was quite easy in my mind about him, for I had seen this condition before. In the morning he would be as stiff as a poker, but recovered.

'Now I'm off for St Anton,' I said. 'I must get there tonight.'

John Buchan

'You are the hardy one,' the man laughed. 'I will show you the quick road to Grunewald, where is the railway. With good fortune you may get the last train.'

I gave him fifty francs on my Herr's behalf, learned his directions for the road, and set off after a draught of goat's milk, munching my last slab of chocolate. I was still strung up to a mechanical activity, and I ran every inch of the three miles to the Staubthal without consciousness of fatigue. I was twenty minutes too soon for the train, and, as I sat on a bench on the platform, my energy suddenly ebbed away. That is what happens after a great exertion. I longed to sleep, and when the train arrived I crawled into a carriage like a man with a stroke. There seemed to be no force left in my limbs. I realized that I was leg-weary, which is a thing you see sometimes with horses, but not often with men.

All the journey I lay like a log in a kind of coma, and it was with difficulty that I recognized my destination, and stumbled out of the train. But I had no sooner emerged from the station of St Anton than I got my second wind. Much snow had fallen since yesterday, but it had stopped now, the sky was clear, and the moon was riding. The sight of the familiar place brought back all my anxieties. The day on the Col of the Swallows was wiped out of my memory, and I saw only the inn at Santa Chiara, and heard Wake's hoarse voice speaking of Mary. The lights were twinkling from the village below, and on the right I saw the clump of trees which held the Pink Chalet.

I took a short cut across the fields, avoiding the little town. I ran hard, stumbling often, for though I had got my mental energy back my legs were still precarious. The station clock had told me that it was nearly half-past nine.

Soon I was on the high-road, and then at the Chalet gates. I heard as in a dream what seemed to be three shrill blasts on a whistle. Then a big car passed me, making for St Anton. For a second I would have hailed it, but it was past me and away. But I had a conviction that my business lay in the house, for I thought Ivery was there, and Ivery was what mattered.

I marched up the drive with no sort of plan in my head, only a blind rushing on fate. I remembered dimly that I had still three cartridges in my revolver.

The front door stood open and I entered and tiptoed down the passage to the room where I had found the Portuguese Jew. No one hindered me, but it was not for lack of servants. I had the impression that there were people near me in the darkness, and I thought I heard German softly spoken. There was someone ahead of me, perhaps the speaker, for I could hear careful footsteps. It was very dark, but a ray of light came from below the door of the room. Then behind me I heard the hall door clang, and the noise of a key turned in its lock. I had walked straight into a trap and all retreat was cut off.

My mind was beginning to work more clearly, though my purpose was still vague. I wanted to get at Ivery and I believed that he was somewhere in front of me. And then I thought of the door which led from the chamber where I had been imprisoned. If I could enter that way I would have the advantage of surprise.

I groped on the right-hand side of the passage and found a handle. It opened upon what seemed to be a dining-room, for there was a faint smell of food. Again I had the impression of people near, who for some unknown reason did not molest me. At the far end I found another door, which led to a second room, which I guessed to be adjacent to the library. Beyond it again must lie the passage from the chamber with the rack. The whole place was as quiet as a shell.

I had guessed right. I was standing in the passage where I stood the night before. In front of me was the library, and there was the same chink of light showing. Very softly I turned the handle and opened it a crack ...

The first thing that caught my eye was the profile of Ivery. He was looking towards the writing-table, where someone was sitting.

CHAPTER EIGHTEEN

THE UNDERGROUND RAILWAY

This is the story which I heard later from Mary ...

She was at Milan with the new Anglo-American hospital when she got Blenkiron's letter. Santa Chiara had always been the place agreed upon, and this message mentioned specifically Santa Chiara, and fixed a date for her presence there. She was a little puzzled by it, for she had not yet had a word from Ivery, to whom she had written twice by the roundabout address in France which Bommaerts had given her. She did not believe that he would come to Italy in the ordinary course of things, and she wondered at Blenkiron's certainty about the date.

The following morning came a letter from Ivery in which he ardently pressed for a meeting. It was the first of several, full of strange talk about some approaching crisis, in which the forebodings of the prophet were mingled with the solicitude of a lover.

'The storm is about to break,' he wrote, 'and I cannot think only of my own fate. I have something to tell you which vitally concerns yourself. You say you are in Lombardy. The Chiavagno valley is within easy reach, and at its head is the inn of Santa Chiara, to which I come on the morning of March 19th. Meet me there even if only for half an hour, I implore you. We have already shared hopes and confidences, and I would now share with you a knowledge which I alone in

John Buchan

Europe possess. You have the heart of a lion, my lady, worthy of what I can bring you.'

Wake was summoned from the Croce Rossa unit with which he was working at Vicenza, and the plan arranged by Blenkiron was faithfully carried out. Four officers of the Alpini, in the rough dress of peasants of the hills, met them in Chiavagno on the morning of the 18th. It was arranged that the hostess of Santa Chiara should go on a visit to her sister's son, leaving the inn, now in the shuttered quiet of wintertime, under the charge of two ancient servants. The hour of Ivery's coming on the 19th had been fixed by him for noon, and that morning Mary would drive up the valley, while Wake and the Alpini went inconspicuously by other routes so as to be in station around the place before midday. But on the evening of the 18th at the Hotel of the Four Kings in Chiavagno Mary received another message. It was from me and told her that I was crossing the Staub at midnight and would be at the inn before dawn. It begged her to meet me there, to meet me alone without the others, because I had that to say to her which must be said before Ivery's coming. I have seen the letter. It was written in a hand which I could not have distinguished from my own scrawl. It was not exactly what I would myself have written, but there were phrases in it which to Mary's mind could have come only from me. Oh, I admit it was cunningly done, especially the love-making, which was just the kind of stammering thing which I would have achieved if I had tried to put my feelings on paper. Anyhow, Mary had no doubt of its genuineness. She slipped off after dinner, hired a carriage with two broken-winded screws and set off up the valley. She left a line for Wake telling him to follow according to the plan - a line which he never got, for his anxiety when he found she had gone drove him to immediate pursuit.

At about two in the morning of the 19th after a slow and icy journey she arrived at the inn, knocked up the aged servants, made herself a cup of chocolate out of her tea-basket and sat down to wait on my coming.

She has described to me that time of waiting. A home-made candle in a tall earthenware candlestick lit up the little salle-a-manger, which was the one room in use. The world was very quiet, the snow muffled the roads, and it was cold with the penetrating chill of the small hours of a March night. Always, she has told me, will the taste of chocolate and the smell of burning tallow bring back to her that strange place and the flutter of the heart with which she waited. For she was on the eve of the crisis of all our labours, she was very young, and youth has a quick fancy which will not be checked. Moreover, it was I who was coming, and save for the scrawl of the night before, we had had no communication for many weeks ... She tried to distract her mind by repeating poetry, and the thing that came into her head was Keats's 'Nightingale', an odd poem for the time and place.

There was a long wicker chair among the furnishings of the room, and she lay down on it with her fur cloak muffled around her. There were sounds of movement in the inn. The old woman who had let her in, with the scent of intrigue of her kind, had brightened when she heard that another guest was coming. Beautiful women do not travel at midnight for nothing. She also was awake and expectant.

Then quite suddenly came the sound of a car slowing down outside. She sprang to her feet in a tremor of excitement. It was like the Picardy chateau again - the dim room and a friend coming out of the night. She heard the front door open and a step in the little hall ...

She was looking at Ivery. ... He slipped his driving-coat off as he entered, and bowed gravely. He was wearing a green hunting suit which in the dusk seemed like khaki, and, as he was about my own height, for a second she was misled. Then she saw his face and her heart stopped.

'You!' she cried. She had sunk back again on the wicker chair.

'I have come as I promised,' he said, 'but a little earlier. You

John Buchan

will forgive me my eagerness to be with you.'

She did not heed his words, for her mind was feverishly busy. My letter had been a fraud and this man had discovered our plans. She was alone with him, for it would be hours before her friends came from Chiavagno. He had the game in his hands, and of all our confederacy she alone remained to confront him. Mary's courage was pretty near perfect, and for the moment she did not think of herself or her own fate. That came later. She was possessed with poignant disappointment at our failure. All our efforts had gone to the winds, and the enemy had won with contemptuous ease. Her nervousness disappeared before the intense regret, and her brain set coolly and busily to work.

It was a new Ivery who confronted her, a man with vigour and purpose in every line of him and the quiet confidence of power. He spoke with a serious courtesy.

'The time for make-believe is past,' he was saying. 'We have fenced with each other. I have told you only half the truth, and you have always kept me at arm's length. But you knew in your heart, my dearest lady, that there must be the full truth between us some day, and that day has come. I have often told you that I love you. I do not come now to repeat that declaration. I come to ask you to entrust yourself to me, to join your fate to mine, for I can promise you the happiness which you deserve.'

He pulled up a chair and sat beside her. I cannot put down all that he said, for Mary, once she grasped the drift of it, was busy with her own thoughts and did not listen. But I gather from her that he was very candid and seemed to grow as he spoke in mental and moral stature. He told her who he was and what his work had been. He claimed the same purpose as hers, a hatred of war and a passion to rebuild the world into decency. But now he drew a different moral. He was a German: it was through Germany alone that peace and regeneration could come. His country was purged from her faults, and the marvellous German discipline was about to prove itself in the eye of gods and men. He told her what he had told me in the room at the Pink Chalet, but with another colouring. Germany was not vengeful or vainglorious, only patient and merciful. God was about to give her the power to decide the world's fate, and it was for him and his kind to see that the decision was beneficent. The greater task of his people was only now beginning.

That was the gist of his talk. She appeared to listen, but her mind was far away. She must delay him for two hours, three hours, four hours. If not, she must keep beside him. She was the only one of our company left in touch with the enemy ...

'I go to Germany now,' he was saying. 'I want you to come with me - to be my wife.'

He waited for an answer, and got it in the form of a startled question.

'To Germany? How?'

'It is easy,' he said, smiling. 'The car which is waiting outside is the first stage of a system of travel which we have perfected.' Then he told her about the Underground Railway - not as he had told it to me, to scare, but as a proof of power and forethought.

His manner was perfect. He was respectful, devoted, thoughtful of all things. He was the suppliant, not the master. He offered her power and pride, a dazzling career, for he had deserved well of his country, the devotion of the faithful lover. He would take her to his mother's house, where she would be welcomed like a princess. I have no doubt he was sincere, for he had many moods, and the libertine whom he had revealed to me at the Pink Chalet had given place to the honourable gentleman. He could play all parts well because he could believe in himself in them all.

Then he spoke of danger, not so as to slight her courage, but to emphasize his own thoughtfulness. The world in which she had lived was crumbling, and he alone could offer a refuge. She felt the steel gauntlet through the texture of the velvet glove.

All the while she had been furiously thinking, with her chin in her hand in the old way ... She might refuse to go. He could compel her, no doubt, for there was no help to be got from the old servants. But it might be difficult to carry an unwilling woman over the first stages of the Underground Railway. There might be chances ... Supposing he accepted her refusal and left her. Then indeed he would be gone for ever and our game would have closed with a fiasco. The great antagonist of England would go home rejoicing, taking his sheaves with him.

At this time she had no personal fear of him. So curious a thing is the human heart that her main preoccupation was with our mission, not with her own fate. To fail utterly seemed too bitter. Supposing she went with him. They had still to get out of Italy and cross Switzerland. If she were with him she would be an emissary of the Allies in the enemy's camp. She asked herself what could she do, and told herself 'Nothing.' She felt like a small bird in a very large trap, and her chief sensation was that of her own powerlessness. But she had learned Blenkiron's gospel and knew that Heaven sends amazing chances to the bold. And, even as she made her decision, she was aware of a dark shadow lurking at the back of her mind, the shadow of the fear which she knew was awaiting her. For she was going into the unknown with a man whom she hated, a man who claimed to be her lover. It was the bravest thing I have ever heard of, and I have lived my life among brave men.

'I will come with you,' she said. 'But you mustn't speak to me, please. I am tired and troubled and I want peace to think.'

As she rose weakness came over her and she swayed till his arm caught her. 'I wish I could let you rest for a little,' he said tenderly, 'but time presses. The car runs smoothly and you can sleep there.'

He summoned one of the servants to whom he handed Mary. 'We leave in ten minutes,' he said, and he went out to see to the car.

Mary's first act in the bedroom to which she was taken was to bathe her eyes and brush her hair. She felt dimly that she must keep her head clear. Her second was to scribble a note to Wake, telling him what had happened, and to give it to the servant with a tip.

'The gentleman will come in the morning,' she said. 'You must give it him at once, for it concerns the fate of your country.' The woman grinned and promised. It was not the first time she had done errands for pretty ladies.

Ivery settled her in the great closed car with much solicitude, and made her comfortable with rugs. Then he went back to the inn for a second, and she saw a light move in the salle-a-manger. He returned and spoke to the driver in German, taking his seat beside him.

But first he handed Mary her note to Wake. 'I think you left this behind you,' he said. He had not opened it.

Alone in the car Mary slept. She saw the figures of Ivery and the chauffeur in the front seat dark against the headlights, and then they dislimned into dreams. She had undergone a greater strain than she knew, and was sunk in the heavy sleep of weary nerves.

When she woke it was daylight. They were still in Italy, as her first glance told her, so they could not have taken the Staub route. They seemed to be among the foothills, for there was little snow, but now and then up tributary valleys she had glimpses of the high peaks. She tried hard to think what it

John Buchan

could mean, and then remembered the Marjolana. Wake had laboured to instruct her in the topography of the Alps, and she had grasped the fact of the two open passes. But the Marjolana meant a big circuit, and they would not be in Switzerland till the evening. They would arrive in the dark, and pass out of it in the dark, and there would be no chance of succour. She felt very lonely and very weak.

Throughout the morning her fear grew. The more hopeless her chance of defeating Ivery became the more insistently the dark shadow crept over her mind. She tried to steady herself by watching the show from the windows. The car swung through little villages, past vineyards and pine-woods and the blue of lakes, and over the gorges of mountain streams. There seemed to be no trouble about passports. The sentries at the controls waved a reassuring hand when they were shown some card which the chauffeur held between his teeth. In one place there was a longish halt, and she could hear Ivery talking Italian with two officers of Bersaglieri, to whom he gave cigars. They were fresh-faced, upstanding boys, and for a second she had an idea of flinging open the door and appealing to them to save her. But that would have been futile, for Ivery was clearly amply certificated. She wondered what part he was now playing.

The Marjolana route had been chosen for a purpose. In one town Ivery met and talked to a civilian official, and more than once the car slowed down and someone appeared from the wayside to speak a word and vanish. She was assisting at the last gathering up of the threads of a great plan, before the Wild Birds returned to their nest. Mostly these conferences seemed to be in Italian, but once or twice she gathered from the movement of the lips that German was spoken and that this rough peasant or that black-hatted bourgeois was not of Italian blood.

Early in the morning, soon after she awoke, Ivery had stopped the car and offered her a well-provided luncheon basket. She could eat nothing, and watched him breakfast off sandwiches beside the driver. In the afternoon he asked her permission to sit with her. The car drew up in a lonely place, and a tea-basket was produced by the chauffeur. Ivery made tea, for she seemed too listless to move, and she drank a cup with him. After that he remained beside her.

'In half an hour we shall be out of Italy,' he said. The car was running up a long valley to the curious hollow between snowy saddles which is the crest of the Marjolana. He showed her the place on a road map. As the altitude increased and the air grew colder he wrapped the rugs closer around her and apologized for the absence of a foot-warmer. 'In a little,' he said, 'we shall be in the land where your slightest wish will be law.'

She dozed again and so missed the frontier post. When she woke the car was slipping down the long curves of the Weiss valley, before it narrows to the gorge through which it debouches on Grunewald.

'We are in Switzerland now,' she heard his voice say. It may have been fancy, but it seemed to her that there was a new note in it. He spoke to her with the assurance of possession. They were outside the country of the Allies, and in a land where his web was thickly spread.

'Where do we stop tonight?' she asked timidly.

'I fear we cannot stop. Tonight also you must put up with the car. I have a little errand to do on the way, which will delay us a few minutes, and then we press on. Tomorrow, my fairest one, fatigue will be ended.'

There was no mistake now about the note of possession in his voice. Mary's heart began to beat fast and wild. The trap had closed down on her and she saw the folly of her courage. It had delivered her bound and gagged into the hands of one whom she loathed more deeply every moment, whose proximity was less welcome than a snake's. She had to bite hard on her lip to keep from screaming.

John Buchan

The weather had changed and it was snowing hard, the same storm that had greeted us on the Col of the Swallows. The pace was slower now, and Ivery grew restless. He looked frequently at his watch, and snatched the speaking-tube to talk to the driver. Mary caught the word 'St Anton'.

'Do we go by St Anton?' she found voice to ask. 'Yes, he said shortly.

The word gave her the faintest glimmering of hope, for she knew that Peter and I had lived at St Anton. She tried to look out of the blurred window, but could see nothing except that the twilight was falling. She begged for the road-map, and saw that so far as she could make out they were still in the broad Grunewald valley and that to reach St Anton they had to cross the low pass from the Staubthal. The snow was still drifting thick and the car crawled.

Then she felt the rise as they mounted to the pass. Here the going was bad, very different from the dry frost in which I had covered the same road the night before. Moreover, there seemed to be curious obstacles. Some careless wood-cart had dropped logs on the highway, and more than once both Ivery and the chauffeur had to get out to shift them. In one place there had been a small landslide which left little room to pass, and Mary had to descend and cross on foot while the driver took the car over alone. Ivery's temper seemed to be souring. To the girl's relief he resumed the outside seat, where he was engaged in constant argument with the chauffeur.

At the head of the pass stands an inn, the comfortable hostelry of Herr Kronig, well known to all who clamber among the lesser peaks of the Staubthal. There in the middle of the way stood a man with a lantern.

'The road is blocked by a snowfall,' he cried. 'They are clearing it now. It will be ready in half an hour's time.'

Ivery sprang from his seat and darted into the hotel. His

business was to speed up the clearing party, and Herr Kronig himself accompanied him to the scene of the catastrophe. Mary sat still, for she had suddenly become possessed of an idea. She drove it from her as foolishness, but it kept returning. Why had those tree-trunks been spilt on the road? Why had an easy pass after a moderate snowfall been suddenly closed?

A man came out of the inn-yard and spoke to the chauffeur. It seemed to be an offer of refreshment, for the latter left his seat and disappeared inside. He was away for some time and returned shivering and grumbling at the weather, with the collar of his greatcoat turned up around his ears. A lantern had been hung in the porch and as he passed Mary saw the man. She had been watching the back of his head idly during the long drive, and had observed that it was of the round bullet type, with no nape to the neck, which is common in the Fatherland. Now she could not see his neck for the coat collar, but she could have sworn that the head was a different shape. The man seemed to suffer acutely from the cold, for he buttoned the collar round his chin and pulled his cap far over his brows.

Ivery came back, followed by a dragging line of men with spades and lanterns. He flung himself into the front seat and nodded to the driver to start. The man had his engine going already so as to lose no time. He bumped over the rough debris of the snowfall and then fairly let the car hum. Ivery was anxious for speed, but he did not want his neck broken and he yelled out to take care. The driver nodded and slowed down, but presently he had got up speed again.

If Ivery was restless, Mary was worse. She seemed suddenly to have come on the traces of her friends. In the St Anton valley the snow had stopped and she let down the window for air, for she was choking with suspense. The car rushed past the station, down the hill by Peter's cottage, through the village, and along the lake shore to the Pink Chalet.

Ivery halted it at the gate. 'See that you fill up with petrol,' he told the man. 'Bid Gustav get the Daimler and be ready to follow in half in hour.'

He spoke to Mary through the open window.

'I will keep you only a very little time. I think you had better wait in the car, for it will be more comfortable than a dismantled house. A servant will bring you food and more rugs for the night journey.'

Then he vanished up the dark avenue.

Mary's first thought was to slip out and get back to the village and there to find someone who knew me or could take her where Peter lived. But the driver would prevent her, for he had been left behind on guard. She looked anxiously at his back, for he alone stood between her and liberty.

That gentleman seemed to be intent on his own business. As soon as Ivery's footsteps had grown faint, he had backed the car into the entrance, and turned it so that it faced towards St Anton. Then very slowly it began to move.

At the same moment a whistle was blown shrilly three times. The door on the right had opened and someone who had been waiting in the shadows climbed painfully in. Mary saw that it was a little man and that he was a cripple. She reached a hand to help him, and he fell on to the cushions beside her. The car was gathering speed.

Before she realized what was happening the new-comer had taken her hand and was patting it.

About two minutes later I was entering the gate of the Pink Chalet.

CHAPTER NINETEEN

THE CAGE OF THE WILD BIRDS

'Why, Mr Ivery, come right in,' said the voice at the table. There was a screen before me, stretching from the fireplace to keep off the draught from the door by which I had entered. It stood higher than my head but there were cracks in it through which I could watch the room. I found a little table on which I could lean my back, for I was dropping with fatigue.

Blenkiron sat at the writing-table and in front of him were little rows of Patience cards. Wood ashes still smouldered in the stove, and a lamp stood at his right elbow which lit up the two figures. The bookshelves and the cabinets were in twilight.

'I've been hoping to see you for quite a time.' Blenkiron was busy arranging the little heaps of cards, and his face was wreathed in hospitable smiles. I remember wondering why he should play the host to the true master of the house.

Ivery stood erect before him. He was rather a splendid figure now that he had sloughed all disguises and was on the threshold of his triumph. Even through the fog in which my brain worked it was forced upon me that here was a man born to play a big part. He had a jowl like a Roman king on a coin, and scornful eyes that were used to mastery. He was younger than me, confound him, and now he looked it.

He kept his eyes on the speaker, while a smile played round his

John Buchan

mouth, a very ugly smile.

'So,' he said. 'We have caught the old crow too. I had scarcely hoped for such good fortune, and, to speak the truth, I had not concerned myself much about you. But now we shall add you to the bag. And what a bag of vermin to lay out on the lawn!' He flung back his head and laughed.

'Mr Ivery -' Blenkiron began, but was cut short.

'Drop that name. All that is past, thank God! I am the Graf von Schwabing, an officer of the Imperial Guard. I am not the least of the weapons that Germany has used to break her enemies.'

'You don't say,' drawled Blenkiron, still fiddling with his Patience cards.

The man's moment had come, and he was minded not to miss a jot of his triumph. His figure seemed to expand, his eye kindled, his voice rang with pride. It was melodrama of the best kind and he fairly rolled it round his tongue. I don't think I grudged it him, for I was fingering something in my pocket. He had won all right, but he wouldn't enjoy his victory long, for soon I would shoot him. I had my eye on the very spot above his right ear where I meant to put my bullet ... For I was very clear that to kill him was the only way to protect Mary. I feared the whole seventy millions of Germany less than this man. That was the single idea that remained firm against the immense fatigue that pressed down on me.

'I have little time to waste on you,' said he who had been called Ivery. 'But I will spare a moment to tell you a few truths. Your childish game never had a chance. I played with you in England and I have played with you ever since. You have never made a move but I have quietly countered it. Why, man, you gave me your confidence. The American Mr Donne ...'

'What about Clarence?' asked Blenkiron. His face seemed a

study in pure bewilderment.

'I was that interesting journalist.'

'Now to think of that!' said Blenkiron in a sad, gentle voice. 'I thought I was safe with Clarence. Why, he brought me a letter from old Joe Hooper and he knew all the boys down Emporia way.'

Ivery laughed. 'You have never done me justice, I fear; but I think you will do it now. Your gang is helpless in my hands. General Hannay ...' And I wish I could give you a notion of the scorn with which he pronounced the word 'General'.

'Yes - Dick?' said Blenkiron intently.

'He has been my prisoner for twenty-four hours. And the pretty Miss Mary, too. You are all going with me in a little to my own country. You will not guess how. We call it the Underground Railway, and you will have the privilege of studying its working. ... I had not troubled much about you, for I had no special dislike of you. You are only a blundering fool, what you call in your country easy fruit.'

'I thank you, Graf,' Blenkiron said solemnly.

'But since you are here you will join the others ... One last word. To beat inepts such as you is nothing. There is a far greater thing. My country has conquered. You and your friends will be dragged at the chariot wheels of a triumph such as Rome never saw. Does that penetrate your thick skull? Germany has won, and in two days the whole round earth will be stricken dumb by her greatness.'

As I watched Blenkiron a grey shadow of hopelessness seemed to settle on his face. His big body drooped in his chair, his eyes fell, and his left hand shuffled limply among his Patience cards. I could not get my mind to work, but I puzzled miserably over his amazing blunders. He had walked blindly into the pit his enemies had dug for him. Peter must have failed to get my message to him, and he knew nothing of last night's work or my mad journey to Italy. We had all bungled, the whole wretched bunch of us, Peter and Blenkiron and myself ... I had a feeling at the back of my head that there was something in it all that I couldn't understand, that the catastrophe could not be quite as simple as it seemed. But I had no power to think, with the insolent figure of Ivery dominating the room ... Thank God I had a bullet waiting for him. That was the one fixed point in the chaos of my mind. For the first time in my life I was resolute on killing one particular man, and the purpose gave me a horrid comfort.

Suddenly Ivery's voice rang out sharp. 'Take your hand out of your pocket. You fool, you are covered from three points in the walls. A movement and my men will make a sieve of you. Others before you have sat in that chair, and I am used to take precautions. Quick. Both hands on the table.'

There was no mistake about Blenkiron's defeat. He was done and out, and I was left with the only card. He leaned wearily on his arms with the palms of his hands spread out.

'I reckon you've gotten a strong hand, Graf,' he said, and his voice was flat with despair.

'I hold a royal flush,' was the answer.

And then suddenly came a change. Blenkiron raised his head, and his sleepy, ruminating eyes looked straight at Ivery.

'I call you,' he said.

I didn't believe my ears. Nor did Ivery.

'The hour for bluff is past,' he said.

'Nevertheless I call you.'

At that moment I felt someone squeeze through the door behind me and take his place at my side. The light was so dim that I saw only a short, square figure, but a familiar voice whispered in my ear. 'It's me - Andra Amos. Man, this is a great ploy. I'm here to see the end o't.'

No prisoner waiting on the finding of the jury, no commander expecting news of a great battle, ever hung in more desperate suspense than I did during the next seconds. I had forgotten my fatigue; my back no longer needed support. I kept my eyes glued to the crack in the screen and my ears drank in greedily every syllable.

Blenkiron was now sitting bolt upright with his chin in his hands. There was no shadow of melancholy in his lean face.

'I say I call you, Herr Graf von Schwabing. I'm going to put you wise about some little things. You don't carry arms, so I needn't warn you against monkeying with a gun. You're right in saying that there are three places in these walls from which you can shoot. Well, for your information I may tell you that there's guns in all three, but they're covering you at this moment. So you'd better be good.'

Ivery sprang to attention like a ramrod. 'Karl,' he cried. 'Gustav!'

As if by magic figures stood on either side of him, like warders by a criminal. They were not the sleek German footmen whom I had seen at the Chalet. One I did not recognize. The other was my servant, Geordie Hamilton.

He gave them one glance, looked round like a hunted animal, and then steadied himself. The man had his own kind of courage.

'I've gotten something to say to you,' Blenkiron drawled. 'It's been a tough fight, but I reckon the hot end of the poker is with you. I compliment you on Clarence Donne. You fooled me fine over that business, and it was only by the mercy of God you didn't win out. You see, there was just the one of us who was liable to recognize you whatever way you twisted your face, and that was Dick Hannay. I give you good marks for Clarence ... For the rest, I had you beaten flat.'

He looked steadily at him. 'You don't believe it. Well, I'll give you proof. I've been watching your Underground Railway for quite a time. I've had my men on the job, and I reckon most of the lines are now closed for repairs. All but the trunk line into France. That I'm keeping open, for soon there's going to be some traffic on it.'

At that I saw Ivery's eyelids quiver. For all his self-command he was breaking.

'I admit we cut it mighty fine, along of your fooling me about Clarence. But you struck a bad snag in General Hannay, Graf. Your heart-to-heart talk with him was poor business. You reckoned you had him safe, but that was too big a risk to take with a man like Dick, unless you saw him cold before you left him ... He got away from this place, and early this morning I knew all he knew. After that it was easy. I got the telegram you had sent this morning in the name of Clarence Donne and it made me laugh. Before midday I had this whole outfit under my hand. Your servants have gone by the Underground Railway - to France. Ehrlich - well, I'm sorry about Ehrlich.'

I knew now the name of the Portuguese Jew.

'He wasn't a bad sort of man,' Blenkiron said regretfully, 'and he was plumb honest. I couldn't get him to listen to reason, and he would play with firearms. So I had to shoot.'

'Dead?' asked Ivery sharply.

'Ye-es. I don't miss, and it was him or me. He's under the ice now - where you wanted to send Dick Hannay. He wasn't your kind, Graf, and I guess he has some chance of getting into

Heaven. If I weren't a hard-shell Presbyterian I'd say a prayer for his soul.' I looked only at Ivery. His face had gone very pale, and his eyes were wandering. I am certain his brain was working at lightning speed, but he was a rat in a steel trap and the springs held him. If ever I saw a man going through hell it was now. His pasteboard castle had crumbled about his ears and he was giddy with the fall of it. The man was made of pride, and every proud nerve of him was caught on the raw.

'So much for ordinary business,' said Blenkiron. 'There's the matter of a certain lady. You haven't behaved over-nice about her, Graf, but I'm not going to blame you. You maybe heard a whistle blow when you were coming in here? No! Why, it sounded like Gabriel's trump. Peter must have put some lung power into it. Well, that was the signal that Miss Mary was safe in your car ... but in our charge. D'you comprehend?'

He did. The ghost of a flush appeared in his cheeks.

'You ask about General Hannay? I'm not just exactly sure where Dick is at the moment, but I opine he's in Italy.'

I kicked aside the screen, thereby causing Amos almost to fall on his face.

'I'm back,' I said, and pulled up an arm-chair, and dropped into it.

I think the sight of me was the last straw for Ivery. I was a wild enough figure, grey with weariness, soaked, dirty, with the clothes of the porter Joseph Zimmer in rags from the sharp rocks of the Schwarzsteinthor. As his eyes caught mine they wavered, and I saw terror in them. He knew he was in the presence of a mortal enemy.

'Why, Dick,' said Blenkiron with a beaming face, 'this is mighty opportune. How in creation did you get here?'

'I walked,' I said. I did not want to have to speak, for I was too tired. I wanted to watch Ivery's face.

Blenkiron gathered up his Patience cards, slipped them into a little leather case and put it in his pocket.

'I've one thing more to tell you. The Wild Birds have been summoned home, but they won't ever make it. We've gathered them in - Pavia, and Hofgaard, and Conradi. Ehrlich is dead. And you are going to join the rest in our cage.'

As I looked at my friend, his figure seemed to gain in presence. He sat square in his chair with a face like a hanging judge, and his eyes, sleepy no more, held Ivery as in a vice. He had dropped, too, his drawl and the idioms of his ordinary speech, and his voice came out hard and massive like the clash of granite blocks.

'You're at the bar now, Graf von Schwabing. For years you've done your best against the decencies of life. You have deserved well of your country, I don't doubt it. But what has your country deserved of the world? One day soon Germany has to do some heavy paying, and you are the first instalment.'

'I appeal to the Swiss law. I stand on Swiss soil, and I demand that I be surrendered to the Swiss authorities.' Ivery spoke with dry lips and the sweat was on his brow.

'Oh, no, no,' said Blenkiron soothingly. 'The Swiss are a nice people, and I would hate to add to the worries of a poor little neutral state ... All along both sides have been outside the law in this game, and that's going to continue. We've abode by the rules and so must you ... For years you've murdered and kidnapped and seduced the weak and ignorant, but we're not going to judge your morals. We leave that to the Almighty when you get across Jordan. We're going to wash our hands of you as soon as we can. You'll travel to France by the Underground Railway and there be handed over to the French Government. From what I know they've enough against you to shoot you every hour of the day for a twelvemonth.'

I think he had expected to be condemned by us there and then and sent to join Ehrlich beneath the ice. Anyhow, there came a flicker of hope into his eyes. I daresay he saw some way to dodge the French authorities if he once got a chance to use his miraculous wits. Anyhow, he bowed with something very like self-possession, and asked permission to smoke. As I have said, the man had his own courage.

'Blenkiron,' I cried, 'we're going to do nothing of the kind.'

He inclined his head gravely towards me. 'What's your notion, Dick?'

'We've got to make the punishment fit the crime,' I said. I was so tired that I had to form my sentences laboriously, as if I were speaking a half-understood foreign tongue.

'Meaning?'

'I mean that if you hand him over to the French he'll either twist out of their hands somehow or get decently shot, which is far too good for him. This man and his kind have sent millions of honest folk to their graves. He has sat spinning his web like a great spider and for every thread there has been an ocean of blood spilled. It's his sort that made the war, not the brave, stupid, fighting Boche. It's his sort that's responsible for all the clotted beastliness ... And he's never been in sight of a shell. I'm for putting him in the front line. No, I don't mean any Uriah the Hittite business. I want him to have a sporting chance, just what other men have. But, by God, he's going to learn what is the upshot of the strings he's been pulling so merrily ... He told me in two days' time Germany would smash our armies to hell. He boasted that he would be mostly responsible for it. Well, let him be there to see the smashing.'

'I reckon that's just,' said Blenkiron.

Ivery's eyes were on me now, fascinated and terrified like those of a bird before a rattlesnake. I saw again the shapeless features

John Buchan

of the man in the Tube station, the residuum of shrinking mortality behind his disguises. He seemed to be slipping something from his pocket towards his mouth, but Geordie Hamilton caught his wrist.

'Wad ye offer?' said the scandalized voice of my servant. 'Sirr, the prisoner would appear to be trying to puishon hisself. Wull I search him?'

After that he stood with each arm in the grip of a warder.

'Mr Ivery,' I said, 'last night, when I was in your power, you indulged your vanity by gloating over me. I expected it, for your class does not breed gentlemen. We treat our prisoners differently, but it is fair that you should know your fate. You are going into France, and I will see that you are taken to the British front. There with my old division you will learn something of the meaning of war. Understand that by no conceivable chance can you escape. Men will be detailed to watch you day and night and to see that you undergo the full rigour of the battlefield. You will have the same experience as other people, no more, no less. I believe in a righteous God and I know that sooner or later you will find death - death at the hands of your own people - an honourable death which is far beyond your deserts. But before it comes you will have understood the hell to which you have condemned honest men.'

In moments of great fatigue, as in moments of great crisis, the mind takes charge and may run on a track independent of the will. It was not myself that spoke, but an impersonal voice which I did not know, a voice in whose tones rang a strange authority. Ivery recognized the icy finality of it, and his body seemed to wilt, and droop. Only the hold of the warders kept him from falling.

I, too, was about at the end of my endurance. I felt dimly that the room had emptied except for Blenkiron and Amos, and that the former was trying to make me drink brandy from the cup of a flask. I struggled to my feet with the intention of going to Mary, but my legs would not carry me ... I heard as in a dream Amos giving thanks to an Omnipotence in whom he officially disbelieved. 'What's that the auld man in the Bible said? Now let thou thy servant depart in peace. That's the way I'm feelin' mysel'.' And then slumber came on me like an armed man, and in the chair by the dying wood-ash I slept off the ache of my limbs, the tension of my nerves, and the confusion of my brain.

CHAPTER TWENTY

THE STORM BREAKS IN THE WEST

The following evening - it was the 20th day of March - I started for France after the dark fell. I drove Ivery's big closed car, and within sat its owner, bound and gagged, as others had sat before him on the same errand. Geordie Hamilton and Amos were his companions. From what Blenkiron had himself discovered and from the papers seized in the Pink Chalet I had full details of the road and its mysterious stages. It was like the journey of a mad dream. In a back street of a little town I would exchange passwords with a nameless figure and be given instructions. At a wayside inn at an appointed hour a voice speaking a thick German would advise that this bridge or that railway crossing had been cleared. At a hamlet among pine woods an unknown man would clamber up beside me and take me past a sentry-post. Smooth as clockwork was the machine, till in the dawn of a spring morning I found myself dropping into a broad valley through little orchards just beginning to blossom, and I knew that I was in France. After that, Blenkiron's own arrangements began, and soon I was drinking coffee with a young lieutenant of Chasseurs, and had taken the gag from Ivery's mouth. The bluecoats looked curiously at the man in the green ulster whose face was the colour of clay and who lit cigarette from cigarette with a shaky hand.

The lieutenant rang up a General of Division who knew all about us. At his headquarters I explained my purpose, and he telegraphed to an Army Headquarters for a permission which was granted. It was not for nothing that in January I had seen certain great personages in Paris, and that Blenkiron had wired ahead of me to prepare the way. Here I handed over Ivery and his guard, for I wanted them to proceed to Amiens under French supervision, well knowing that the men of that great army are not used to let slip what they once hold.

It was a morning of clear spring sunlight when we breakfasted in that little red-roofed town among vineyards with a shining river looping at our feet. The General of Division was an Algerian veteran with a brush of grizzled hair, whose eye kept wandering to a map on the wall where pins and stretched thread made a spider's web.

'Any news from the north?' I asked.

'Not yet,' he said. 'But the attack comes soon. It will be against our army in Champagne.' With a lean finger he pointed out the enemy dispositions.

'Why not against the British?' I asked. With a knife and fork I made a right angle and put a salt dish in the centre. 'That is the German concentration. They can so mass that we do not know which side of the angle they will strike till the blow falls.'

'It is true,' he replied. 'But consider. For the enemy to attack towards the Somme would be to fight over many miles of an old battle-ground where all is still desert and every yard of which you British know. In Champagne at a bound he might enter unbroken country. It is a long and difficult road to Amiens, but not so long to Chilons. Such is the view of Petain. Does it convince you?'

'The reasoning is good. Nevertheless he will strike at Amiens, and I think he will begin today.'

He laughed and shrugged his shoulders. 'Nous verrons. You are obstinate, my general, like all your excellent countrymen.'

But as I left his headquarters an aide-de-camp handed him a message on a pink slip. He read it, and turned to me with a grave face.

'You have a flair, my friend. I am glad we did not wager. This morning at dawn there is great fighting around St Quentin. Be comforted, for they will not pass. Your Marechal will hold them.'

That was the first news I had of the battle.

At Dijon according to plan I met the others. I only just caught the Paris train, and Blenkiron's great wrists lugged me into the carriage when it was well in motion. There sat Peter, a docile figure in a carefully patched old R.F.C. uniform. Wake was reading a pile of French papers, and in a corner Mary, with her feet up on the seat, was sound asleep.

We did not talk much, for the life of the past days had been so hectic that we had no wish to recall it. Blenkiron's face wore an air of satisfaction, and as he looked out at the sunny spring landscape he hummed his only tune. Even Wake had lost his restlessness. He had on a pair of big tortoiseshell reading glasses, and when he looked up from his newspaper and caught my eye he smiled. Mary slept like a child, delicately flushed, her breath scarcely stirring the collar of the greatcoat which was folded across her throat. I remember looking with a kind of awe at the curve of her young face and the long lashes that lay so softly on her cheek, and wondering how I had borne the anxiety of the last months. Wake raised his head from his reading, glanced at Mary and then at me, and his eyes were kind, almost affectionate. He seemed to have won peace of mind among the hills.

Only Peter was out of the picture. He was a strange, disconsolate figure, as he shifted about to ease his leg, or gazed incuriously from the window. He had shaved his beard again, but it did not make him younger, for his face was too lined and his eyes too old to change. When I spoke to him he looked towards Mary and held up a warning finger.

'I go back to England,' he whispered. 'Your little mysie is going to take care of me till I am settled. We spoke of it yesterday at my cottage. I will find a lodging and be patient till the war is over. And you, Dick?'

'Oh, I rejoin my division. Thank God, this job is over. I have an easy trund now and can turn my attention to straight-forward soldiering. I don't mind telling you that I'll be glad to think that you and Mary and Blenkiron are safe at home. What about you, Wake?'

'I go back to my Labour battalion,' he said cheerfully. 'Like you, I have an easier mind.'

I shook my head. 'We'll see about that. I don't like such sinful waste. We've had a bit of campaigning together and I know your quality.'

'The battalion's quite good enough for me,' and he relapsed into a day-old Temps.

Mary had suddenly woke, and was sitting upright with her fists in her eyes like a small child. Her hand flew to her hair, and her eyes ran over us as if to see that we were all there. As she counted the four of us she seemed relieved.

'I reckon you feel refreshed, Miss Mary,' said Blenkiron. 'It's good to think that now we can sleep in peace, all of us. Pretty soon you'll be in England and spring will be beginning, and please God it'll be the start of a better world. Our work's over, anyhow.'

'I wonder,' said the girl gravely. 'I don't think there's any discharge in this war. Dick, have you news of the battle? This was the day.'

'It's begun,' I said, and told them the little I had learned from the French General. 'I've made a reputation as a prophet, for he thought the attack was coming in Champagne. It's St Quentin right enough, but I don't know what has happened. We'll hear in Paris.'

Mary had woke with a startled air as if she remembered her old instinct that our work would not be finished without a sacrifice, and that sacrifice the best of us. The notion kept recurring to me with an uneasy insistence. But soon she appeared to forget her anxiety. That afternoon as we journeyed through the pleasant land of France she was in holiday mood, and she forced all our spirits up to her level. It was calm, bright weather, the long curves of ploughland were beginning to quicken into green, the catkins made a blue mist on the willows by the watercourses, and in the orchards by the red-roofed hamlets the blossom was breaking. In such a scene it was hard to keep the mind sober and grey, and the pall of war slid from us. Mary cosseted and fussed over Peter like an elder sister over a delicate little boy. She made him stretch his bad leg full length on the seat, and when she made tea for the party of us it was a protesting Peter who had the last sugar biscuit. Indeed, we were almost a merry company, for Blenkiron told stories of old hunting and engineering days in the West, and Peter and I were driven to cap them, and Mary asked provo-cative questions, and Wake listened with amused interest. It was well that we had the carriage to ourselves, for no queerer rigs were ever assembled. Mary, as always, was neat and workmanlike in her dress; Blenkiron was magnificent in a suit of russet tweed with a pale-blue shirt and collar, and well-polished brown shoes; but Peter and Wake were in uniforms which had seen far better days, and I wore still the boots and the shapeless and ragged clothes of Joseph Zimmer, the porter from Arosa.

We appeared to forget the war, but we didn't, for it was in the background of all our minds. Somewhere in the north there was raging a desperate fight, and its issue was the true test of our success or failure. Mary showed it by bidding me ask for news at every stopping-place. I asked gendarmes and

Permissionnaires, but I learned nothing. Nobody had ever heard of the battle. The upshot was that for the last hour we all fell silent, and when we reached Paris about seven o'clock my first errand was to the bookstall.

I bought a batch of evening papers, which we tried to read in the taxis that carried us to our hotel. Sure enough there was the announcement in big headlines. The enemy had attacked in great strength from south of Arras to the Oise; but everywhere he had been repulsed and held in our battle-zone. The leading articles were confident, the notes by the various military critics were almost braggart. At last the German had been driven to an offensive, and the Allies would have the opportunity they had longed for of proving their superior fighting strength. It was, said one and all, the opening of the last phase of the war.

I confess that as I read my heart sank. If the civilians were so over-confident, might not the generals have fallen into the same trap? Blenkiron alone was unperturbed. Mary said nothing, but she sat with her chin in her hands, which with her was a sure sign of deep preoccupation.

Next morning the papers could tell us little more. The main attack had been on both sides of St Quentin, and though the British had given ground it was only the outposts line that had gone. The mist had favoured the enemy, and his bombardment had been terrific, especially the gas shells. Every journal added the old old comment - that he had paid heavily for his temerity, with losses far exceeding those of the defence.

Wake appeared at breakfast in his private's uniform. He wanted to get his railway warrant and be off at once, but when I heard that Amiens was his destination I ordered him to stay and travel with me in the afternoon. I was in uniform myself now and had taken charge of the outfit. I arranged that Blenkiron, Mary, and Peter should go on to Boulogne and sleep the night there, while Wake and I would be dropped at Amiens to await instructions.

I spent a busy morning. Once again I visited with Blenkiron the little cabinet in the Boulevard St Germain, and told in every detail our work of the past two months. Once again I sat in the low building beside the Invalides and talked to staff officers. But some of the men I had seen on the first visit were not there. The chiefs of the French Army had gone north.

We arranged for the handling of the Wild Birds, now safely in France, and sanction was given to the course I had proposed to adopt with Ivery. He and his guard were on their way to Amiens, and I would meet them there on the morrow. The great men were very complimentary to us, so complimentary that my knowledge of grammatical French ebbed away and I could only stutter in reply. That telegram sent by Blenkiron on the night of the 18th, from the information given me in the Pink Chalet, had done wonders in clearing up the situation.

But when I asked them about the battle they could tell me little. It was a very serious attack in tremendous force, but the British line was strong and the reserves were believed to be sufficient. Petain and Foch had gone north to consult with Haig. The situation in Champagne was still obscure, but some French reserves were already moving thence to the Somme sector. One thing they did show me, the British dispositions. As I looked at the plan I saw that my old division was in the thick of the fighting.

'Where do you go now?' I was asked.

'To Amiens, and then, please God, to the battle front,' I said.

'Good fortune to you. You do not give body or mind much rest, my general.'

After that I went to the Mission Anglaise, but they had nothing beyond Haig's communique and a telephone message from G.H.Q. that the critical sector was likely to be that between St Quentin and the Oise. The northern pillar of our defence, south of Arras, which they had been nervous about, had stood like a rock. That pleased me, for my old battalion of the Lennox Highlanders was there.

Crossing the Place de la Concorde, we fell in with a British staff officer of my acquaintance, who was just starting to motor back to G.H.Q. from Paris leave. He had a longer face than the people at the Invalides.

'I don't like it, I tell you,' he said. 'It's this mist that worries me. I went down the whole line from Arras to the Oise ten days ago. It was beautifully sited, the cleverest thing you ever saw. The outpost line was mostly a chain of blobs - redoubts, you know, with machine-guns - so arranged as to bring flanking fire to bear on the advancing enemy. But mist would play the devil with that scheme, for the enemy would be past the place for flanking fire before we knew it... Oh, I know we had good warning, and had the battle-zone manned in time, but the outpost line was meant to hold out long enough to get everything behind in apple-pie order, and I can't see but how big chunks of it must have gone in the first rush. ... Mind you, we've banked everything on that battle-zone. It's damned good, but if it's gone -'He flung up his hands.

'Have we good reserves?' I asked.

He shrugged his shoulders.

'Have we positions prepared behind the battle-zone?'

'I didn't notice any,' he said dryly, and was off before I could get more out of him.

'You look rattled, Dick,' said Blenkiron as we walked to the hotel.

'I seem to have got the needle. It's silly, but I feel worse about this show than I've ever felt since the war started. Look at this city here. The papers take it easily, and the people are walking about as if nothing was happening. Even the soldiers aren't worried. You may call me a fool to take it so hard, but I've a sense in my bones that we're in for the bloodiest and darkest fight of our lives, and that soon Paris will be hearing the Boche guns as she did in 1914.'

'You're a cheerful old Jeremiah. Well, I'm glad Miss Mary's going to be in England soon. Seems to me she's right and that this game of ours isn't quite played out yet. I'm envying you some, for there's a place waiting for you in the fighting line.'

'You've got to get home and keep people's heads straight there. That's the weak link in our chain and there's a mighty lot of work before you.'

'Maybe,' he said abstractedly, with his eye on the top of the Vendome column.

The train that afternoon was packed with officers recalled from leave, and it took all the combined purchase of Blenkiron and myself to get a carriage reserved for our little party. At the last moment I opened the door to admit a warm and agitated captain of the R.F.C. in whom I recognized my friend and benefactor, Archie Roylance.

'Just when I was gettin' nice and clean and comfy a wire comes tellin' me to bundle back, all along of a new battle. It's a cruel war, Sir.' The afflicted young man mopped his forehead, grinned cheerfully at Blenkiron, glanced critically at Peter, then caught sight of Mary and grew at once acutely conscious of his appearance. He smoothed his hair, adjusted his tie and became desperately sedate.

I introduced him to Peter and he promptly forgot Mary's existence. If Peter had had any vanity in him it would have been flattered by the frank interest and admiration in the boy's eyes. 'I'm tremendously glad to see you safe back, sir. I've always hoped I might have a chance of meeting you. We want you badly now on the front. Lensch is gettin' a bit uppish.'

Then his eye fell on Peter's withered leg and he saw that he had blundered. He blushed scarlet and looked his apologies. But they weren't needed, for it cheered Peter to meet someone who talked of the possibility of his fighting again. Soon the two were deep in technicalities, the appalling technicalities of the airman. It was no good listening to their talk, for you could make nothing of it, but it was bracing up Peter like wine. Archie gave him a minute description of Lensch's latest doings and his new methods. He, too, had heard the rumour that Peter had mentioned to me at St Anton, of a new Boche plane, with mighty engines and stumpy wings cunningly cambered, which was a devil to climb; but no specimens had yet appeared over the line. They talked of Bali, and Rhys Davids, and Bishop, and McCudden, and all the heroes who had won their spurs since the Somme, and of the new British makes, most of which Peter had never seen and had to have explained to him.

Outside a haze had drawn over the meadows with the twilight. I pointed it out to Blenkiron.

'There's the fog that's doing us. This March weather is just like October, mist morning and evening. I wish to Heaven we could have some good old drenching spring rain.'

Archie was discoursing of the Shark-Gladas machine.

'I've always stuck to it, for it's a marvel in its way, but it has my heart fairly broke. The General here knows its little tricks. Don't you, sir? Whenever things get really excitin', the engine's apt to quit work and take a rest.'

'The whole make should be publicly burned,' I said, with gloomy recollections.

'I wouldn't go so far, sir. The old Gladas has surprisin' merits. On her day there's nothing like her for pace and climbing-power, and she steers as sweet as a racin' cutter. The trouble about her is she's too complicated. She's like some breeds of

John Buchan

car - you want to be a mechanical genius to understand her ... If they'd only get her a little simpler and safer, there wouldn't be her match in the field. I'm about the only man that has patience with her and knows her merits, but she's often been nearly the death of me. All the same, if I were in for a big fight against some fellow like Lensch, where it was neck or nothing, I'm hanged if I wouldn't pick the Gladas.'

Archie laughed apologetically. 'The subject is banned for me in our mess. I'm the old thing's only champion, and she's like a mare I used to hunt that loved me so much she was always tryin' to chew the arm off me. But I wish I could get her a fair trial from one of the big pilots. I'm only in the second class myself after all.'

We were running north of St Just when above the rattle of the train rose a curious dull sound. It came from the east, and was like the low growl of a veld thunderstorm, or a steady roll of muffled drums.

'Hark to the guns!' cried Archie. 'My aunt, there's a tidy bombardment goin' on somewhere.'

I had been listening on and off to guns for three years. I had been present at the big preparations before Loos and the Somme and Arras, and I had come to accept the racket of artillery as something natural and inevitable like rain or sunshine. But this sound chilled me with its eeriness, I don't know why. Perhaps it was its unexpectedness, for I was sure that the guns had not been heard in this area since before the Marne. The noise must be travelling down the Oise valley, and I judged there was big fighting somewhere about Chauny or La Fere. That meant that the enemy was pressing hard on a huge front, for here was clearly a great effort on his extreme left wing. Unless it was our counter-attack. But somehow I didn't think so.

I let down the window and stuck my head into the night. The fog had crept to the edge of the track, a gossamer mist through which houses and trees and cattle could be seen dim in the moonlight. The noise continued - not a mutter, but a steady rumbling flow as solid as the blare of a trumpet. Presently, as we drew nearer Amiens, we left it behind us, for in all the Somme valley there is some curious configuration which blankets sound. The countryfolk call it the 'Silent Land', and during the first phase of the Somme battle a man in Amiens could not hear the guns twenty miles off at Albert.

As I sat down again I found that the company had fallen silent, even the garrulous Archie. Mary's eyes met mine, and in the indifferent light of the French railway-carriage I could see excitement in them - I knew it was excitement, not fear. She had never heard the noise of a great barrage before. Blenkiron was restless, and Peter was sunk in his own thoughts. I was growing very depressed, for in a little I would have to part from my best friends and the girl I loved. But with the depression was mixed an odd expectation, which was almost pleasant. The guns had brought back my profession to me, I was moving towards their thunder, and God only knew the end of it. The happy dream I had dreamed of the Cotswolds and a home with Mary beside me seemed suddenly to have fallen away to an infinite distance. I felt once again that I was on the razor-edge of life.

The last part of the journey I was casting back to rake up my knowledge of the countryside. I saw again the stricken belt from Serre to Combles where we had fought in the summer of '17. I had not been present in the advance of the following spring, but I had been at Cambrai and I knew all the down country from Lagnicourt to St Quentin. I shut my eyes and tried to picture it, and to see the roads running up to the line, and wondered just at what points the big pressure had come. They had told me in Paris that the British were as far south as the Oise, so the bombardment we had heard must be directed to our address. With Passchendaele and Cambrai in my mind, and some notion of the difficulties we had always had in getting drafts, I was puzzled to think where we could have found the troops to man the new front. We must be unholily

John Buchan

thin on that long line. And against that awesome bombard-ment! And the masses and the new tactics that Ivery had bragged of!

When we ran into the dingy cavern which is Amiens station I seemed to note a new excitement. I felt it in the air rather than deduced it from any special incident, except that the platform was very crowded with civilians, most of them with an extra amount of baggage. I wondered if the place had been bombed the night before.

'We won't say goodbye yet,' I told the others. 'The train doesn't leave for half an hour. I'm off to try and get news.' Accompanied by Archie, I hunted out an R.T.O. of my acqu-aintance. To my questions he responded cheerfully.

'Oh, we're doing famously, sir. I heard this afternoon from a man in Operations that G.H.Q. was perfectly satisfied. We've killed a lot of Huns and only lost a few kilometres of ground ... You're going to your division? Well, it's up Peronne way, or was last night. Cheyne and Dunthorpe came back from leave and tried to steal a car to get up to it ... Oh, I'm having the deuce of a time. These blighted civilians have got the wind up, and a lot are trying to clear out. The idiots say the Huns will be in Amiens in a week. What's the phrase? "Pourvu que les civils tiennent." 'Fraid I must push on, Sir.'

I sent Archie back with these scraps of news and was about to make a rush for the house of one of the Press officers, who would, I thought, be in the way of knowing things, when at the station entrance I ran across Laidlaw. He had been B.G.G.S. in the corps to which my old brigade belonged, and was now on the staff of some army. He was striding towards a car when I grabbed his arm, and he turned on me a very sick face.

'Good Lord, Hannay! Where did you spring from? The news, you say?' He sank his voice, and drew me into a quiet corner. 'The news is hellish.'

'They told me we were holding,' I observed.

'Holding be damned! The Boche is clean through on a broad front. He broke us today at Maissemy and Essigny. Yes, the battle-zone. He's flinging in division after division like the blows of a hammer. What else could you expect?' And he clutched my arm fiercely. 'How in God's name could eleven divisions hold a front of forty miles? And against four to one in numbers? It isn't war, it's naked lunacy.'

I knew the worst now, and it didn't shock me, for I had known it was coming. Laidlaw's nerves were pretty bad, for his face was pale and his eyes bright like a man with a fever.

'Reserves!' and he laughed bitterly. 'We have three infantry divisions and two cavalry. They're into the mill long ago. The French are coming up on our right, but they've the devil of a way to go. That's what I'm down here about. And we're getting help from Horne and Plumer. But all that takes days, and meantime we're walking back like we did at Mons. And at this time of day, too ... Oh, yes, the whole line's retreating. Parts of it were pretty comfortable, but they had to get back or be put in the bag. I wish to Heaven I knew where our right divisions have got to. For all I know they're at Compiegne by now. The Boche was over the canal this morning, and by this time most likely he's across the Somme.'

At that I exclaimed. 'D'you mean to tell me we're going to lose Peronne?'

'Peronne!' he cried. 'We'll be lucky not to lose Amiens! ... And on the top of it all I've got some kind of blasted fever. I'll be raving in an hour.'

He was rushing off, but I held him.

'What about my old lot?' I asked.

'Oh, damned good, but they're shot all to bits. Every division did well. It's a marvel they weren't all scuppered, and it'll be a flaming miracle if they find a line they can stand on. Westwater's got a leg smashed. He was brought down this evening, and you'll find him in the hospital. Fraser's killed and Lefroy's a prisoner - at least, that was my last news. I don't know who's got the brigades, but Masterton's carrying on with the division ... You'd better get up the line as fast as you can and take over from him. See the Army Commander. He'll be in Amiens tomorrow morning for a pow-wow.'

Laidlaw lay wearily back in his car and disappeared into the night, while I hurried to the train.

The others had descended to the platform and were grouped round Archie, who was discoursing optimistic nonsense. I got them into the carriage and shut the door.

'It's pretty bad,' I said. 'The front's pierced in several places and we're back to the Upper Somme. I'm afraid it isn't going to stop there. I'm off up the line as soon as I can get my orders. Wake, you'll come with me, for every man will be wanted. Blenkiron, you'll see Mary and Peter safe to England. We're just in time, for tomorrow it mightn't be easy to get out of Amiens.'

I can see yet the anxious faces in that ill-lit compartment. We said goodbye after the British style without much to-do. I remember that old Peter gripped my hand as if he would never release it, and that Mary's face had grown very pale. If I delayed another second I should have howled, for Mary's lips were trembling and Peter had eyes like a wounded stag. 'God bless you,' I said hoarsely, and as I went off I heard Peter's voice, a little cracked, saying 'God bless you, my old friend.'

I spent some weary hours looking for Westwater. He was not in the big clearing station, but I ran him to earth at last in the new hospital which had just been got going in the Ursuline convent. He was the most sterling little man, in ordinary life rather dry and dogmatic, with a trick of taking you up sharply which didn't make him popular. Now he was lying very stiff and quiet in the hospital bed, and his blue eyes were solemn and pathetic like a sick dog's.

'There's nothing much wrong with me,' he said, in reply to my question. 'A shell dropped beside me and damaged my foot. They say they'll have to cut it off ... I've an easier mind now you're here, Hannay. Of course you'll take over from Masterton. He's a good man but not quite up to his job. Poor Fraser - you've heard about Fraser. He was done in at the very start. Yes, a shell. And Lefroy. If he's alive and not too badly smashed the Hun has got a troublesome prisoner.'

He was too sick to talk, but he wouldn't let me go.

'The division was all right. Don't you believe anyone who says we didn't fight like heroes. Our outpost line held up the Hun for six hours, and only about a dozen men came back. We could have stuck it out in the battle-zone if both flanks hadn't been turned. They got through Crabbe's left and came down the Verey ravine, and a big wave rushed Shropshire Wood ... We fought it out yard by yard and didn't budge till we saw the Plessis dump blazing in our rear. Then it was about time to go ... We haven't many battalion commanders left. Watson, Endicot, Crawshay ...' He stammered out a list of gallant fellows who had gone.

'Get back double quick, Hannay. They want you. I'm not happy about Masterton. He's too young for the job.' And then a nurse drove me out, and I left him speaking in the strange forced voice of great weakness.

At the foot of the staircase stood Mary.

'I saw you go in,' she said, 'so I waited for you.'

'Oh, my dear,' I cried, 'you should have been in Boulogne by now. What madness brought you here?'

'They know me here and they've taken me on. You couldn't expect me to stay behind. You said yourself everybody was wanted, and I'm in a Service like you. Please don't be angry, Dick.'

I wasn't angry, I wasn't even extra anxious. The whole thing seemed to have been planned by fate since the creation of the world. The game we had been engaged in wasn't finished and it was right that we should play it out together. With that feeling came a conviction, too, of ultimate victory. Somehow or sometime we should get to the end of our pilgrimage. But I remembered Mary's forebodings about the sacrifice required. The best of us. That ruled me out, but what about her?

I caught her to my arms. 'Goodbye, my very dearest. Don't worry about me, for mine's a soft job and I can look after my skin. But oh! take care of yourself, for you are all the world to me.'

She kissed me gravely like a wise child.

'I am not afraid for you,' she said. 'You are going to stand in the breach, and I know - I know you will win. Remember that there is someone here whose heart is so full of pride of her man that it hasn't room for fear.'

As I went out of the convent door I felt that once again I had been given my orders.

It did not surprise me that, when I sought out my room on an upper floor of the Hotel de France, I found Blenkiron in the corridor. He was in the best of spirits.

'You can't keep me out of the show, Dick,' he said, 'so you needn't start arguing. Why, this is the one original chance of a lifetime for John S. Blenkiron. Our little fight at Erzerum was only a side-show, but this is a real high-class Armageddon. I guess I'll find a way to make myself useful.'

I had no doubt he would, and I was glad he had stayed behind. But I felt it was hard on Peter to have the job of returning to England alone at such a time, like useless flotsam washed up by a flood.

'You needn't worry,' said Blenkiron. 'Peter's not making England this trip. To the best of my knowledge he has beat it out of this township by the eastern postern. He had some talk with Sir Archibald Roylance, and presently other gentlemen of the Royal Flying Corps appeared, and the upshot was that Sir Archibald hitched on to Peter's grip and departed without saying farewell. My notion is that he's gone to have a few words with his old friends at some flying station. Or he might have the idea of going back to England by aeroplane, and so having one last flutter before he folds his wings. Anyhow, Peter looked a mighty happy man. The last I saw he was smoking his pipe with a batch of young lads in a Flying Corps waggon and heading straight for Germany.'

CHAPTER TWENTY-ONE

HOW AN EXILE RETURNED TO HIS OWN PEOPLE

Next morning I found the Army Commander on his way to Doullens.

'Take over the division?' he said. 'Certainly. I'm afraid there isn't much left of it. I'll tell Carr to get through to the Corps Headquarters, when he can find them. You'll have to nurse the remnants, for they can't be pulled out yet - not for a day or two. Bless me, Hannay, there are parts of our line which we're holding with a man and a boy. You've got to stick it out till the French take over. We're not hanging on by our eyelids - it's our eyelashes now.'

'What about positions to fall back on, sir?' I asked.

'We're doing our best, but we haven't enough men to prepare them.' He plucked open a map. 'There we're digging a line - and there. If we can hold that bit for two days we shall have a fair line resting on the river. But we mayn't have time.'

Then I told him about Blenkiron, whom of course he had heard of. 'He was one of the biggest engineers in the States, and he's got a nailing fine eye for country. He'll make good somehow if you let him help in the job.'

'The very fellow,' he said, and he wrote an order. 'Take this to Jacks and he'll fix up a temporary commission. Your man can find a uniform somewhere in Amiens.'

After that I went to the detail camp and found that Ivery had duly arrived.

'The prisoner has given no trouble, sir,' Hamilton reported. 'But he's a wee thing peevish. They're saying that the Gairmans is gettin' on fine, and I was tellin' him that he should be proud of his ain folk. But he wasn't verra weel pleased.'

Three days had wrought a transformation in Ivery. That face, once so cool and capable, was now sharpened like a hunted beast's. His imagination was preying on him and I could picture its torture. He, who had been always at the top directing the machine, was now only a cog in it. He had never in his life been anything but powerful; now he was impotent. He was in a hard, unfamiliar world, in the grip of something which he feared and didn't understand, in the charge of men who were in no way amenable to his persuasiveness. It was like a proud and bullying manager suddenly forced to labour in a squad of navvies, and worse, for there was the gnawing physical fear of what was coming.

He made an appeal to me.

'Do the English torture their prisoners?' he asked. 'You have beaten me. I own it, and I plead for mercy. I will go on my knees if you like. I am not afraid of death - in my own way.'

'Few people are afraid of death - in their own way.'

'Why do you degrade me? I am a gentleman.'

'Not as we define the thing,' I said.

His jaw dropped. 'What are you going to do with me?' he quavered.

John Buchan

'You have been a soldier,' I said. 'You are going to see a little fighting - from the ranks. There will be no brutality, you will be armed if you want to defend yourself, you will have the same chance of survival as the men around you. You may have heard that your countrymen are doing well. It is even possible that they may win the battle. What was your forecast to me? Amiens in two days, Abbeville in three. Well, you are a little behind scheduled time, but still you are prospering. You told me that you were the chief architect of all this, and you are going to be given the chance of seeing it, perhaps of sharing in it - from the other side. Does it not appeal to your sense of justice?' He groaned and turned away. I had no more pity for him than I would have had for a black mamba that had killed my friend and was now caught to a cleft tree. Nor, oddly enough, had Wake. If we had shot Ivery outright at St Anton, I am certain that Wake would have called us murderers. Now he was in complete agreement. His passionate hatred of war made him rejoice that a chief contriver of war should be made to share in its terrors.

'He tried to talk me over this morning,' he told me. 'Claimed he was on my side and said the kind of thing I used to say last year. It made me rather ashamed of some of my past performances to hear that scoundrel imitating them ... By the way, Hannay, what are you going to do with me?'

'You're coming on my staff. You're a stout fellow and I can't do without you.'

'Remember I won't fight.'

'You won't be asked to. We're trying to stem the tide which wants to roll to the sea. You know how the Boche behaves in occupied country, and Mary's in Amiens.'

At that news he shut his lips.

'Still -'he began.

Still" I said. 'I don't ask you to forfeit one of your blessed principles. You needn't fire a shot. But I want a man to carry orders for me, for we haven't a line any more, only a lot of blobs like quicksilver. I want a clever man for the job and a brave one, and I know that you're not afraid.'

'No,' he said. 'I don't think I am - much. Well. I'm content!'

I started Blenkiron off in a car for Corps Headquarters, and in the afternoon took the road myself. I knew every inch of the country - the lift of the hill east of Amiens, the Roman highway that ran straight as an arrow to St Quentin, the marshy lagoons of the Somme, and that broad strip of land wasted by battle between Dompierre and Peronne. I had come to Amiens through it in January, for I had been up to the line before I left for Paris, and then it had been a peaceful place, with peasants tilling their fields, and new buildings going up on the old battle-field, and carpenters busy at cottage roofs, and scarcely a transport waggon on the road to remind one of war. Now the main route was choked like the Albert road when the Somme battle first began - troops going up and troops coming down, the latter in the last stage of weariness; a ceaseless traffic of ambulances one way and ammunition waggons the other; busy staff cars trying to worm a way through the mass; strings of gun horses, oddments of cavalry, and here and there blue French uniforms. All that I had seen before; but one thing was new to me. Little country carts with sad-faced women and mystified children in them and piles of household plenishing were creeping westward, or stood waiting at village doors. Beside these tramped old men and boys, mostly in their Sunday best as if they were going to church. I had never seen the sight before, for I had never seen the British Army falling back. The dam which held up the waters had broken and the dwellers in the valley were trying to save their pitiful little treasures. And over everything, horse and man, cart and wheelbarrow, road and tillage, lay the white March dust, the sky was blue as June, small birds were busy in the copses, and in the corners of abandoned gardens I had a glimpse of the first violets.

Presently as we topped a rise we came within full noise of the guns. That, too, was new to me, for it was no ordinary bombardment. There was a special quality in the sound, something ragged, straggling, intermittent, which I had never heard before. It was the sign of open warfare and a moving battle.

At Peronne, from which the newly returned inhabitants had a second time fled, the battle seemed to be at the doors. There I had news of my division. It was farther south towards St Christ. We groped our way among bad roads to where its headquarters were believed to be, while the voice of the guns grew louder. They turned out to be those of another division, which was busy getting ready to cross the river. Then the dark fell, and while airplanes flew west into the sunset there was a redder sunset in the east, where the unceasing flashes of gunfire were pale against the angry glow of burning dumps. The sight of the bonnet-badge of a Scots Fusilier made me halt, and the man turned out to belong to my division. Half an hour later I was taking over from the much-relieved Masterton in the ruins of what had once been a sugar-beet factory.

There to my surprise I found Lefroy. The Boche had held him prisoner for precisely eight hours. During that time he had been so interested in watching the way the enemy handled an attack that he had forgotten the miseries of his position. He described with blasphemous admiration the endless wheel by which supplies and reserve troops move up, the silence, the smoothness, the perfect discipline. Then he had realized that he was a captive and unwounded, and had gone mad. Being a heavy-weight boxer of note, he had sent his two guards spinning into a ditch, dodged the ensuing shots, and found shelter in the lee of a blazing ammunition dump where his pursuers hesitated to follow. Then he had spent an anxious hour trying to get through an outpost line, which he thought was Boche. Only by overhearing an exchange of oaths in the accents of Dundee did he realize that it was our own ... It was a comfort to have Lefroy back, for he was both stout-hearted and resourceful. But I found that I had a division only on paper. It was about the strength of a brigade, the brigades battalions, and the battalions companies.

This is not the place to write the story of the week that followed. I could not write it even if I wanted to, for I don't know it. There was a plan somewhere, which you will find in the history books, but with me it was blank chaos. Orders came, but long before they arrived the situation had changed, and I could no more obey them than fly to the moon. Often I had lost touch with the divisions on both flanks. Intelligence arrived erratically out of the void, and for the most part we worried along without it. I heard we were under the French - first it was said to be Foch, and then Fayolle, whom I had met in Paris. But the higher command seemed a million miles away, and we were left to use our mother wits. My problem was to give ground as slowly as possible and at the same time not to delay too long, for retreat we must, with the Boche sending in brand-new divisions each morning. It was a kind of war worlds distant from the old trench battles, and since I had been taught no other I had to invent rules as I went along. Looking back, it seems a miracle that any of us came out of it. Only the grace of God and the uncommon toughness of the British soldier bluffed the Hun and prevented him pouring through the breach to Abbeville and the sea. We were no better than a mosquito curtain stuck in a doorway to stop the advance of an angry bull.

The Army Commander was right; we were hanging on with our eyelashes. We must have been easily the weakest part of the whole front, for we were holding a line which was never less than two miles and was often, as I judged, nearer five, and there was nothing in reserve to us except some oddments of cavalry who chased about the whole battle-field under vague orders. Mercifully for us the Boche blundered. Perhaps he did not know our condition, for our airmen were magnificent and you never saw a Boche plane over our line by day, though they bombed us merrily by night. If he had called our bluff we should have been done, but he put his main strength to the north and the south of us. North he pressed hard on the Third

Army, but he got well hammered by the Guards north of Bapaume and he could make no headway at Arras. South he drove at the Paris railway and down the Oise valley, but there Petain's reserves had arrived, and the French made a noble stand.

Not that he didn't fight hard in the centre where we were, but he hadn't his best troops, and after we got west of the bend of the Somme he was outrunning his heavy guns. Still, it was a desperate enough business, for our flanks were all the time falling back, and we had to conform to movements we could only guess at. After all, we were on the direct route to Amiens, and it was up to us to yield slowly so as to give Haig and Petain time to get up supports. I was a miser about every yard of ground, for every yard and every minute were precious. We alone stood between the enemy and the city, and in the city was Mary.

If you ask me about our plans I can't tell you. I had a new one every hour. I got instructions from the Corps, but, as I have said, they were usually out of date before they arrived, and most of my tactics I had to invent myself. I had a plain task, and to fulfil it I had to use what methods the Almighty allowed me. I hardly slept, I ate little, I was on the move day and night, but I never felt so strong in my life. It seemed as if I couldn't tire, and, oddly enough, I was happy. If a man's whole being is focused on one aim, he has no time to worry ... I remember we were all very gentle and soft-spoken those days. Lefroy, whose tongue was famous for its edge, now cooed like a dove. The troops were on their uppers, but as steady as rocks. We were against the end of the world, and that stiffens a man ...

Day after day saw the same performance. I held my wavering front with an outpost line which delayed each new attack till I could take its bearings. I had special companies for counter-attack at selected points, when I wanted time to retire the rest of the division. I think we must have fought more than a dozen of such little battles. We lost men all the time, but the enemy made no big scoop, though he was always on the edge of one. Looking back, it seems like a succession of miracles. Often I was in one end of a village when the Boche was in the other. Our batteries were always on the move, and the work of the gunners was past praising. Sometimes we faced east, sometimes north, and once at a most critical moment due south, for our front waved and blew like a flag at a masthead ... Thank God, the enemy was getting away from his big engine, and his ordinary troops were fagged and poor in quality. It was when his fresh shock battalions came on that I held my breath ... He had a heathenish amount of machine-guns and he used them beautifully. Oh, I take my hat off to the Boche performance. He was doing what we had tried to do at the Somme and the Aisne and Arras and Ypres, and he was more or less succeeding. And the reason was that he was going bald-headed for victory.

The men, as I have said, were wonderfully steady and patient under the fiercest trial that soldiers can endure. I had all kinds in the division - old army, new army, Territorials - and you couldn't pick and choose between them. They fought like Trojans, and, dirty, weary, and hungry, found still some salt of humour in their sufferings. It was a proof of the rock-bottom sanity of human nature. But we had one man with us who was hardly sane. ...

In the hustle of those days I now and then caught sight of Ivery. I had to be everywhere at all hours, and often visited that remnant of Scots Fusiliers into which the subtlest brain in Europe had been drafted. He and his keepers were never on outpost duty or in any counter-attack. They were part of the mass whose only business was to retire discreetly. This was child's play to Hamilton, who had been out since Mons; and Amos, after taking a day to get used to it, wrapped himself in his grim philosophy and rather enjoyed it. You couldn't surprise Amos any more than a Turk. But the man with them, whom they never left - that was another matter.

'For the first wee bit,' Hamilton reported, 'we thocht he was

John Buchan

gaun daft. Every shell that came near he jumped like a young horse. And the gas! We had to tie on his mask for him, for his hands were fushionless. There was whiles when he wadna be hindered from standin' up and talkin' to hisself, though the bullets was spittin'. He was what ye call demoralized ... Syne he got as though he didna hear or see onything. He did what we tell't him, and when we let him be he sat down and grat. He's aye greetin' ... Queer thing, sirr, but the Gairmans canna hit him. I'm aye shakin' bullets out o' my claes, and I've got a hole in my shoulder, and Andra took a bash on his tin that wad hae felled onybody that hadna a heid like a stot. But, sirr, the prisoner taks no scaith. Our boys are feared of him. There was an Irishman says to me that he had the evil eye, and ye can see for yerself that he's no canny.'

I saw that his skin had become like parchment and that his eyes were glassy. I don't think he recognized me.

'Does he take his meals?' I asked.

'He doesna eat muckle. But he has an unco thirst. Ye canna keep him off the men's water-bottles.'

He was learning very fast the meaning of that war he had so confidently played with. I believe I am a merciful man, but as I looked at him I felt no vestige of pity. He was dreeing the weird he had prepared for others. I thought of Scudder, of the thousand friends I had lost, of the great seas of blood and the mountains of sorrow this man and his like had made for the world. Out of the corner of my eye I could see the long ridges above Combles and Longueval which the salt of the earth had fallen to win, and which were again under the hoof of the Boche. I thought of the distracted city behind us and what it meant to me, and the weak, the pitifully weak screen which was all its defence. I thought of the foul deeds which had made the German name to stink by land and sea, foulness of which he was the arch-begetter. And then I was amazed at our forbearance. He would go mad, and madness for him was more decent than sanity.

I had another man who wasn't what you might call normal, and that was Wake. He was the opposite of shell-shocked, if you understand me. He had never been properly under fire before, but he didn't give a straw for it. I had known the same thing with other men, and they generally ended by crumpling up, for it isn't natural that five or six feet of human flesh shouldn't be afraid of what can torture and destroy it. The natural thing is to be always a little scared, like me, but by an effort of the will and attention to work to contrive to forget it. But Wake apparently never gave it a thought. He wasn't foolhardy, only indifferent. He used to go about with a smile on his face, a smile of contentment. Even the horrors - and we had plenty of them - didn't affect him. His eyes, which used to be hot, had now a curious open innocence like Peter's. I would have been happier if he had been a little rattled.

One night, after we had had a bad day of anxiety, I talked to him as we smoked in what had once been a French dug-out. He was an extra right arm to me, and I told him so. 'This must be a queer experience for you,' I said.

'Yes,' he replied, 'it is very wonderful. I did not think a man could go through it and keep his reason. But I know many things I did not know before. I know that the soul can be reborn without leaving the body.'

I stared at him, and he went on without looking at me.

'You're not a classical scholar, Hannay? There was a strange cult in the ancient world, the worship of Magna Mater - the Great Mother. To enter into her mysteries the votary passed through a bath of blood - I think I am passing through that bath. I think that like the initiate I shall be renatus in aeternum - reborn into the eternal.'

I advised him to have a drink, for that talk frightened me. It looked as if he were becoming what the Scots call 'fey'. Lefroy noticed the same thing and was always speaking about it. He was as brave as a bull himself, and with very much the same kind of courage; but Wake's gallantry perturbed him. 'I can't make the chap out,' he told me. 'He behaves as if his mind was too full of better things to give a damn for Boche guns. He doesn't take foolish risks - I don't mean that, but he behaves as if risks didn't signify. It's positively eerie to see him making notes with a steady hand when shells are dropping like hailstones and we're all thinking every minute's our last. You've got to be careful with him, sir. He's a long sight too valuable for us to spare.'

Lefroy was right about that, for I don't know what I should have done without him. The worst part of our job was to keep touch with our flanks, and that was what I used Wake for. He covered country like a moss-trooper, sometimes on a rusty bicycle, oftener on foot, and you couldn't tire him. I wonder what other divisions thought of the grimy private who was our chief means of communication. He knew nothing of military affairs before, but he got the hang of this rough-and-tumble fighting as if he had been born for it. He never fired a shot; he carried no arms; the only weapons he used were his brains. And they were the best conceivable. I never met a staff officer who was so quick at getting a point or at sizing up a situation. He had put his back into the business, and first-class talent is not common anywhere. One day a G. S. O. from a neighbouring division came to see me. 'Where on earth did you pick up that man Wake?' he asked.

'He's a conscientious objector and a non-combatant,' I said.

'Then I wish to Heaven we had a few more conscientious objectors in this show. He's the only fellow who seems to know anything about this blessed battle. My general's sending you a chit about him.'

'No need,' I said, laughing. 'I know his value. He's an old friend of mine.'

I used Wake as my link with Corps Headquarters, and especially with Blenkiron. For about the sixth day of the show

I was beginning to get rather desperate. This kind of thing couldn't go on for ever. We were miles back now, behind the old line ⁰Of '17, and, as we rested one flank on the river, the immediate situation was a little easier. But I had lost a lot of men, and those that were left were blind with fatigue. The big bulges of the enemy to north and south had added to the length of the total front, and I found I had to fan out my thin ranks. The Boche was still pressing on, though his impetus was slacker. If he knew how little there was to stop him in my section he might make a push which would carry him to Amiens. Only the magnificent work of our airmen had prevented him getting that knowledge, but we couldn't keep the secrecy up for ever. Some day an enemy plane would get over, and it only needed the drive of a fresh storm-battalion or two to scatter us. I wanted a good prepared position, with sound trenches and decent wiring. Above all I wanted reserves - reserves. The word was on my lips all day and it haunted my dreams. I was told that the French were to relieve us, but when - when? My reports to Corps Headquarters were one long wail for more troops. I knew there was a position prepared behind us, but I needed men to hold it.

Wake brought in a message from Blenkiron. 'We're waiting for you, Dick,' he wrote, 'and we've gotten quite a nice little home ready for you. This old man hasn't hustled so hard since he struck copper in Montana in '92. We've dug three lines of trenches and made a heap of pretty redoubts, and I guess they're well laid out, for the Army staff has supervised them and they're no slouches at this brand of engineering. You would have laughed to see the labour we employed. We had all breeds of Dago and Chinaman, and some of your own South African blacks, and they got so busy on the job they forgot about bedtime. I used to be reckoned a bit of a slave driver, but my special talents weren't needed with this push. I'm going to put a lot of money into foreign missions henceforward.'

I wrote back: 'Your trenches are no good without men. For God's sake get something that can hold a rifle. My lot are done to the world.'

Then I left Lefroy with the division and went down on the back of an ambulance to see for myself. I found Blenkiron, some of the Army engineers, and a staff officer from Corps Headquarters, and I found Archie Roylance.

They had dug a mighty good line and wired it nobly. It ran from the river to the wood of La Bruyere on the little hill above the Ablain stream. It was desperately long, but I saw at once it couldn't well be shorter, for the division on the south of us had its hands full with the fringe of the big thrust against the French.

'It's no good blinking the facts,' I told them. 'I haven't a thousand men, and what I have are at the end of their tether. If you put 'em in these trenches they'll go to sleep on their feet. When can the French take over?'

I was told that it had been arranged for next morning, but that it had now been put off twenty-four hours. It was only a temporary measure, pending the arrival of British divisions from the north.

Archie looked grave. 'The Boche is pushin' up new troops in this sector. We got the news before I left squadron head-quarters. It looks as if it would be a near thing, sir.'

'It won't be a near thing. It's an absolute black certainty. My fellows can't carry on as they are another day. Great God, they've had a fortnight in hell! Find me more men or we buckle up at the next push.' My temper was coming very near its limits.

'We've raked the country with a small-tooth comb, sir,' said one of the staff officers. 'And we've raised a scratch pack. Best part of two thousand. Good men, but most of them know nothing about infantry fighting. We've put them into platoons, and done our best to give them some kind of training. There's one thing may cheer you. We've plenty of machine-guns. There's a machine-gun school near by and we got all the men who were taking the course and all the plant.'

I don't suppose there was ever such a force put into the field before. It was a wilder medley than Moussy's camp-followers at First Ypres. There was every kind of detail in the shape of men returning from leave, representing most of the regiments in the army. There were the men from the machine-gun school. There were Corps troops - sappers and A.S.C., and a handful of Corps cavalry. Above all, there was a batch of American engineers, fathered by Blenkiron. I inspected them where they were drilling and liked the look of them. 'Forty-eight hours,' I said to myself. 'With luck we may just pull it off.'

Then I borrowed a bicycle and went back to the division. But before I left I had a word with Archie. 'This is one big game of bluff, and it's you fellows alone that enable us to play it. Tell your people that everything depends on them. They mustn't stint the planes in this sector, for if the Boche once suspicions how little he's got before him the game's up. He's not a fool and he knows that this is the short road to Amiens, but he imagines we're holding it in strength. If we keep up the fiction for another two days the thing's done. You say he's pushing up troops?'

'Yes, and he's sendin' forward his tanks.'

'Well, that'll take time. He's slower now than a week ago and he's got a deuce of a country to march over. There's still an outside chance we may win through. You go home and tell the R.F.C. what I've told you.'

He nodded. 'By the way, sir, Pienaar's with the squadron. He would like to come up and see you.'

'Archie,' I said solemnly, 'be a good chap and do me a favour. If I think Peter's anywhere near the line I'll go off my head with worry. This is no place for a man with a bad leg. He should have been in England days ago. Can't you get him off - to Amiens, anyhow?'

'We scarcely like to. You see, we're all desperately sorry for him, his fun gone and his career over and all that. He likes bein' with us and listenin' to our yarns. He has been up once or twice too. The Shark-Gladas. He swears it's a great make, and certainly he knows how to handle the little devil.'

'Then for Heaven's sake don't let him do it again. I look to you, Archie, remember. Promise.'

'Funny thing, but he's always worryin' about you. He has a map on which he marks every day the changes in the position, and he'd hobble a mile to pump any of our fellows who have been up your way.'

That night under cover of darkness I drew back the division to the newly prepared lines. We got away easily, for the enemy was busy with his own affairs. I suspected a relief by fresh troops.

There was no time to lose, and I can tell you I toiled to get things straight before dawn. I would have liked to send my own fellows back to rest, but I couldn't spare them yet. I wanted them to stiffen the fresh lot, for they were veterans. The new position was arranged on the same principles as the old front which had been broken on March 21st. There was our forward zone, consisting of an outpost line and redoubts, very cleverly sited, and a line of resistance. Well behind it were the trenches which formed the battle-zone. Both zones were heavily wired, and we had plenty of machine-guns; I wish I could say we had plenty of men who knew how to use them. The outposts were merely to give the alarm and fall back to the line of resistance which was to hold out to the last. In the forward zone I put the freshest of my own men, the units being brought up to something like strength by the details returning from leave that the Corps had commandeered. With them I put the American engineers, partly in the redoubts and partly in companies for counter-attack. Blenkiron had reported that they could shoot like Dan'l Boone, and were simply spoiling for a fight. The rest of the force was in the battle-zone, which was our last hope. If that went the Boche had a clear walk to Amiens. Some additional field batteries had been brought up to support our very weak divisional artillery. The front was so long that I had to put all three of my emaciated brigades in the line, so I had nothing to speak of in reserve. It was a most almighty gamble.

We had found shelter just in time. At 6.30 next day - for a change it was a clear morning with clouds beginning to bank up from the west - the Boche let us know he was alive. He gave us a good drenching with gas shells which didn't do much harm, and then messed up our forward zone with his trench mortars. At 7.20 his men began to come on, first little bunches with machine-guns and then the infantry in waves. It was clear they were fresh troops, and we learned afterwards from prisoners that they were Bavarians - 6th or 7th, I forget which, but the division that hung us up at Monchy. At the same time there was the sound of a tremendous bombardment across the river. It looked as if the main battle had swung from Albert and Montdidier to a direct push for Amiens. I have often tried to write down the events of that day. I tried it in my report to the Corps; I tried it in my own diary; I tried it because Mary wanted it; but I have never been able to make any story that hung together. Perhaps I was too tired for my mind to retain clear impressions, though at the time I was not conscious of special fatigue. More likely it is because the fight itself was so confused, for nothing happened according to the books and the orderly soul of the Boche must have been scarified ... At first it went as I expected. The outpost line was pushed in, but the fire from the redoubts broke up the advance, and enabled the line of resistance in the forward zone to give a good account of itself. There was a check, and then another big wave, assisted by a barrage from field-guns brought far forward. This time the line of resistance gave at several points, and Lefroy flung in the Americans in a counter-attack. That was a mighty performance. The engineers, yelling like

John Buchan

dervishes, went at it with the bayonet, and those that preferred swung their rifles as clubs. It was terribly costly fighting and all wrong, but it succeeded. They cleared the Boche out of a ruined farm he had rushed, and a little wood, and re-established our front. Blenkiron, who saw it all, for he went with them and got the tip of an ear picked off by a machine-gun bullet, hadn't any words wherewith to speak of it. 'And I once said those boys looked puffy,' he moaned.

The next phase, which came about midday, was the tanks. I had never seen the German variety, but had heard that it was speedier and heavier than ours, but unwieldy. We did not see much of their speed, but we found out all about their clumsiness. Had the things been properly handled they should have gone through us like rotten wood. But the whole outfit was bungled. It looked good enough country for the use of them, but the men who made our position had had an eye to this possibility. The great monsters, mounting a field-gun besides other contrivances, wanted something like a highroad to be happy in. They were useless over anything like difficult ground. The ones that came down the main road got on well enough at the start, but Blenkiron very sensibly had mined the highway, and we blew a hole like a diamond pit. One lay helpless at the foot of it, and we took the crew prisoner; another stuck its nose over and remained there till our field-guns got the range and knocked it silly. As for the rest - there is a marshy lagoon called the Patte d'Oie beside the farm of Gavrelle, which runs all the way north to the river, though in most places it only seems like a soft patch in the meadows. This the tanks had to cross to reach our line, and they never made it. Most got bogged, and made pretty targets for our gunners; one or two returned; and one the Americans, creeping forward under cover of a little stream, blew up with a time fuse.

By the middle of the afternoon I was feeling happier. I knew the big attack was still to come, but I had my forward zone intact and I hoped for the best. I remember I was talking to Wake, who had been going between the two zones, when I got the first warning of a new and unexpected peril. A dud shell plumped down a few yards from me.

'Those fools across the river are firing short and badly off the straight,' I said.

Wake examined the shell. 'No, it's a German one,' he said.

Then came others, and there could be no mistake about the direction - followed by a burst of machine-gun fire from the same quarter. We ran in cover to a point from which we could see the north bank of the river, and I got my glass on it. There was a lift of land from behind which the fire was coming. We looked at each other, and the same conviction stood in both faces. The Boche had pushed down the northern bank, and we were no longer in line with our neighbours. The enemy was in a situation to catch us with his fire on our flank and left rear. We couldn't retire to conform, for to retire meant giving up our prepared position.

It was the last straw to all our anxieties, and for a moment I was at the end of my wits. I turned to Wake, and his calm eyes pulled me together.

'If they can't retake that ground, we're fairly carted,' I said.

'We are. Therefore they must retake it.'

'I must get on to Mitchinson.' But as I spoke I realized the futility of a telephone message to a man who was pretty hard up against it himself. Only an urgent appeal could effect anything ... I must go myself ... No, that was impossible. I must send Lefroy ... But he couldn't be spared. And all my staff officers were up to their necks in the battle. Besides, none of them knew the position as I knew it ... And how to get there? It was a long way round by the bridge at Loisy.

Suddenly I was aware of Wake's voice. 'You had better send me,' he was saying. 'There's only one way - to swim the river a little lower down.'

'That's too damnably dangerous. I won't send any man to certain death.'

'But I volunteer,' he said. 'That, I believe, is always allowed in war.'

'But you'll be killed before you can cross.'

'Send a man with me to watch. If I get over, you may be sure I'll get to General Mitchinson. If not, send somebody else by Loisy. There's desperate need for hurry, and you see yourself it's the only way.'

The time was past for argument. I scribbled a line to Mitchinson as his credentials. No more was needed, for Wake knew the position as well as I did. I sent an orderly to accompany him to his starting-place on the bank.

'Goodbye,' he said, as we shook hands. 'You'll see, I'll come back all right.' His face, I remember, looked singularly happy. Five minutes later the Boche guns opened for the final attack.

I believe I kept a cool head; at least so Lefroy and the others reported. They said I went about all afternoon grinning as if I liked it, and that I never raised my voice once. (It's rather a fault of mine that I bellow in a scrap.) But I know I was feeling anything but calm, for the problem was ghastly. It all depended on Wake and Mitchinson. The flanking fire was so bad that I had to give up the left of the forward zone, which caught it fairly, and retire the men there to the battle-zone. The latter was better protected, for between it and the river was a small wood and the bank rose into a bluff which sloped inwards towards us. This withdrawal meant a switch, and a switch isn't a pretty thing when it has to be improvised in the middle of a battle.

The Boche had counted on that flanking fire. His plan was to break our two wings - the old Boche plan which crops up in every fight. He left our centre at first pretty well alone, and thrust along the river bank and to the wood of La Bruyère, where we linked up with the division on our right. Lefroy was in the first area, and Masterton in the second, and for three hours it was as desperate a business as I have ever faced ... The improvised switch went, and more and more of the forward zone disappeared. It was a hot, clear spring afternoon, and in the open fighting the enemy came on like troops at manoeuvres. On the left they got into the battle-zone, and I can see yet Lefroy's great figure leading a counter-attack in person, his face all puddled with blood from a scalp wound ...

I would have given my soul to be in two places at once, but I had to risk our left and keep close to Masterton, who needed me most. The wood of La Bruyère was the maddest sight. Again and again the Boche was almost through it. You never knew where he was, and most of the fighting there was duels between machine-gun parties. Some of the enemy got round behind us, and only a fine performance of a company of Cheshires saved a complete breakthrough.

As for Lefroy, I don't know how he stuck it out, and he doesn't know himself, for he was galled all the time by that accursed flanking fire. I got a note about half past four saying that Wake had crossed the river, but it was some weary hours after that before the fire slackened. I tore back and forward between my wings, and every time I went north I expected to find that Lefroy had broken. But by some miracle he held. The Boches were in his battle-zone time and again, but he always flung them out. I have a recollection of Blenkiron, stark mad, encouraging his Americans with strange tongues. Once as I passed him I saw that he had his left arm tied up. His blackened face grinned at me. 'This bit of landscape's mighty unsafe for democracy,' he croaked. 'For the love of Mike get your guns on to those devils across the river. They're plaguing my boys too bad.'

It was about seven o'clock, I think, when the flanking fire

slacked off, but it was not because of our divisional guns. There was a short and very furious burst of artillery fire on the north bank, and I knew it was British. Then things began to happen. One of our planes - they had been marvels all day, swinging down like hawks for machine-gun bouts with the Boche infantry - reported that Mitchinson was attacking hard and getting on well. That eased my mind, and I started off for Masterton, who was in greater straits than ever, for the enemy seemed to be weakening on the river bank and putting his main strength in against our right ... But my G.S.O.2 stopped me on the road. 'Wake,' he said. 'He wants to see you.'

'Not now,' I cried.

'He can't live many minutes.'

I turned and followed him to the ruinous cowshed which was my divisional headquarters. Wake, as I heard later, had swum the river opposite to Mitchinson's right, and reached the other shore safely, though the current was whipped with bullets. But he had scarcely landed before he was badly hit by shrapnel in the groin. Walking at first with support and then carried on a stretcher, he managed to struggle on to the divisional headquarters, where he gave my message and explained the situation. He would not let his wound be looked to till his job was done. Mitchinson told me afterwards that with a face grey from pain he drew for him a sketch of our position and told him exactly how near we were to our end ... After that he asked to be sent back to me, and they got him down to Loisy in a crowded ambulance, and then up to us in a returning empty. The M.O. who looked at his wound saw that the thing was hopeless, and did not expect him to live beyond Loisy. He was bleeding internally and no surgeon on earth could have saved him.

When he reached us he was almost pulseless, but he recovered for a moment and asked for me.

I found him, with blue lips and a face drained of blood, lying on my camp bed. His voice was very small and far away.

'How goes it?' he asked.

'Please God, we'll pull through ... thanks to you, old man.'

'Good,' he said and his eyes shut.

He opened them once again.

'Funny thing life. A year ago I was preaching peace ... I'm still preaching it ... I'm not sorry.'

I held his hand till two minutes later he died.

In the press of a fight one scarcely realizes death, even the death of a friend. It was up to me to make good my assurance to Wake, and presently I was off to Masterton. There in that shambles of La Bruyere, while the light faded, there was a desperate and most bloody struggle. It was the last lap of the contest. Twelve hours now, I kept telling myself, and the French will be here and we'll have done our task. Alas! how many of us would go back to rest? ... Hardly able to totter, our counter-attacking companies went in again. They had gone far beyond the limits of mortal endurance, but the human spirit can defy all natural laws. The balance trembled, hung, and then dropped the right way. The enemy impetus weakened, stopped, and the ebb began.

I wanted to complete the job. Our artillery put up a sharp barrage, and the little I had left comparatively fresh I sent in for a counter-stroke. Most of the men were untrained, but there was that in our ranks which dispensed with training, and we had caught the enemy at the moment of lowest vitality. We pushed him out of La Bruyere, we pushed him back to our old forward zone, we pushed him out of that zone to the position from which he had begun the day.

But there was no rest for the weary. We had lost at least a third

John Buchan

of our strength, and we had to man the same long line. We consolidated it as best we could, started to replace the wiring that had been destroyed, found touch with the division on our right, and established outposts. Then, after a conference with my brigadiers, I went back to my headquarters, too tired to feel either satisfaction or anxiety. In eight hours the French would be here. The words made a kind of litany in my ears.

In the cowshed where Wake had lain, two figures awaited me. The talc-enclosed candle revealed Hamilton and Amos, dirty beyond words, smoke-blackened, blood-stained, and intricately bandaged. They stood stiffly to attention.

'Sirr, the prisoner,' said Hamilton. 'I have to report that the prisoner is deid.'

I stared at them, for I had forgotten Ivery. He seemed a creature of a world that had passed away.

'Sirr, it was like this. Ever sin' this mornin', the prisoner seemed to wake up. Ye'll mind that he was in a kind of dream all week. But he got some new notion in his heid, and when the battle began he exheebited signs of restlessness. Whiles he wad lie doun in the trench, and whiles he was wantin' back to the dug-out. Accordin' to instructions I provided him wi' a rifle, but he didna seem to ken how to handle it. It was your orders, sirr, that he was to have means to defend hisself if the enemy cam on, so Amos gie'd him a trench knife. But verra soon he looked as if he was ettlin' to cut his throat, so I deprived him of it.'

Hamilton stopped for breath. He spoke as if he were reciting a lesson, with no stops between the sentences.

'I jaloused, sirr, that he wadna last oot the day, and Amos here was of the same opinion. The end came at twenty minutes past three - I ken the time, for I had just compared my watch with Amos. Ye'll mind that the Gairmans were beginning a big attack. We were in the front trench of what they ca' the battle-zone, and Amos and me was keepin' oor eyes on the enemy, who could be obsairved dribblin' ower the open. just then the prisoner catches sight of the enemy and jumps up on the top. Amos tried to hold him, but he kicked him in the face. The next we kenned he was runnin' verra fast towards the enemy, holdin' his hands ower his heid and crying out loud in a foreign langwidge.'

'It was German,' said the scholarly Amos through his broken teeth.

'It was Gairman,' continued Hamilton. 'It seemed as if he was appealin' to the enemy to help him. But they paid no attention, and he cam under the fire of their machine-guns. We watched him spin round like a teetotum and kenned that he was bye with it.'

'You are sure he was killed?' I asked.

'Yes, sirr. When we counter-attacked we fund his body.'

There is a grave close by the farm of Gavrelle, and a wooden cross at its head bears the name of the Graf von Schwabing and the date of his death. The Germans took Gavrelle a little later. I am glad to think that they read that inscription.

John Buchan

CHAPTER TWENTY-TWO

THE SUMMONS COMES FOR MR STANDFAST

I slept for one and three-quarter hours that night, and when I awoke I seemed to emerge from deeps of slumber which had lasted for days. That happens sometimes after heavy fatigue and great mental strain. Even a short sleep sets up a barrier between past and present which has to be elaborately broken down before you can link on with what has happened before. As my wits groped at the job some drops of rain splashed on my face through the broken roof. That hurried me out-of-doors. It was just after dawn and the sky was piled with thick clouds, while a wet wind blew up from the southwest. The long-prayed-for break in the weather seemed to have come at last. A deluge of rain was what I wanted, something to soak the earth and turn the roads into water-courses and clog the enemy transport, something above all to blind the enemy's eyes ... For I remembered what a preposterous bluff it all had been, and what a piteous broken handful stood between the Germans and their goal. If they knew, if they only knew, they would brush us aside like flies.

As I shaved I looked back on the events of yesterday as on something that had happened long ago. I seemed to judge them impersonally, and I concluded that it had been a pretty good fight. A scratch force, half of it dog-tired and half of it untrained, had held up at least a couple of fresh divisions ... But we couldn't do it again, and there were still some hours before us of desperate peril. When had the Corps said that the

French would arrive? ... I was on the point of shouting for Hamilton to get Wake to ring up Corps Headquarters, when I remembered that Wake was dead. I had liked him and greatly admired him, but the recollection gave me scarcely a pang. We were all dying, and he had only gone on a stage ahead.

There was no morning strafe, such as had been our usual fortune in the past week. I went out-of-doors and found a noiseless world under the lowering sky. The rain had stopped falling, the wind of dawn had lessened, and I feared that the storm would be delayed. I wanted it at once to help us through the next hours of tension. Was it in six hours that the French were coming? No, it must be four. It couldn't be more than four, unless somebody had made an infernal muddle. I wondered why everything was so quiet. It would be breakfast time on both sides, but there seemed no stir of man's presence in that ugly strip half a mile off. Only far back in the German hinterland I seemed to hear the rumour of traffic.

An unslept and unshaven figure stood beside me which revealed itself as Archie Roylance.

'Been up all night,' he said cheerfully, lighting a cigarette. 'No, I haven't had breakfast. The skipper thought we'd better get another anti-aircraft battery up this way, and I was superintendin' the job. He's afraid of the Hun gettin' over your lines and spying out the nakedness of the land. For, you know, we're uncommon naked, sir. Also,' and Archie's face became grave, 'the Hun's pourin' divisions down on this sector. As I judge, he's blowin' up for a thunderin' big drive on both sides of the river. Our lads yesterday said all the country back of Peronne was lousy with new troops. And he's gettin' his big guns forward, too. You haven't been troubled with them yet, but he has got the roads mended and the devil of a lot of new light railways, and any moment we'll have the five-point-nines sayin' Good-mornin' ... Pray Heaven you get relieved in time, sir. I take it there's not much risk of another push this mornin'?'

'I don't think so. The Boche took a nasty knock yesterday, and he must fancy we're pretty strong after that counter-attack. I don't think he'll strike till he can work both sides of the river, and that'll take time to prepare. That's what his fresh divisions are for ... But remember, he can attack now, if he likes. If he knew how weak we were he's strong enough to send us all to glory in the next three hours. It's just that knowledge that you fellows have got to prevent his getting. If a single Hun plane crosses our lines and returns, we're wholly and utterly done. You've given us splendid help since the show began, Archie. For God's sake keep it up to the finish and put every machine you can spare in this sector.'

'We're doin' our best,' he said. 'We got some more fightin' scouts down from the north, and we're keepin' our eyes skinned. But you know as well as I do, sir, that it's never an ab-so-lute certainty. If the Hun sent over a squadron we might beat 'em all down but one, and that one might do the trick. It's a matter of luck. The Hun's got the wind up all right in the air just now and I don't blame the poor devil. I'm inclined to think we haven't had the pick of his push here. Jennings says he's doin' good work in Flanders, and they reckon there's the deuce of a thrust comin' there pretty soon. I think we can manage the kind of footler he's been sendin' over here lately, but if Lensch or some lad like that were to choose to turn up I wouldn't say what might happen. The air's a big lottery,' and Archie turned a dirty face skyward where two of our planes were moving very high towards the east.

The mention of Lensch brought Peter to mind, and I asked if he had gone back.

'He won't go,' said Archie, 'and we haven't the heart to make him. He's very happy, and plays about with the Gladas single-seater. He's always speakin' about you, sir, and it'd break his heart if we shifted him.'

I asked about his health, and was told that he didn't seem to have much pain.

'But he's a bit queer,' and Archie shook a sage head. 'One of the reasons why he won't budge is because he says God has some work for him to do. He's quite serious about it, and ever since he got the notion he has perked up amazin'. He's always askin' about Lensch, too - not vindictive like, you understand, but quite friendly. Seems to take a sort of proprietary interest in him. I told him Lensch had had a far longer spell of first-class fightin' than anybody else and was bound by the law of averages to be downed soon, and he was quite sad about it.'

I had no time to worry about Peter. Archie and I swallowed breakfast and I had a pow-wow with my brigadiers. By this time I had got through to Corps H.Q. and got news of the French. It was worse than I expected. General Peguy would arrive about ten o'clock, but his men couldn't take over till well after midday. The Corps gave me their whereabouts and I found it on the map. They had a long way to cover yet, and then there would be the slow business of relieving. I looked at my watch. There were still six hours before us when the Boche might knock us to blazes, six hours of maddening anxiety ... Lefroy announced that all was quiet on the front, and that the new wiring at the Bois de la Bruyere had been completed. Patrols had reported that during the night a fresh German division seemed to have relieved that which we had punished so stoutly yesterday. I asked him if he could stick it out against another attack. 'No,' he said without hesitation. 'We're too few and too shaky on our pins to stand any more. I've only a man to every three yards.' That impressed me, for Lefroy was usually the most devil-may-care optimist.

'Curse it, there's the sun,' I heard Archie cry. It was true, for the clouds were rolling back and the centre of the heavens was a patch of blue. The storm was coming - I could smell it in the air - but probably it wouldn't break till the evening. Where, I wondered, would we be by that time?

It was now nine o'clock, and I was keeping tight hold on myself, for I saw that I was going to have hell for the next hours. I am a pretty stolid fellow in some ways, but I have

John Buchan

always found patience and standing still the most difficult job to tackle, and my nerves were all tattered from the long strain of the retreat. I went up to the line and saw the battalion commanders. Everything was unwholesomely quiet there. Then I came back to my headquarters to study the reports that were coming in from the air patrols. They all said the same thing - abnormal activity in the German back areas. Things seemed shaping for a new 21st of March, and, if our luck were out, my poor little remnant would have to take the shock. I telephoned to the Corps and found them as nervous as me. I gave them the details of my strength and heard an agonized whistle at the other end of the line. I was rather glad I had companions in the same purgatory.

I found I couldn't sit still. If there had been any work to do I would have buried myself in it, but there was none. Only this fearsome job of waiting. I hardly ever feel cold, but now my blood seemed to be getting thin, and I astonished my staff by putting on a British warm and buttoning up the collar. Round that derelict farm I ranged like a hungry wolf, cold at the feet, queasy in the stomach, and mortally edgy in the mind.

Then suddenly the cloud lifted from me, and the blood seemed to run naturally in my veins. I experienced the change of mood which a man feels sometimes when his whole being is fined down and clarified by long endurance. The fight of yesterday revealed itself as something rather splendid. What risks we had run and how gallantly we had met them! My heart warmed as I thought of that old division of mine, those ragged veterans that were never beaten as long as breath was left them. And the Americans and the boys from the machine-gun school and all the oddments we had commandeered! And old Blenkiron raging like a good-tempered lion! It was against reason that such fortitude shouldn't win out. We had snarled round and bitten the Boche so badly that he wanted no more for a little. He would come again, but presently we should be relieved and the gallant blue-coats, fresh as paint and burning for revenge, would be there to worry him.

I had no new facts on which to base my optimism, only a changed point of view. And with it came a recollection of other things. Wake's death had left me numb before, but now the thought of it gave me a sharp pang. He was the first of our little confederacy to go. But what an ending he had made, and how happy he had been in that mad time when he had come down from his pedestal and become one of the crowd! He had found himself at the last, and who could grudge him such happiness? If the best were to be taken, he would be chosen first, for he was a big man, before whom I uncovered my head. The thought of him made me very humble. I had never had his troubles to face, but he had come clean through them, and reached a courage which was for ever beyond me. He was the Faithful among us pilgrims, who had finished his journey before the rest. Mary had foreseen it. 'There is a price to be paid,' she had said -'the best of us.'

And at the thought of Mary a flight of warm and happy hopes seemed to settle on my mind. I was looking again beyond the war to that peace which she and I would some day inherit. I had a vision of a green English landscape, with its far-flung scents of wood and meadow and garden ... And that face of all my dreams, with the eyes so childlike and brave and honest, as if they, too, saw beyond the dark to a radiant country. A line of an old song, which had been a favourite of my father's, sang itself in my ears:

> There's an eye that ever weeps and a fair face will be fain
> When I ride through Annan Water wi' my bonny bands again!

We were standing by the crumbling rails of what had once been the farm sheepfold. I looked at Archie and he smiled back at me, for he saw that my face had changed. Then he turned his eyes to the billowing clouds.

I felt my arm clutched.

'Look there!' said a fierce voice, and his glasses were

John Buchan

turned upward.

I looked, and far up in the sky saw a thing like a wedge of wild geese flying towards us from the enemy's country. I made out the small dots which composed it, and my glass told me they were planes. But only Archie's practised eye knew that they were enemy.

'Boche?' I asked.

'Boche,' he said. 'My God, we're for it now.' My heart had sunk like a stone, but I was fairly cool. I looked at my watch and saw that it was ten minutes to eleven.

'How many?'

'Five,' said Archie. 'Or there may be six - not more.'

'Listen!' I said. 'Get on to your headquarters. Tell them that it's all up with us if a single plane gets back. Let them get well over the line, the deeper in the better, and tell them to send up every machine they possess and down them all. Tell them it's life or death. Not one single plane goes back. Quick!'

Archie disappeared, and as he went our anti-aircraft guns broke out. The formation above opened and zigzagged, but they were too high to be in much danger. But they were not too high to see that which we must keep hidden or perish.

The roar of our batteries died down as the invaders passed westward. As I watched their progress they seemed to be dropping lower. Then they rose again and a bank of cloud concealed them.

I had a horrid certainty that they must beat us, that some at any rate would get back. They had seen thin lines and the roads behind us empty of supports. They would see, as they advanced, the blue columns of the French coming up from the south-west, and they would return and tell the enemy that a blow now would open the road to Amiens and the sea. He had plenty of strength for it, and presently he would have overwhelming strength. It only needed a spear-point to burst the jerry-built dam and let the flood through ... They would return in twenty minutes, and by noon we would be broken. Unless - unless the miracle of miracles happened, and they never returned.

Archie reported that his skipper would do his damnedest and that our machines were now going up. 'We've a chance, sir,' he said, 'a good sportin' chance.' It was a new Archie, with a hard voice, a lean face, and very old eyes.

Behind the jagged walls of the farm buildings was a knoll which had once formed part of the high-road. I went up there alone, for I didn't want anybody near me. I wanted a viewpoint, and I wanted quiet, for I had a grim time before me. From that knoll I had a big prospect of country. I looked east to our lines on which an occasional shell was falling, and where I could hear the chatter of machine-guns. West there was peace for the woods closed down on the landscape. Up to the north, I remember, there was a big glare as from a burning dump, and heavy guns seemed to be at work in the Ancre valley. Down in the south there was the dull murmur of a great battle. But just around me, in the gap, the deadliest place of all, there was an odd quiet. I could pick out clearly the different sounds. Somebody down at the farm had made a joke and there was a short burst of laughter. I envied the humorist his composure. There was a clatter and jingle from a battery changing position. On the road a tractor was jolting along - I could hear its driver shout and the screech of its unoiled axle.

My eyes were glued to my glasses, but they shook in my hands so that I could scarcely see. I bit my lip to steady myself, but they still wavered. From time to time I glanced at my watch. Eight minutes gone - ten - seventeen. If only the planes would come into sight! Even the certainty of failure would be better than this harrowing doubt. They should be back by now unless they had swung north across the salient, or unless the miracle

John Buchan

of miracles -

Then came the distant yapping of an anti-aircraft gun, caught up the next second by others, while smoke patches studded the distant blue sky. The clouds were banking in mid-heaven, but to the west there was a big clear space now woolly with shrapnel bursts. I counted them mechanically - one - three - five - nine - with despair beginning to take the place of my anxiety. My hands were steady now, and through the glasses I saw the enemy.

Five attenuated shapes rode high above the bombardment, now sharp against the blue, now lost in a film of vapour. They were coming back, serenely, contemptuously, having seen all they wanted.

The quiet was gone now and the din was monstrous. Anti-aircraft guns, singly and in groups, were firing from every side. As I watched it seemed a futile waste of ammunition. The enemy didn't give a tinker's curse for it ... But surely there was one down. I could only count four now. No, there was the fifth coming out of a cloud. In ten minutes they would be all over the line. I fairly stamped in my vexation. Those guns were no more use than a sick headache. Oh, where in God's name were our own planes?

At that moment they came, streaking down into sight, four fighting-scouts with the sun glinting on their wings and burnishing their metal cowls. I saw clearly the rings of red, white, and blue. Before their downward drive the enemy instantly spread out.

I was watching with bare eyes now, and I wanted companionship, for the time of waiting was over. Automatically I must have run down the knoll, for the next I knew I was staring at the heavens with Archie by my side. The combatants seemed to couple instinctively. Diving, wheeling, climbing, a pair would drop out of the melee or disappear behind a cloud. Even at that height I could hear the methodical rat-tat-tat of the machine-guns. Then there was a sudden flare and wisp of smoke. A plane sank, turning and twisting, to earth.

'Hun!' said Archie, who had his glasses on it.

Almost immediately another followed. This time the pilot recovered himself, while still a thousand feet from the ground, and started gliding for the enemy lines. Then he wavered, plunged sickeningly, and fell headlong into the wood behind La Bruyere.

Farther east, almost over the front trenches, a two-seater Albatross and a British pilot were having a desperate tussle. The bombardment had stopped, and from where we stood every movement could be followed. First one, then another, climbed uppermost and dived back, swooped out and wheeled in again, so that the two planes seemed to clear each other only by inches. Then it looked as if they closed and interlocked. I expected to see both go crashing, when suddenly the wings of one seemed to shrivel up, and the machine dropped like a stone.

'Hun,' said Archie. 'That makes three. Oh, good lads! Good lads!'

Then I saw something which took away my breath. Sloping down in wide circles came a German machine, and, following, a little behind and a little above, a British. It was the first surrender in mid-air I had seen. In my amazement I watched the couple right down to the ground, till the enemy landed in a big meadow across the high-road and our own man in a field nearer the river.

When I looked back into the sky, it was bare. North, south, east, and west, there was not a sign of aircraft, British or German.

A violent trembling took me. Archie was sweeping the heavens with his glasses and muttering to himself. Where was the fifth man? He must have fought his way through, and it was too late.

But was it? From the toe of a great rolling cloud-bank a flame shot earthwards, followed by a V-shaped trail of smoke. British or Boche? British or Boche? I didn't wait long for an answer. For, riding over the far end of the cloud, came two of our fighting scouts.

I tried to be cool, and snapped my glasses into their case, though the reaction made me want to shout. Archie turned to me with a nervous smile and a quivering mouth. 'I think we have won on the post,' he said.

He reached out a hand for mine, his eyes still on the sky, and I was grasping it when it was torn away. He was staring upwards with a white face.

We were looking at the sixth enemy plane.

It had been behind the others and much lower, and was making straight at a great speed for the east. The glasses showed me a different type of machine - a big machine with short wings, which looked menacing as a hawk in a covey of grouse. It was under the cloud-bank, and above, satisfied, easing down after their fight, and unwitting of this enemy, rode the two British craft.

A neighbouring anti-aircraft gun broke out into a sudden burst, and I thanked Heaven for its inspiration. Curious as to this new development, the two British turned, caught sight of the Boche, and dived for him.

What happened in the next minutes I cannot tell. The three seemed to be mixed up in a dog fight, so that I could not distinguish friend from foe. My hands no longer trembled; I was too desperate. The patter of machine-guns came down to us, and then one of the three broke clear and began to climb. The others strained to follow, but in a second he had risen beyond their fire, for he had easily the pace of them. Was it the Hun?

Archie's dry lips were talking.

'It's Lensch,' he said.

'How d'you know?' I gasped angrily.

'Can't mistake him. Look at the way he slipped out as he banked. That's his patent trick.'

In that agonizing moment hope died in me. I was perfectly calm now, for the time for anxiety had gone. Farther and farther drifted the British pilots behind, while Lensch in the completeness of his triumph looped more than once as if to cry an insulting farewell. In less than three minutes he would be safe inside his own lines, and he carried the knowledge which for us was death.

 Someone was bawling in my ear, and pointing upward. It was Archie and his face was wild. I looked and gasped - seized my glasses and looked again.

A second before Lensch had been alone; now there were two machines.

I heard Archie's voice. 'My God, it's the Gladas - the little Gladas.' His fingers were digging into my arm and his face was against my shoulder. And then his excitement sobered into an awe which choked his speech, as he stammered -'It's old -'

But I did not need him to tell me the name, for I had divined it when I first saw the new plane drop from the clouds. I had that queer sense that comes sometimes to a man that a friend is present when he cannot see him. Somewhere up in the void two heroes were fighting their last battle - and one of them had a crippled leg.

I had never any doubt about the result, though Archie told me later that he went crazy with suspense. Lensch was not aware of his opponent till he was almost upon him, and I wonder if by any freak of instinct he recognized his greatest antagonist. He never fired a shot, nor did Peter ... I saw the German twist and side-slip as if to baffle the fate descending upon him. I saw Peter veer over vertically and I knew that the end had come. He was there to make certain of victory and he took the only way. The machines closed, there was a crash which I felt though I could not hear it, and next second both were hurtling down, over and over, to the earth.

They fell in the river just short of the enemy lines, but I did not see them, for my eyes were blinded and I was on my knees.

After that it was all a dream. I found myself being embraced by a French General of Division, and saw the first companies of the cheerful bluecoats whom I had longed for. With them came the rain , and it was under a weeping April sky that early in the night I marched what was left of my division away from the battle-field. The enemy guns were starting to speak behind us, but I did not heed them. I knew that now there were warders at the gate, and I believed that by the grace of God that gate was barred for ever.

They took Peter from the wreckage with scarcely a scar except his twisted leg. Death had smoothed out some of the age in him, and left his face much as I remembered it long ago in the Mashonaland hills. In his pocket was his old battered Pilgrim's Progress. It lies before me as I write, and beside it - for I was his only legatee - the little case which came to him weeks later, containing the highest honour that can be bestowed upon a soldier of Britain. It was from the Pilgrim's Progress that I read next morning, when in the lee of an apple-orchard Mary and Blenkiron and I stood in the soft spring rain beside his grave. And what I read was the tale in the end not of Mr Standfast, whom he had singled out for his counterpart, but of Mr Valiant-for-Truth whom he had not hoped to emulate. I set down the words as a salute and a farewell:

Then said he, 'I am going to my Father's; and though with great difficulty I am got hither, yet now I do not repent me of all the trouble I have been at to arrive where I am. My sword I give to him that shall succeed me in my pilgrimage, and my courage and skill to him that can get it. My marks and scars I carry with me, to be a witness for me that I have fought His battles who now will be my rewarder.'

So he passed over, and all the trumpets sounded for him on the other side.

John Buchan

Choose from Thousands of 1stWorldLibrary Classics By

A. M. Barnard
Ada Leverson
Adolphus William Ward
Aesop
Agatha Christie
Alexander Aaronsohn
Alexander Kielland
Alexandre Dumas
Alfred Gatty
Alfred Ollivant
Alice Duer Miller
Alice Turner Curtis
Alice Dunbar
Allen Chapman
Alleyne Ireland
Ambrose Bierce
Amelia E. Barr
Amory H. Bradford
Andrew Lang
Andrew McFarland Davis
Andy Adams
Angela Brazil
Anna Alice Chapin
Anna Sewell
Annie Besant
Annie Hamilton Donnell
Annie Payson Call
Annie Roe Carr
Annonaymous
Anton Chekhov
Archibald Lee Fletcher
Arnold Bennett
Arthur C. Benson
Arthur Conan Doyle
Arthur M. Winfield
Arthur Ransome
Arthur Schnitzler
Arthur Train
Atticus
B.H. Baden-Powell
B. M. Bower
B. C. Chatterjee
Baroness Emmuska Orczy
Baroness Orczy
Basil King
Bayard Taylor
Ben Macomber
Bertha Muzzy Bower
Bjornstjerne Bjornson

Booth Tarkington
Boyd Cable
Bram Stoker
C. Collodi
C. E. Orr
C. M. Ingleby
Carolyn Wells
Catherine Parr Traill
Charles A. Eastman
Charles Amory Beach
Charles Dickens
Charles Dudley Warner
Charles Farrar Browne
Charles Ives
Charles Kingsley
Charles Klein
Charles Hanson Towne
Charles Lathrop Pack
Charles Romyn Dake
Charles Whibley
Charles Willing Beale
Charlotte M. Braeme
Charlotte M. Yonge
Charlotte Perkins Stetson
Clair W. Hayes
Clarence Day Jr.
Clarence E. Mulford
Clemence Housman
Confucius
Coningsby Dawson
Cornelis DeWitt Wilcox
Cyril Burleigh
D. H. Lawrence
Daniel Defoe
David Garnett
Dinah Craik
Don Carlos Janes
Donald Keyhoe
Dorothy Kilner
Dougan Clark
Douglas Fairbanks
E. Nesbit
E. P. Roe
E. Phillips Oppenheim
E. S. Brooks
Earl Barnes
Edgar Rice Burroughs
Edith Van Dyne
Edith Wharton

Edward Everett Hale
Edward J. O'Biren
Edward S. Ellis
Edwin L. Arnold
Eleanor Atkins
Eleanor Hallowell Abbott
Eliot Gregory
Elizabeth Gaskell
Elizabeth McCracken
Elizabeth Von Arnim
Ellem Key
Emerson Hough
Emilie F. Carlen
Emily Bronte
Emily Dickinson
Enid Bagnold
Enilor Macartney Lane
Erasmus W. Jones
Ernie Howard Pie
Ethel May Dell
Ethel Turner
Ethel Watts Mumford
Eugene Sue
Eugenie Foa
Eugene Wood
Eustace Hale Ball
Evelyn Everett-green
Everard Cotes
F. H. Cheley
F. J. Cross
F. Marion Crawford
Fannie E. Newberry
Federick Austin Ogg
Ferdinand Ossendowski
Fergus Hume
Florence A. Kilpatrick
Fremont B. Deering
Francis Bacon
Francis Darwin
Frances Hodgson Burnett
Frances Parkinson Keyes
Frank Gee Patchin
Frank Harris
Frank Jewett Mather
Frank L. Packard
Frank V. Webster
Frederic Stewart Isham
Frederick Trevor Hill
Frederick Winslow Taylor

Friedrich Kerst
Friedrich Nietzsche
Fyodor Dostoyevsky
G.A. Henty
G.K. Chesterton
Gabrielle E. Jackson
Garrett P. Serviss
Gaston Leroux
George A. Warren
George Ade
Geroge Bernard Shaw
George Cary Eggleston
George Durston
George Ebers
George Eliot
George Gissing
George MacDonald
George Meredith
George Orwell
George Sylvester Viereck
George Tucker
George W. Cable
George Wharton James
Gertrude Atherton
Gordon Casserly
Grace E. King
Grace Gallatin
Grace Greenwood
Grant Allen
Guillermo A. Sherwell
Gulielma Zollinger
Gustav Flaubert
H. A. Cody
H. B. Irving
H.C. Bailey
H. G. Wells
H. H. Munro
H. Irving Hancock
H. R. Naylor
H. Rider Haggard
H. W. C. Davis
Haldeman Julius
Hall Caine
Hamilton Wright Mabie
Hans Christian Andersen
Harold Avery
Harold McGrath
Harriet Beecher Stowe
Harry Castlemon
Harry Coghill
Harry Houidini

Hayden Carruth
Helent Hunt Jackson
Helen Nicolay
Hendrik Conscience
Hendy David Thoreau
Henri Barbusse
Henrik Ibsen
Henry Adams
Henry Ford
Henry Frost
Henry James
Henry Jones Ford
Henry Seton Merriman
Henry W Longfellow
Herbert A. Giles
Herbert Carter
Herbert N. Casson
Herman Hesse
Hildegard G. Frey
Homer
Honore De Balzac
Horace B. Day
Horace Walpole
Horatio Alger Jr.
Howard Pyle
Howard R. Garis
Hugh Lofting
Hugh Walpole
Humphry Ward
Ian Maclaren
Inez Haynes Gillmore
Irving Bacheller
Isabel Cecilia Williams
Isabel Hornibrook
Israel Abrahams
Ivan Turgenev
J.G.Austin
J. Henri Fabre
J. M. Barrie
J. M. Walsh
J. Macdonald Oxley
J. R. Miller
J. S. Fletcher
J. S. Knowles
J. Storer Clouston
J. W. Duffield
Jack London
Jacob Abbott
James Allen
James Andrews
James Baldwin

James Branch Cabell
James DeMille
James Joyce
James Lane Allen
James Lane Allen
James Oliver Curwood
James Oppenheim
James Otis
James R. Driscoll
Jane Abbott
Jane Austen
Jane L. Stewart
Janet Aldridge
Jens Peter Jacobsen
Jerome K. Jerome
Jessie Graham Flower
John Buchan
John Burroughs
John Cournos
John F. Kennedy
John Gay
John Glasworthy
John Habberton
John Joy Bell
John Kendrick Bangs
John Milton
John Philip Sousa
John Taintor Foote
Jonas Lauritz Idemil Lie
Jonathan Swift
Joseph A. Altsheler
Joseph Carey
Joseph Conrad
Joseph E. Badger Jr
Joseph Hergesheimer
Joseph Jacobs
Jules Vernes
Julian Hawthrone
Julie A Lippmann
Justin Huntly McCarthy
Kakuzo Okakura
Karle Wilson Baker
Kate Chopin
Kenneth Grahame
Kenneth McGaffey
Kate Langley Bosher
Kate Langley Bosher
Katherine Cecil Thurston
Katherine Stokes
L. A. Abbot
L. T. Meade

L. Frank Baum
Latta Griswold
Laura Dent Crane
Laura Lee Hope
Laurence Housman
Lawrence Beasley
Leo Tolstoy
Leonid Andreyev
Lewis Carroll
Lewis Sperry Chafer
Lilian Bell
Lloyd Osbourne
Louis Hughes
Louis Joseph Vance
Louis Tracy
Louisa May Alcott
Lucy Fitch Perkins
Lucy Maud Montgomery
Luther Benson
Lydia Miller Middleton
Lyndon Orr
M. Corvus
M. H. Adams
Margaret E. Sangster
Margret Howth
Margaret Vandercook
Margaret W. Hungerford
Margret Penrose
Maria Edgeworth
Maria Thompson Daviess
Mariano Azuela
Marion Polk Angellotti
Mark Overton
Mark Twain
Mary Austin
Mary Catherine Crowley
Mary Cole
Mary Hastings Bradley
Mary Roberts Rinehart
Mary Rowlandson
M. Wollstonecraft Shelley
Maud Lindsay
Max Beerbohm
Myra Kelly
Nathaniel Hawthrone
Nicolo Machiavelli
O. F. Walton
Oscar Wilde

Owen Johnson
P.G. Wodehouse
Paul and Mabel Thorne
Paul G. Tomlinson
Paul Severing
Percy Brebner
Percy Keese Fitzhugh
Peter B. Kyne
Plato
Quincy Allen
R. Derby Holmes
R. L. Stevenson
R. S. Ball
Rabindranath Tagore
Rahul Alvares
Ralph Bonehill
Ralph Henry Barbour
Ralph Victor
Ralph Waldo Emmerson
Rene Descartes
Ray Cummings
Rex Beach
Rex E. Beach
Richard Harding Davis
Richard Jefferies
Richard Le Gallienne
Robert Barr
Robert Frost
Robert Gordon Anderson
Robert L. Drake
Robert Lansing
Robert Lynd
Robert Michael Ballantyne
Robert W. Chambers
Rosa Nouchette Carey
Rudyard Kipling
Saint Augustine
Samuel B. Allison
Samuel Hopkins Adams
Sarah Bernhardt
Sarah C. Hallowell
Selma Lagerlof
Sherwood Anderson
Sigmund Freud
Standish O'Grady
Stanley Weyman
Stella Benson
Stella M. Francis

Stephen Crane
Stewart Edward White
Stijn Streuvels
Swami Abhedananda
Swami Parmananda
T. S. Ackland
T. S. Arthur
The Princess Der Ling
Thomas A. Janvier
Thomas A Kempis
Thomas Anderton
Thomas Bailey Aldrich
Thomas Bulfinch
Thomas De Quincey
Thomas Dixon
Thomas H. Huxley
Thomas Hardy
Thomas More
Thornton W. Burgess
U. S. Grant
Upton Sinclair
Valentine Williams
Various Authors
Vaughan Kester
Victor Appleton
Victor G. Durham
Victoria Cross
Virginia Woolf
Wadsworth Camp
Walter Camp
Walter Scott
Washington Irving
Wilbur Lawton
Wilkie Collins
Willa Cather
Willard F. Baker
William Dean Howells
William le Queux
W. Makepeace Thackeray
William W. Walter
William Shakespeare
Winston Churchill
Yei Theodora Ozaki
Yogi Ramacharaka
Young E. Allison
Zane Grey

Printed in the United States
93475LV00002B/128/A